Real life thank yous go out to everybody involved in the marathon production of Be Dangerous On Rock Guitar. I will start with the irrepressible Tom Miller who spent a lot of the summer meticulously printing the half-tones found in this book. All typesetting was done by Horizon Printing and Graphics, Newark, DE. So, thanks again to Barbara for the long haul. And to Betsy, who did so much of the work on the transcriptions, for seeing it through to the end with me. And to my Mom and Dad, for their endless proofreading and support, and for making my first book, The Heavy Guitar Bible, possible. And to drummer Tim (who knows the true meaning of heavy metal), guitarist Phil, bassist Tris and photographer Bill Harrison for coming over and putting up with all of the bright lights, high volume and late hours. And to Rob Rage (and all the boys in the band) for knowing that it would work all along. And to the people at Minuteman Press on the corner of Main and Chapel Streets in Newark, DE, for putting up with me ten times a day for the two years that it took to make all the little pieces the right size. Special thanks to Lauren and Company at Cherry Lane Music of Port Chester, NY, for once more allowing it all to happen, and for taking Be Dangerous to the far corners of the United States, and beyond.

Be Dangerous On Rock Guitar was independently produced by The Heavy Guitar Company, Great Falls, VA 22066. All text, page design, layout, ink drawing and technical diagrams were provided by the author.

Reprinted 3/96

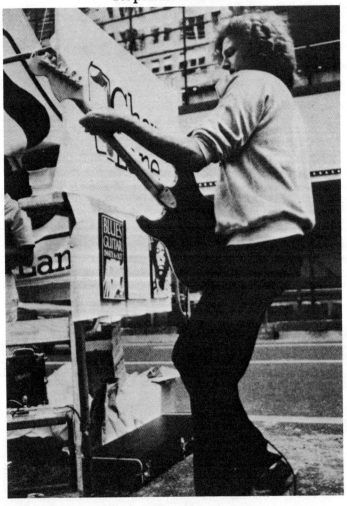

WINDOWS

Roadmap
to Be Dangerous On Rock Guitar

First of all, Be Dangerous On Rock Guitar is a multimedia package which consists of four interrelated parts:

A. <u>This Book</u> . . . . printed word, guitar graphics, transcriptions, various charts, pictures, drawings.

B. <u>Six one-hour Cassette Tapes</u> . . spoken word, guitar technique examples, aural effects, tuning frequency, recorded transcriptions.

C. <u>One Wall Poster</u> . . . . 12 full size fretboard charts, the four part *Universal Diagram* series, facts and figures.

D. Helpful Fretboard Dots . . . . . . hundreds of small adhesive fretboard marking dots.

The diverse nature of the information provided by these four separate parts are brought together by numbered sections called WINDOWS, which appear both *in the book* and *on the tapes*. We are, of course, trying to capture the feel of playing live stage guitar. That's a tall order which requires a vehicle somewhat *wider in concept* than a simple book chapter. So get ready to travel through 24 WINDOWS, one at a time, starting with WINDOW 1. Next we will cover a few specific points about the difference between the WINDOWS you <u>see in the book</u> and those you <u>hear on the tapes</u>.

Characteristics of WINDOWS found in the book:

A. Each WINDOW is clearly identified by name and number.

B. At the beginning of each WINDOW, a <u>Primary Objective Statement</u> is printed. This short account states the directive of the WINDOW in a nutshell.

C. The first paragraph of each WINDOW outlines the subject at hand; then fretboard diagrams, guitar transcriptions, charts, and occasional text follow. The text of the book, and the text of the tape frequently run in parallel.

Characteristics of WINDOWS found on the tape:

A. Each WINDOW opens with the sounding of an <u>A 440 tuning fork</u>.

B. Each WINDOW is then verbally identified by <u>name and number</u>.

C. You then hear the reading of the <u>Primary Objective Statement</u>.

Now that we have *that* cleared up, there's a little more dirty work ahead as we take a closer look at the various graphic systems that you will find, and have to deal with, inside the WINDOWS of Be Dangerous On Rock Guitar. We start with the six line guitar staff, commonly called *tab*, which is used to transcribe all guitar passages.

The Six Line Guitar Staff

The special six line guitar staff that you see used in this book is no accident. It was designed after strict consideration was given to the true needs of the rock guitarist. *What are those needs?* First, you need a system that can pinpoint a position, or precisely spell out a line of the board. Second, you need a vehicle that provides a rough blueprint *on paper*, that you can use to duplicate a short passage provided on *the cassette*. The six line guitar staff is great for showing precise fretboard position, fingering, note sequence, duration of note (dot size), etc. It also provides you with a working approximation of fluid, improvised guitarwork.

The word *transcription* is used to indicate an example given on the six line staff. All transcriptions are numbered consecutively and labeled for key. The example below shows the sequence of notes that result when an E major chord is strummed from the low E string to the high E string. *Symbols* that are placed over certain notes to indicate a particular technique, and various *dot sizes* indicate relative time values.

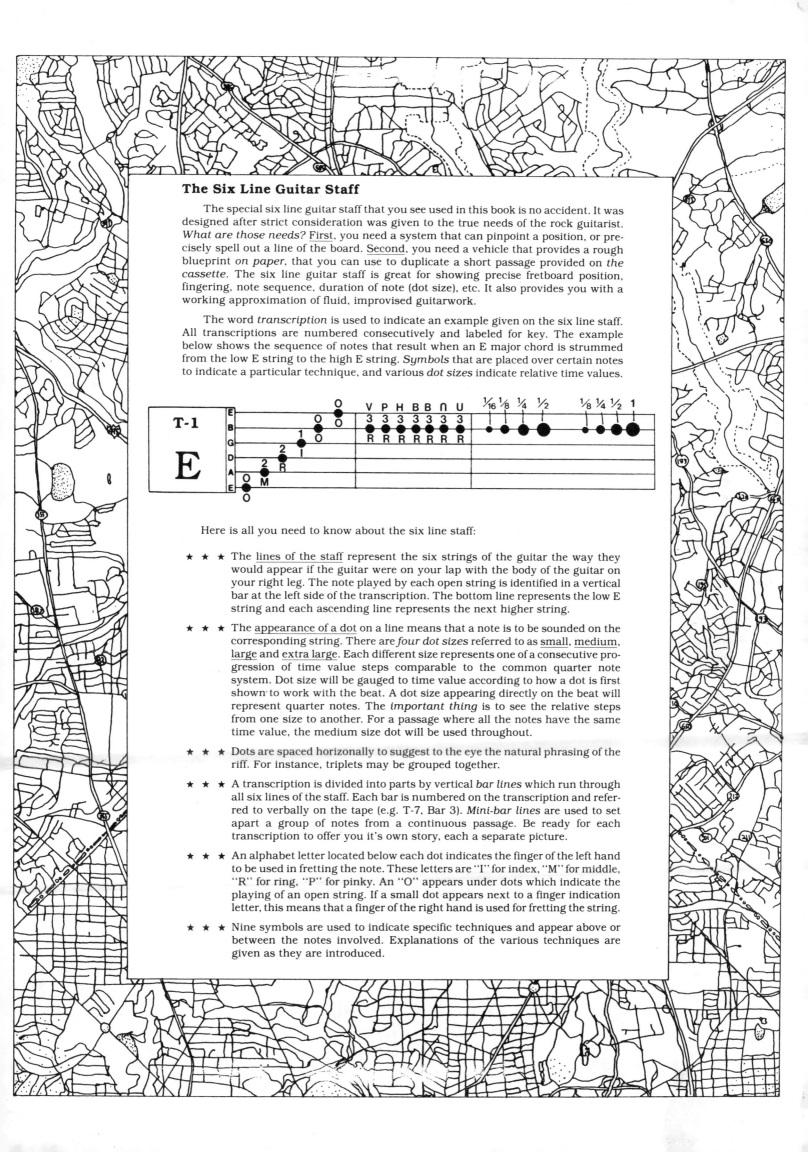

Here is all you need to know about the six line staff:

★ ★ ★ The <u>lines of the staff</u> represent the six strings of the guitar the way they would appear if the guitar were on your lap with the body of the guitar on your right leg. The note played by each open string is identified in a vertical bar at the left side of the transcription. The bottom line represents the low E string and each ascending line represents the next higher string.

★ ★ ★ The <u>appearance of a dot</u> on a line means that a note is to be sounded on the corresponding string. There are *four dot sizes* referred to as <u>small</u>, <u>medium</u>, <u>large</u> and <u>extra large</u>. Each different size represents one of a consecutive progression of time value steps comparable to the common quarter note system. Dot size will be gauged to time value according to how a dot is first shown to work with the beat. A dot size appearing directly on the beat will represent quarter notes. The *important thing* is to see the relative steps from one size to another. For a passage where all the notes have the same time value, the medium size dot will be used throughout.

★ ★ ★ Dots are spaced horizonally to suggest to the eye the natural phrasing of the riff. For instance, triplets may be grouped together.

★ ★ ★ A transcription is divided into parts by vertical *bar lines* which run through all six lines of the staff. Each bar is numbered on the transcription and referred to verbally on the tape (e.g. T-7, Bar 3). *Mini-bar lines* are used to set apart a group of notes from a continuous passage. Be ready for each transcription to offer you it's own story, each a separate picture.

★ ★ ★ An alphabet letter located below each dot indicates the finger of the left hand to be used in fretting the note. These letters are "I" for index, "M" for middle, "R" for ring, "P" for pinky. An "O" appears under dots which indicate the playing of an open string. If a small dot appears next to a finger indication letter, this means that a finger of the right hand is used for fretting the string.

★ ★ ★ Nine symbols are used to indicate specific techniques and appear above or between the notes involved. Explanations of the various techniques are given as they are introduced.

These symbols appear between or above the lines of the six line staff

Symbol	Technique
P	Pull
H	Hammer
RH	Repeat Hammer
V	Vibrato
HRM	Harmonic
B	Bend half step
•B	Bend whole step
U	Slide up
∩	Slide down

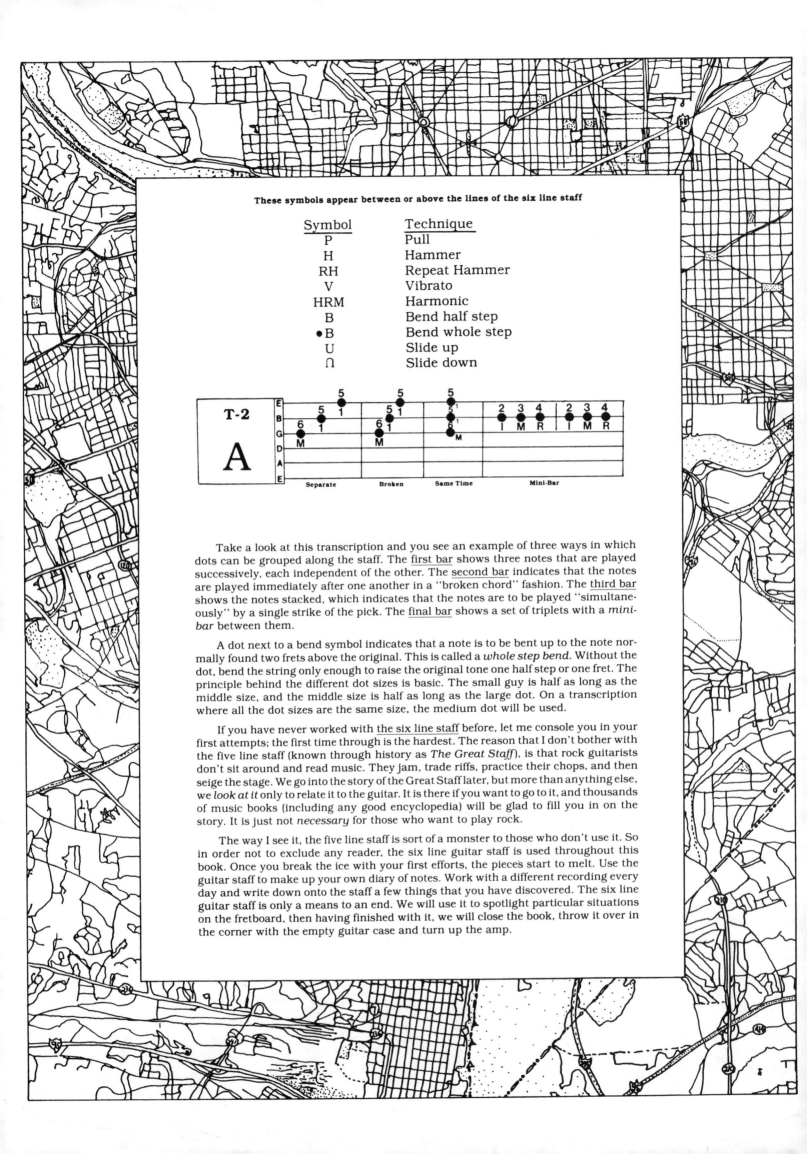

Take a look at this transcription and you see an example of three ways in which dots can be grouped along the staff. The <u>first bar</u> shows three notes that are played successively, each independent of the other. The <u>second bar</u> indicates that the notes are played immediately after one another in a "broken chord" fashion. The <u>third bar</u> shows the notes stacked, which indicates that the notes are to be played "simultaneously" by a single strike of the pick. The <u>final bar</u> shows a set of triplets with a *mini-bar* between them.

A dot next to a bend symbol indicates that a note is to be bent up to the note normally found two frets above the original. This is called a *whole step bend*. Without the dot, bend the string only enough to raise the original tone one half step or one fret. The principle behind the different dot sizes is basic. The small guy is half as long as the middle size, and the middle size is half as long as the large dot. On a transcription where all the dot sizes are the same size, the medium dot will be used.

If you have never worked with <u>the six line staff</u> before, let me console you in your first attempts; the first time through is the hardest. The reason that I don't bother with the five line staff (known through history as *The Great Staff*), is that rock guitarists don't sit around and read music. They jam, trade riffs, practice their chops, and then seige the stage. We go into the story of the Great Staff later, but more than anything else, we *look at it* only to relate it to the guitar. It is there if you want to go to it, and thousands of music books (including any good encyclopedia) will be glad to fill you in on the story. It is just not *necessary* for those who want to play rock.

The way I see it, the five line staff is sort of a monster to those who don't use it. So in order not to exclude any reader, the six line guitar staff is used throughout this book. Once you break the ice with your first efforts, the pieces start to melt. Use the guitar staff to make up your own diary of notes. Work with a different recording every day and write down onto the staff a few things that you have discovered. The six line guitar staff is only a means to an end. We will use it to spotlight particular situations on the fretboard, then having finished with it, we will close the book, throw it over in the corner with the empty guitar case and turn up the amp.

Next . . . Fretboard Diagrams

Fretboards are represented in a variety of ways. Whole board diagrams (24 frets) are used on occasion, but the real work horse is the twelve fret variety. These guys show a sweet octave on each of the six strings between the nut and the double dot twelfth fret. You also see plenty of shots down on the open strings showing only the first five frets, while partial shots spotlight just a few chosen frets. All fretboard diagrams show chosen notes on the low E string with tiny letters.

The *Universal Diagram* series along with full size fretboard representations appear on the Be Dangerous wall poster.

Twelve fret

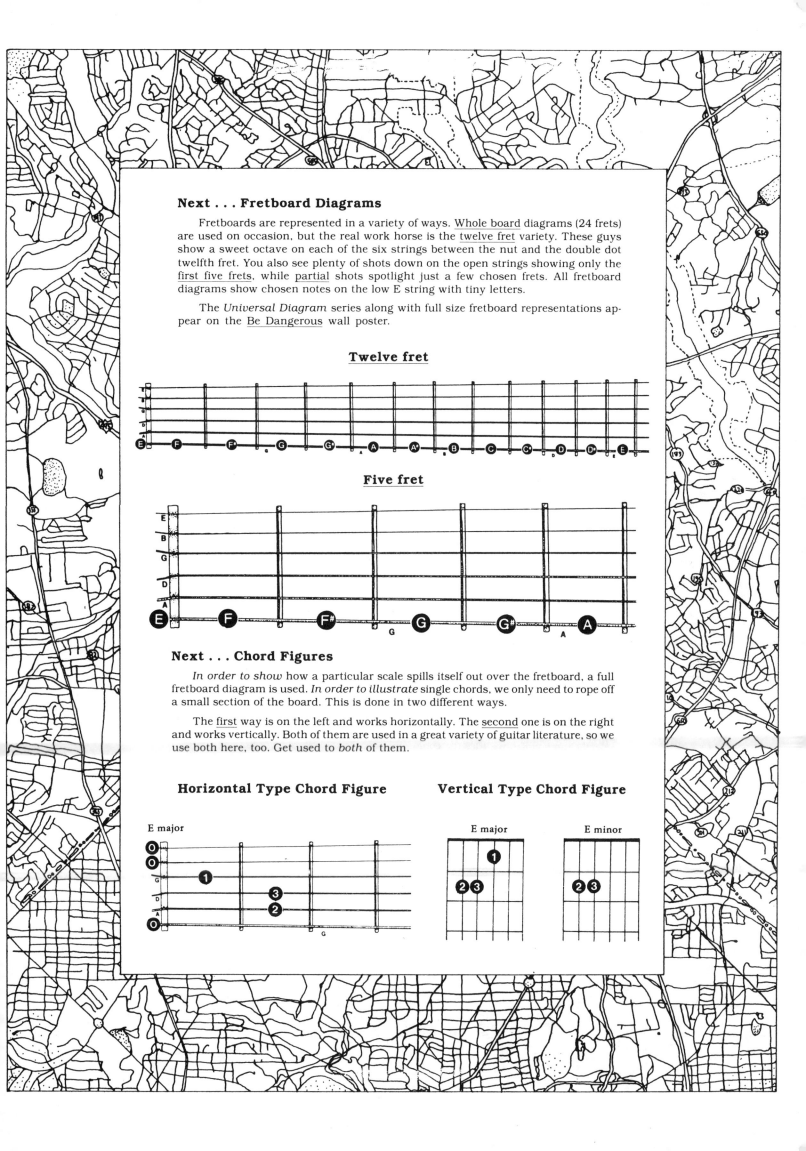

Five fret

Next . . . Chord Figures

In order to show how a particular scale spills itself out over the fretboard, a full fretboard diagram is used. *In order to illustrate* single chords, we only need to rope off a small section of the board. This is done in two different ways.

The first way is on the left and works horizontally. The second one is on the right and works vertically. Both of them are used in a great variety of guitar literature, so we use both here, too. Get used to *both* of them.

Horizontal Type Chord Figure

E major

Vertical Type Chord Figure

E major   E minor

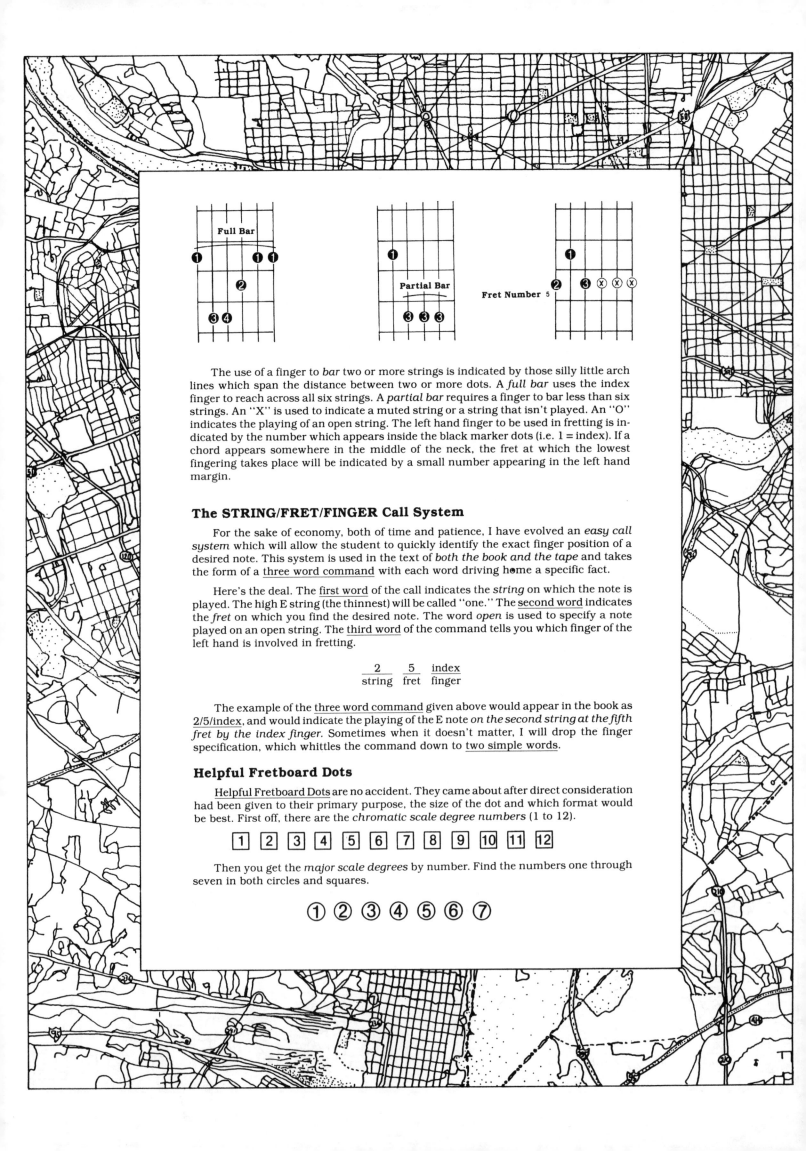

The use of a finger to *bar* two or more strings is indicated by those silly little arch lines which span the distance between two or more dots. A *full bar* uses the index finger to reach across all six strings. A *partial bar* requires a finger to bar less than six strings. An "X" is used to indicate a muted string or a string that isn't played. An "O" indicates the playing of an open string. The left hand finger to be used in fretting is indicated by the number which appears inside the black marker dots (i.e. 1 = index). If a chord appears somewhere in the middle of the neck, the fret at which the lowest fingering takes place will be indicated by a small number appearing in the left hand margin.

The STRING/FRET/FINGER Call System

For the sake of economy, both of time and patience, I have evolved an *easy call system* which will allow the student to quickly identify the exact finger position of a desired note. This system is used in the text of *both the book and the tape* and takes the form of a three word command with each word driving home a specific fact.

Here's the deal. The first word of the call indicates the *string* on which the note is played. The high E string (the thinnest) will be called "one." The second word indicates the *fret* on which you find the desired note. The word *open* is used to specify a note played on an open string. The third word of the command tells you which finger of the left hand is involved in fretting.

$$\frac{2}{\text{string}} \quad \frac{5}{\text{fret}} \quad \frac{\text{index}}{\text{finger}}$$

The example of the three word command given above would appear in the book as 2/5/index, and would indicate the playing of the E note *on the second string at the fifth fret by the index finger*. Sometimes when it doesn't matter, I will drop the finger specification, which whittles the command down to two simple words.

Helpful Fretboard Dots

Helpful Fretboard Dots are no accident. They came about after direct consideration had been given to their primary purpose, the size of the dot and which format would be best. First off, there are the *chromatic scale degree numbers* (1 to 12).

1 2 3 4 5 6 7 8 9 10 11 12

Then you get the *major scale degrees* by number. Find the numbers one through seven in both circles and squares.

① ② ③ ④ ⑤ ⑥ ⑦

Then the *five note blues scale degrees* are identified by their relation to the major scale degrees.

① ③ ④ ⑤ ⑦

And don't forget the *symbols to understand.*

🌙 ★ ▲ ◆ ■

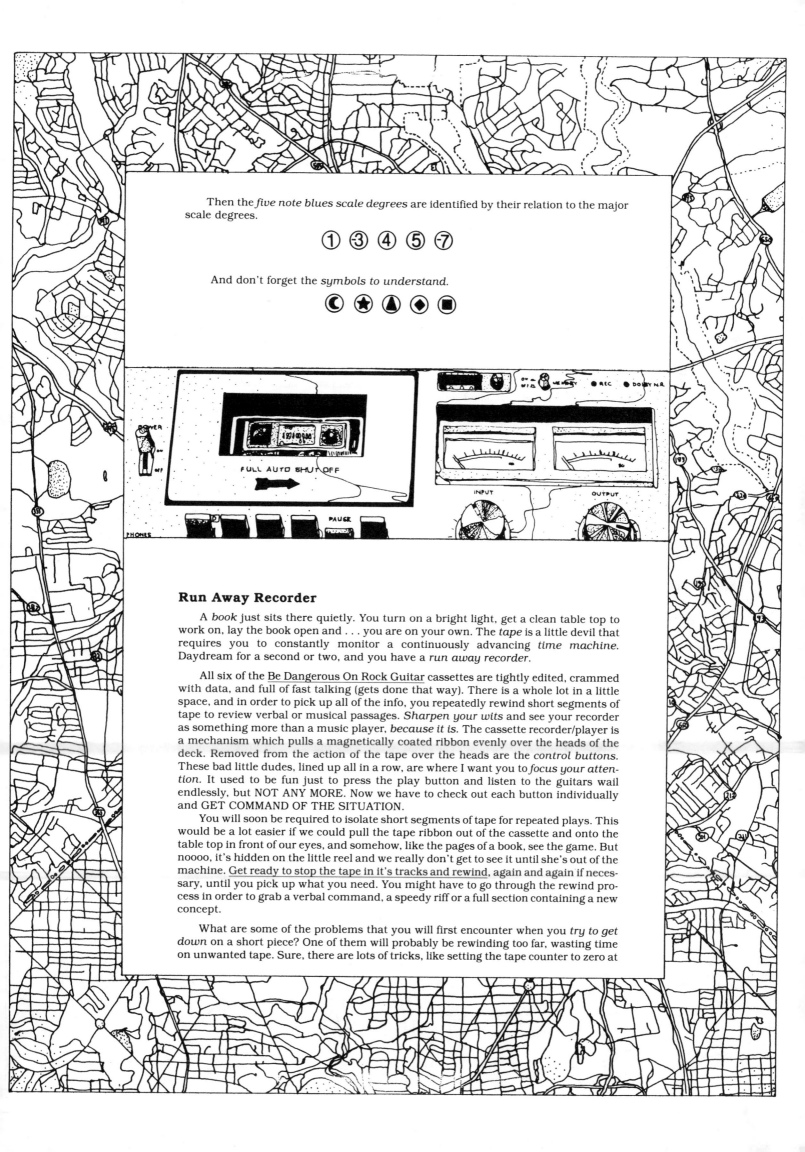

Run Away Recorder

A *book* just sits there quietly. You turn on a bright light, get a clean table top to work on, lay the book open and . . . you are on your own. The *tape* is a little devil that requires you to constantly monitor a continuously advancing *time machine*. Daydream for a second or two, and you have a *run away recorder.*

All six of the Be Dangerous On Rock Guitar cassettes are tightly edited, crammed with data, and full of fast talking (gets done that way). There is a whole lot in a little space, and in order to pick up all of the info, you repeatedly rewind short segments of tape to review verbal or musical passages. *Sharpen your wits* and see your recorder as something more than a music player, *because it is.* The cassette recorder/player is a mechanism which pulls a magnetically coated ribbon evenly over the heads of the deck. Removed from the action of the tape over the heads are the *control buttons.* These bad little dudes, lined up all in a row, are where I want you to *focus your attention.* It used to be fun just to press the play button and listen to the guitars wail endlessly, but NOT ANY MORE. Now we have to check out each button individually and GET COMMAND OF THE SITUATION.

You will soon be required to isolate short segments of tape for repeated plays. This would be a lot easier if we could pull the tape ribbon out of the cassette and onto the table top in front of our eyes, and somehow, like the pages of a book, see the game. But noooo, it's hidden on the little reel and we really don't get to see it until she's out of the machine. Get ready to stop the tape in it's tracks and rewind, again and again if necessary, until you pick up what you need. You might have to go through the rewind process in order to grab a verbal command, a speedy riff or a full section containing a new concept.

What are some of the problems that you will first encounter when you *try to get down* on a short piece? One of them will probably be rewinding too far, wasting time on unwanted tape. Sure, there are lots of tricks, like setting the tape counter to zero at the desired moment. But here are the chips . . . YOU GOT TO USE TO GET USED TO. That's right, the only answer is to develop your touch on the control buttons. Get tough with it. Send out the signal to the circuits to *get to work* for you. They will if you do.

Any cassette player will suffice, but some are better than others *for withstanding the abuse* that repeated rewinding offers to the poor little machine. Get a portable model by all means. The stereo component models are designed for the long haul of reproducing albums and are not best suited for our purposes. You'll see what I mean if you try to do it on the wrong cat. Anyway, the *all-in-one battery bad boys* stand up to the movable equipment scene, which has always been part of the rock. Plus, they have some excellent features for a guitarist intent on hunting down riffs. And that, my friend, is what you got.

Yes, advanced features built right into the deck can really help the cause. Light touch "Cue Review" buttons allow the user to *rewind* in short bursts without breaking the machine out of the play mode. Cue review can also be used in the same way *to advance* the tape if you find yourself in the middle. "Auto search" is another modern feature that can help you *in and around* short segments of tape. This feature automatically spins the tape in forward or reverse to the next blank spot on the tape. This is particularly useful to find the end (or beginning) of a musical passage.

The bottom line: get the best machine that you can. If money is a no no, then get the cheapest one you can find. It will do. So here's to all those cassette players out there, and to their little speakers that move the air.

Many Things

Just picture what it must have been like back in the middle ages when some young boy had to learn the ways of the keyboard under the watchful eye of some old rough, tough teacher that *just would not give up* until the boy could, one fine day, inherit the position of *MAIN KEYBOARD DUDE* for the cathedral. I'm sure that *more than once* the student thought to tell the teacher off, and pull down a few Ray Charles licks.

The basic reason that the old fashion "crack your knuckles with a stick" approach will not work for rock guitar instruction is that rock guitarists simply *play too loose* to get caught up in all that mumbo jumbo. One of the problems with the rigid approach is that it works great for the basics, but is lacking when it comes to exploring the multi-colored moods of a diverse beast like rock music. Finger exercises, endless scale climbing, structured practice sessions, *all of that stuff is fine in its place*, but is not an end unto itself.

Be Dangerous On Rock Guitar is meant to provide you with a *ticket to the world of rock guitar* by bringing together the best of two diverse worlds. Firstly, it will teach you about music in general. The guitar is, after all, a musical instrument. Secondly, it will spotlight a spectrum of details, each one a different slant on attacking the board. *Many things*, some presenting overlapping theories and concepts, will be independently studied.

The regemented approach works fine if you are training for the Olympic Games, but the subject of rock guitar is too emotional, too dimensional to fully categorize. Oh, you'll get your share of straight facts and figures (witness the wall poster), but they will never overshadow the delicate, intangible side of rock which provides us all with so much magic.

Take your time to see the music in its component parts. Look closely at what is involved in a single technique. Make a discovery, then run it down the board in a few variations, committing it to memory for subsequent execution. After a while, you draw a circle around the whole game, and *many things* seem as one. Your axe gets sharper and your choice turns to whim. Without realizing it, you are submerged in your own music, free to wander.

WINDOW #1

The Big Picture

Primary Objective Statement

To present the elements of modern music

Gravity is funny stuff. It pulls a stack of Marshall amps smack down onto the planks of the stage, keeps a rowdy crowd glued to their seats, holds the beer to the bottom of your cup, while at the same time, allows eccentric, world-famous rock guitarists to daringly leap into the air without worrying if they are ever going to come down again. They always do. Gravity pulls the river to the sea, the car to the road and the leaf to the ground, but if you dig down and try to find it – YOU'RE WASTING YOUR TIME.

You see, there are four specific natural forces in the universe; strong nuclear, weak nuclear, electro-magnetic, and gravitational. Yes, gravity is an invisible *force* created by an accumulation of mass. In our specific case, the mass of the earth (6.5×10^{21} tons) is pulling everything that's loose on and above the crust of the planet (cars, air, rivers, rock stars, etc.) towards the center of the globe with the accustomed force of 1 G (one gravitational unit). Now it just so happens that our planet sustains a phenomenon known to all as an atmosphere, which is a gaseous mass surrounding a celestial body. Because molecules of air are invisible to the eye, we cannot bear witness to their constant violent interaction with each other. They can't escape because they are pulled by gravity toward the center of the planet. They fight with all their little might to cram up next to the surface, and in the process form a delicate, thin veil which covers the outer crust. The resulting molecular traffic jam is referred to as atmospheric pressure. The air we breathe is a mixture of gases composed of 78% nitrogen, 21% oxygen, .9% argon and several other trace gases.

The reason that we don't seem to feel atmospheric pressure is because we grew up in it. The ear is, however, extremely sensitive to quick changes above or below atmospheric pressure. It is for this reason that we can hear sounds, which invariably cause fluctuations in the pressure of the air, even when they are created at a considerable distance.

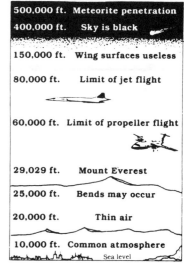

500,000 ft.	Meteorite penetration
400,000 ft.	Sky is black
150,000 ft.	Wing surfaces useless
80,000 ft.	Limit of jet flight
60,000 ft.	Limit of propeller flight
29,029 ft.	Mount Everest
25,000 ft.	Bends may occur
20,000 ft.	Thin air
10,000 ft.	Common atmosphere
	Sea level

The ear is a complex transducer which transforms acoustic energy into mechanical vibrations by scooping up invisible sound waves with the outer ear and funneling them into the auditory canal which runs to the eardrum. This eardrum is a thin membrane which vibrates from the impact of sound waves, and is connected in the middle ear to three tiny bones called the auditory ossicles. These little dudes transmit the vibration from the eardrum to a small snail-like organ called the cochlea, located in the inner ear. The amazing thing about this guy is that it is filled with *liquid* which, through pressure waves, passes on the vibration to tiny sensory hairs growing out of specialized cells which line the inside of the fluid-filled sack. The deformation of the hairs causes the sending of an electrical impulse to the brain. While certain hairs respond to certain frequencies, loud sounds cause more stimulation, which in turn is interpreted in the brain as increased loudness. So, the next time you reach for the volume knob, *have mercy on those little hairs.*

As you can imagine, sound is perceived differently by every person. It is not like a coin on the table that you can plainly see and examine. It is invisible, intangible, travels by means of air pressure waves, quivering membranes, shaking bones, pulsating fluid and lightning quick electrical impulses before it creates a shimmering, fleeting impression in the listener's mind. No wonder music is so hard to pin down!!!

ACOUSTICS (Greek, Hearing)

Acoustics is the science of sound. The fundamental laws of acoustics apply to all sounds; high or low, loud or soft, musical or otherwise as they pass through gas, liquid or solid. In order to get a rounded picture of this diverse subject, you have to consider the <u>generation</u> of sound from a source, the <u>transmission</u> of a sound wave through a medium, and the <u>reception</u> of the wave by a receiver.

Transmission

Generation

Reception

Spherical Emission

THE NATURE OF THE SOUND WAVE

A simple sound, such as the snapping of fingers, is carried through the air on a single pressure shock wave. When your fingers come together, that last bit of air between the two surfaces is *forced out* against the surrounding air. This is the first domino. The wave thus formed is both <u>compressional</u> (depends on the elasticity of the air) and <u>longitudinal</u> (particles of the medium vibrate in the direction of the line of advance of the wave). How doth it spread? Unless otherwise directed, a free sound wave will spread out in an ever-increasing spherical wavefront, which diminishes as it progresses. A sound wave is thus a vehicle for the *transmission of mechanical energy* along a distinctly shaped, ever-advancing front, which, with the exception of its volume, remains fundamentally unchanged throughout its propogation — AMEN.

The speed at which sound travels (commonly about 760 MPH at the surface of the earth) will be affected by changes in the <u>density</u>, <u>pressure</u> and <u>temperature</u> of the air. Sound travels slower as the *pressure* and *density* of the air increases. A greater number of molecules per cubic inch means a slowing of the forward movement of the wave. *Humidity* always increases the density of the air, slowing sound down. Like crossing a crowded room, it takes a little longer. Inversely, supersonic aircraft pilots prefer flying in the upper reaches of the atmosphere because they can fly faster without breaking the *speed of sound.* Breaking the speed of sound turns the airship into a tremendous sound source.

Now . . . changes in *temperature* affect the elasticity of the air. An increase in heat will excite the molecules of the air, enabling a sound wave to travel faster and with more clarity. Why did your band sound so great that clear hot night, and so crudy that cool wet night in the basement? Think about it.

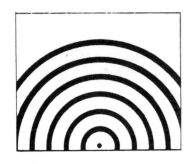

Sound travels through water 4 times faster than air, and 15 times faster through steel than air.

Air Temp.	Speed of Sound
32°F.	740 M.P.H.
68°F.	758 M.P.H.
77°F.	771 M.P.H.
212°F.	839 M.P.H.

THE CHARACTERISTICS OF MUSICAL SOUND

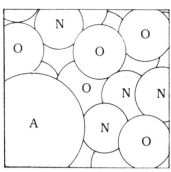

The Random House Dictionary defines *duration* as "the length of time during which something continues or exists." It is the fact that musical sounds *continue in time* that distinguishes them from single sounds which occur only once and are carried on a single wavefront. During the creation of a musical sound, the air is compressed repeatedly by the continued vibration of an elastic body. What is meant by an "elastic body?" Any musical sound source will do; a stretched string, a tuning fork, a set of vocal cords or the two 12" speakers of a Fender Twin Reverb amp. Once some form of mechanical energy (the picking of a string, a forced stream of air, magnetic oscillation, etc.) is applied to the "elastic body," it becomes distorted from its relaxed state, and is set into regular vibratory motion. This creates an oscillating disturbance in the air, *a train of sound waves*, which are similar in character, equally timed alike to form and travel through the air with the same velocity. In other words — each periodic disturbance is the same.

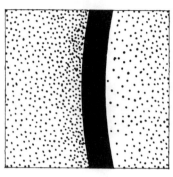

Scientists always strive to make what is *out there* comprehendible to us by visual charts which serve to represent some complex natural action in understandable, measurable terms. This is the case with the two dimentional *sine wave* which is used to represent the pressure oscillation of a sound wave. Below is a demonstration of how a sine wave can be obtained from a singing tuning fork if a drawing point is fixed on one of the forks, and the fork itself is moved evenly across the page.

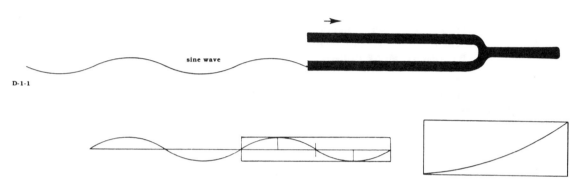

sine wave

D-1-1

Even though the sine wave has its limitations for describing the sound wave, it is good enough. What we are going to do now is take a look at the different ways we can *graphically represent* the characteristics of a musical tone. It seems analytical, and I *know*, it's not music. Not yet at least. In just a minute though, we will get to the part where the sounds go pop, bang, *you're a star*. At that time, we will have made our arrival in that far away land, that place where the troubled world melts away and we can all have fun playing loud heavy rock guitar. That glorious realm where power chords rule all, and cascading lead breaks tumble down, down. But for now, in order to know all, we will determine the essential features of the musical tone.

A pure tone is the simplest musical sound and is characterized by it's singular frequency and distinct monotone. After a silence, if a pure tone is sounded, its properties become immediately evident. The pure tone emitted from a struck tuning fork has a certain mysterious singularity, a hypnotic type of drone which sort of stays with you a little after the fork is stopped. Truly pure tones are rarely found in music because practically all instruments produce complex sounds, even when they are seemingly playing a single note. *Harmonic* interplay, the simultaneous playing of two or more notes, also has its consequences, forming relationships where single notes can no longer be objectively heard by the listener.

FREQUENCY

Frequency is the number of sound waves per second produced by a sounding body. Each periodic oscillation of a tuning fork produces one sound wave consisting of one zone of air compression and one zone of air rarefaction. The rate at which sound waves are produced relates directly to the *highness* or *lowness* of a note, a quality referred to as the *pitch* of a note. A sound of fixed pitch is called a *tone*. The frequency of sound waves is generally measured in cycles per second (cps) or in the identically measured hertz (hz). Accordingly, 440 cps is the same thing as 440 hz, but for larger numbered frequencies, the term kilohertz (Khz) is used to indicate 1000 hz. So much for terms.

Further down the line we will look deeper into the specific range of the guitar, octave ranges, voice ranges, overtones, scale degree determination and more, but for right now, here is the most important concept for you to grasp; *every note that you hear has a corresponding frequency*. A particular note may be loud or soft, used in simultaneous harmony with another note, used as a component of a chord, or quickly employed as a grace note; doesn't matter that much people — *each note still has its own special frequency*. Each identifiable tone or note occupies a certain point somewhere in the usable music range. Larger than the usable music range is the full spectral range of human hearing, called the audible range, which sweeps the tremendous span between 20 hz and 20,000 hz. Just for a minute, think of this range as an unbroken, all inclusive entity which your ears were designed to accommodate. A musical note exists as a fixed point in this universal range, an infinitesimally minute, one-dimensional blip in an ocean of diversity. Some wierdos can hear below 20 hz but describe what they hear not as a single tone but as a series of "swooshes." The 20,000 hz upper limit of hearing represents an awesomely shrill treble tone, way out of the usable music range, yet the ear reports the sound to the brain. The word *infrasonic* refers to sound waves produced below the 20 hz mark, below the threshold of human hearing. The word *ultrasonic* refers to sound waves produced above the 20,000 hz frequency mark, above the human hearing range. Bats and dolphin emit sonic waves of a frequency upward of 150,000 hz, and through a sophisticated system of ultrasonic echolocation, can use their sense of hearing to "see" what is around them.

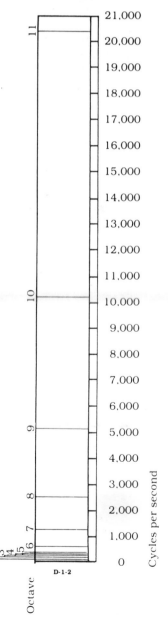

D-1-2

Octave

Cycles per second

Octave

1	2	3	4	5	6	7	8	9	10	11
20	40	80	160	320	640	1280	2560	5120	10,240	20,480

Cycles per second

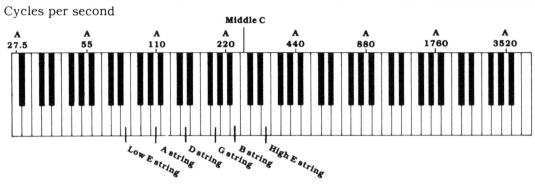

The 88-key piano provides a rough idea of the frequency extremes of the usable music range. The lowest key plays an A note of 27.5 hz, while the highest key plays a C note of 4186 hz. Middle C, that lukewarm mid-range tone that separates the treble range from the bass range, checks in at 261.63 hz. This note is found on the guitar on the second string at the second fret. The highest and lowest open strings of the guitar are E — 82.41 hz and E — 329.63 hz respectively. Because of the need to establish a single point of reference for the building of musical scales throughout the music range, the A note above middle C was established at 440 hz by an international conference of musicians in 1955. This is the note most common tuning forks are manufactured to produce and can be played on the guitar on the first string at the fifth fret. You will hear this special *tuning frequency* open each of the Windows on the Be Dangerous On Rock Guitar cassette tape series.

Each note has a specific frequency. It is not important to know the frequency numbers of particular notes. What is important is *realizing* that all of that guitar work that we hear on all of those albums *that we love so much* is actually composed of NOTES, NOTES and more NOTES, each with an identifiable position in the sweeping range. If we know this, and really believe it, then we should be able, with effort, to figure out what we hear on any record, and then play it on our guitar. In other words — TEACH YOURSELF GUITAR FROM FINISHED RECORDINGS. This is precisely the purpose of Window #23 Copy any Riff, Off any Record, Note for Note. It boils down to a process of identification, pure and simple. More later.

The term *absolute pitch* refers to the uncanny ability of some persons to immediately identify a single musical note, *upon blindly hearing the note sounded.* Also applies to those who can sing any note in the common musical range at will. You hear a lot of people who don't know what they're talking about say so-and-so has perfect pitch. Doubt it until you see so-and-so, with their back to the piano, identify a random note played from the piano keyboard. Yea means Yea.

The term *relative pitch* refers to the more common, and musically more valuable gift of being able to identify the pitch of one note in relation to another. This is the ability to determine intervals, the distance between notes, when you hear them. To the musician, relative pitch is just a few words that indicate a person's ability to know how to *bring in* the correct note (on a non-fixed note instrument, or with the voice) above or below notes already sounded. Once a song starts, you are in a particular key anyway, so relative pitch has to do with *where you finally decide* to place notes relative to the key note of the song. How close your choices are to the acoustically perfect points determines the first fiddler. A mark of the natural musician, having good relative pitch helps a bunch when it comes time to attempt the tuning of the six-string guitar. When you got it, you got it. When you don't got it, you can develop it. Practice makes perfect.

One more time, before we move on, *frequency* is the number of times per second that a sound-producing body vibrates, resulting in a train of pressure waves. *Melody* is a succession of musical tones. *Harmony* is the simultaneous occurance of musical tones. Most instruments produce, when sounding a seemingly single tone, a complex tone which is actually the *fundamental tone* (the one identified as the single tone, measured in hz) along with several *overtones* (higher exact multiples of the fundamental). *White noise* is the extremely complex sounding of multiple frequencies, whereby no single pitch is decernible and appears as a simple hiss to the human ear.

WAVELENGTH

The distance from a point in one compressional impulse, to the corresponding point in the next impulse is called the wavelength of a sound wave. Every different frequency level has its own corresponding wavelength. The formula for the numerical determination of the *actual physical dimension* of the sound-waves which are all around us is shown below. Hint: the lower the frequency, the longer the wavelength.

Speed of Sound ÷ Frequency = Wavelength

1100 ft/sec ÷ 440 cycles/sec = 2.5 feet/cycle (wavelength)

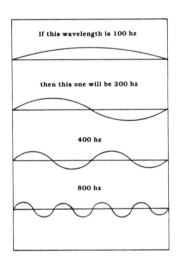

Every given pitch has its own specific wavelength, measured from one compressional peak to the next following peak.

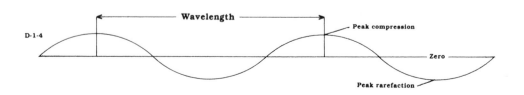

THE SIX OPEN STRINGS OF THE GUITAR

Alphabet Name	E	A	D	G	B	E
String Number	6	5	4	3	2	1
Frequency	82.41 hz	110.00 hz	146.83 hz	196.00 hz	246.94 hz	329.63 hz
Wavelength	13.34 ft.	10.00 ft.	7.49 ft.	5.61 ft.	4.45 ft.	3.33 ft.

Other Guys	Frequency	Wavelength
Low E String of Bass Guitar	41.20 hz	26.69 ft.
Middle C	261.63 hz	4.20 ft.
Universal Tuning A Note	440.00 hz	2.5 ft.
E Note on 1st String, 12th fret	659.26 hz	1.66 ft.
High Key Piano	4,186.01 hz	.26 ft.
Bat Echolocation	150,000.00 hz	.08 in.

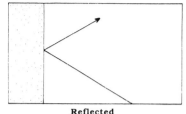

Reflected

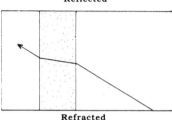

Refracted

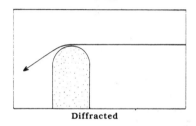

Diffracted

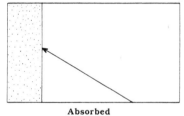

Absorbed

See what I mean now, your infiniteness? Each determined frequency level, each note, is really a *substantial invisible train of waves*. A guitar amplifier is, needless to say, a tremendous generator of such waves. Once you start to make them, what happens to them out in the air? For starters, they travel in spherical wavefronts away from the amplifier at the speed of sound. You see, acoustic waves have many of the same properties as a lot of other kinds of waves in this universe. Light waves, water waves, you know — they all have common wave properties. It just so happens that the Beatles, the Stones, Elvis, EVERYBODY, made sounds. Let's look at sound waves and what they do as they carry the message of rock to the receiver.

Sounds from your guitar (and all others) are:

A. Reflected — cast back from a surface
B. Refracted — bent as they pass into another medium
C. Diffracted — bend or spread out around obstacles in their path
D. Absorbed — taken in without echo, recoil or reflection (includes absorption into the air itself)

Sound waves usually do a little of a lot of different things all at once. In addition to the above list, sound waves also exhibit the properties of *constructive reinforcement* and *destructive interference* and are easily focused by their reflection off of a non-absorbing surface. Sound waves can be directed immediately after their emission from the speaker enclosure, or at a distance by a reflective concave wall which will cause the waves to converge. *Reverberation* is a sustaining short range echo effect caused by reflection, especially in large rooms. When specifically directed, high frequency (short wavelength) sounds tend to travel in direct beams, whereas lower frequencies are found to spread out in wide trajectories. If an object is placed in the way of a train of sound waves, some of the sound will be absorbed, some reflected, and some diffracted. If the wavelength of a sound wave is short in comparison with the object, the sound wave will be reflected or absorbed, leaving a ''shadow'' of reduced reception behind the obstacle. If the wavelength of a sound wave is longer than the obstacle, the sound will speed itself around the obstruction without much shadow or reflection. This is why on the way to the party from the car, you just hear the lower frequencies from the band making their way out of the house.

INTENSITY

The intensity, or volume, of a sound wave is measured by the fluctuation in pressure caused by the passing of a sound wave. The louder the sound, the greater the pressure of the wave front on the ear drum. The word *amplitude* is used to indicate the intensity, the wave power, the pressure variation which is translated into the sensation of loudness in the mind. Do remember though, that the pressure wave is carried through the air directly away from the sound source. Out *into* the air. Unlike water waves, whose actual height is measured, the amplitude of a sound wave is measured by the amount of the pressure in a longitudinally moving front.

The louder the sound, the more violent the action of the sound source against the surrounding air. Turn the lights up bright, get your guitar and pluck the low E string very lightly and take a *definite close look* at that wire shake. Stop the string. Hold the guitar so the string is right up in front of your eyes and pluck the string hard. See how the height of the arc of the singing string is *so much greater* when you pluck it hard. Over the twelfth fret, the area in which the string vibrates is clearly 3 or 4 times greater when the string is plucked hard. It also sounds a lot louder. Hmmmm. . . funny thing about that.

Yea, you have *to go to the sound source* in order to get at how intensity works. The louder the sound, the more violent the action of the source. Don't get this action mixed up with frequency. You can pick a guitar string hard or easy, but the frequency output (pitch) remains the same. The same thing goes for a loud speaker. If a speaker is producing a 440 hz tone and the volume knob is turned up, the throw of the speaker cone *in its mount* takes on greater proportions, moving greater amounts of air, but with a constant frequency of 440 cycles per second. The greater the intensity of a sound wave, the further that wave will travel in free air.

Intensity (loudness) is measured in *decibels*. The decibel is the unit of measurement that determines the fluctuation in air pressure caused by sound waves. The *wattage rating* that you find on many guitar amplifiers relates to the potential electrical power which may be used to drive the speakers. A word to the wise — be careful with the volume levels of the band. Don't overexpose yourself to *very loud* sounds lest you damage your ears. At least keep a good distance from all speakers if you have them really cranked. Let's keep it in the safe range, at least guys. O.K.

Amplitude, volume, intensity, call it what you will . . . very little compares to the amplitude of the sound wave created by a volcanic eruption on the island of Krakatoa, off the mainland of Indonesia. When this cat blew its top (1883), it threw rocks 34 miles into the air. And, according to the Guinness Book of World Records, the resulting sound wave was recorded *four hours later* on another island some 2,968 miles away as, now dig this, ''the roar of heavy guns!!!'' We're talking serious volume levels, here. I mean, this leaves Ted Nugent, Blue Cheer, Zepplin and Van Halen with the leaves gently tumbling through the woods.

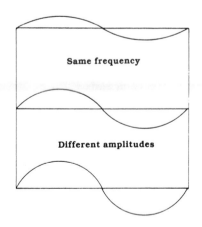

Same frequency

Different amplitudes

Sound Source	Decibles
Quiet whisper	10
Softest violin	25
Conversation	60
Loud factory	90
Thunder crack	110
Too much	120

THE ENVELOPE CURVE

One of the definitions in my dictionary of the word *envelope* reads "to cover entirely." The envelope curve is a charted line, figured on the Cartesian double coordinate system (x, y axis, also used for sine wave representations), which sound engineers use to look at the level of intensity or "tonal response" of a musical sound over its entire duration. The idea is basically to chart a note, or complex musical sound, with the vertical axis measuring the intensity of the sound, with the horizontal axis measuring the passage of time. Even though you can say that all the envelope curve indicates is volume over time, it really does more than that. It describes how the note plays itself out revealing the nature of its manifestation. Below, find a typical envelope curve for a musical sound along with descriptions of its parts.

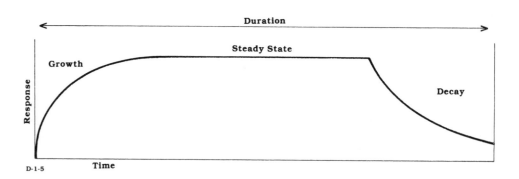

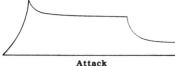

Attack

Delayed Attack

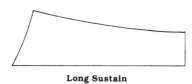

Long Sustain

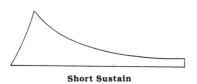

Short Sustain

Overdriven Signal

GROWTH

The growth period is the initial development of the sound, when it first swells into existence. This time interval can vary between immediate and noticeably delayed. This is the character of the response *right off the bat.*

STEADY STATE

This is when the physical energy driving the sound source IS SPENT. Rock guitarists set their amps to just push the constant signal any way — straight across the top. Distortion, sustain and feedback can be a way of life. One note, put a major triad on top of it and you have the components. Steady state, when it is level across the top. A *definite take* on the frequency of the vibration. Guess what's next?

DECAY

Got to get away. Yea, she is falling fast or slow, it all depends on the envelope curve. The intensity of the sound waves produced by an acoustic guitar begin to decay immediately after the first breath breathed into the string from the pick. The electric guitar, at least the way I prefer to play it (through a distortion box through a pignose amp at full volume) does not decay. So there is the difference.

DURATION

Duration is the length of time that a sound continues without interruption in its output. Some instruments can *hold* a note for any chosen time period (violin, saxophone) while others are sounded by the striking or plucking of a string which quickly starts to decay (piano, acoustic guitar). The Axe of Axes (electric guitar) is, naturally, the best of both worlds. Clean at mid-volume, the electric guitar can produce an envelope curve similar to an acoustic guitar. The overdriven electric guitar, the mark of great rock, sustains sounds until the guitarist decides to go on. The envelope curve of a sustained high-gain signal has an immediate growth period with a straight line steady state period. The line drops as quickly as it ascended, not to indicate decay, but the *chosen end.* The standard quarter note system directly ties the duration of a note with the meter or beat of the music.

The variety of possibilities of the envelope curve is staggering, and through necessity and experimentation, is constantly being explored. We have a Casio 1000 keyboard in our music studio and the thing gets 1000 different combinations of tonal quality, including your choice of ten different envelope curves at the press of a button. Obviously, we will be fooling around trying to understand the instrument for quite some time. *How do envelope curves differ?* Well, your guitar sounds different from day to day, *right?* Were you ever disappointed in a live recording because it didn't live up to the studio record? Did you ever consider the artist who can't duplicate it? What a jam, I can't duplicate the sound today!! Not the same envelope curve!!

PORTAMENTO

This is an Italian word that literally means the "act of carrying." To us it means the continuous gliding movement from one tone into another. The graphic representation of portamento shows *frequency* on the vertical axis, with a time line as the horizontal axis. Forget official definitions. Just imagine a note sounding. One easy note. You could take it up to the next note in the scale *on a slide* if you were playing a violin. Sliding trombone, same deal. Electric guitar — sound a fretted note and bend (a half-step is a little, a whole step is a lot, a step-and-a-half is pushing hard). Or if you really want to vary the frequency, hit an open string on the electric, pick up a harmonic, and go down on the *waa bar.* Wow, that's heavy. Sorry, piano players, no go.

Portamento

VIBRATO

Technically, vibrato is the extremely small, yet noticeable, wavering of pitch produced by the quick, regular movement of the left hand finger on the fretted string. Functionally, vibrato is the conscientious rocking of the finger on the singing string along the direction of the string. This causes a delightful fluctuation in both frequency and intensity (between 3 and 6 times a second) which allows artists to demonstrate emotional expression in their playing. Vibrato can add character to the singer's voice if used sparingly, and can bring that special halting, vacillating quality to any musical tone. *Tremolo* is a term that has two different meanings. Firstly, it is used to describe an exaggerated vibrato technique which sounds like a frequency wobble. Secondly, it means the rapid repitition of one note (perhaps with the up and down movement of the pick) sounding the rapid reiteration of a single tone.

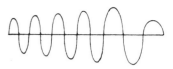

Amplitude modulation

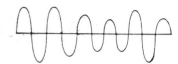

Frequency modulation

TIMBRE

As stated before, pure musical tones are rare. Just like life, musical tones just aren't that simple. Nature always arranges for things to seem simple at first, then upon a second deeper look, perplexingly complex. *Then*, after all the facts are in and considered, the clouds part and it dawns on you that nature builds very complex systems in very simple ways, *always* making the option for the most basic possible way. A light suddenly comes on in your head — *"it's not so confusing after all. I couldn't have thought of a better way myself!!"* So, it is with the way a guitar string vibrates. The vibration of the full length of the string is the primary mode of string vibration referred to as the <u>fundamental</u>. This provides us with the fundamental frequency, which invariably results in the fundamental tone. Seems simple enough. Thing is, in addition to vibrating in its overall length, the singing string also vibrates in halfs, thirds, fourths, fifths, etc. Now comes the part where it seems perplexingly complex. When the string vibrates in half, one half moves up, the other down. Extrapolate this to thirds, fourths, fifths, etc., and consider that all of this vibration takes place on a single string *at the same time*. Talk about complex. And you are stuck with this mess — like it or not. It is the way guitar strings work. Too late now, no way to change it.

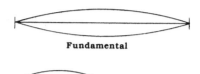

Fundamental

First Overtone

The vibratory modes other than the fundamental are called *overtones, harmonies,* or *upper partials* (more on these later). The frequencies produced by the overtone series are, as you might expect, exact multiples of the fundamental frequency (1F, 2F, 3F, 4F, etc.). Each overtone produces its own subtle tone which is acoustically and mathematically related to the fundamental. Because the intensity of the overtone series is much less than the fundamental, the ear tends to hear all of the string's simultaneously sounding frequencies as a single tone; the fundamental enriched with other natural overtones.

Second Overtone

The way it works out, all musical instruments (wind included, some electronic keyboards excluded) produce complex musical tones which are composite. Each instrument distributes its vibratory energy to produce its own specific variety of overtone volumes. This distinct mixture of overtone soundings gives each instrument its own characteristic *tone color, timbre* or *quality.* Each individual guitar has its own unique timbre. Everything about the guitar makes a difference; the construction, the wood, the hardware, the strings, even the performer and how he fingers the strings, can positively affect the timbre of the note produced. Helps to know your chops, too. More later.

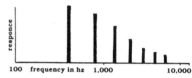

Fundamental with first two overtones

The Overtone Series

That about does it for the characteristics of a musical tone. Just a word before we move on to other pieces of The Big Picture. With the exception of duration, all of the above listed characteristics are constantly influencing each other. These qualities cannot be separated from each other in performance, only in consideration. After all is said and done, it is the sensitivity of the performer that brings all of these qualities together into a useful vehicle. Although it doesn't seem like it, all music has these described characteristics as a common base. The reason I bothered to go over them one by one is so you can now go forth knowing the forces that create all music.

It is not my purpose to teach how to read music, or the elements of the common five line staff. There are hundreds of good music books that already *do just that.* If you are not familiar with the basics (which is all you need here), I would strongly suggest looking up the term *music* in any decent encyclopedia in any library. Just walk into the general reference room and pick up volume M of the *Encyclopedia Britannica,* and for a few dimes, you can Xerox what you need and go home. Here you will find a seemingly endless discourse on clefs, time signatures, notes, rests, accidentals, ties, dots, etc. — all presented in a strictly formal, absolutely correct format, far beyond the capabilities or desires of this old heavy metal barnstormer. While we are on the subject of reference, my highest recommendation goes out to *The Harvard Brief Dictionary of Music.* This gem of a music book has been a tremendous help to me in writing on the subject of music. This little guy, conveniently arranged from A to Z, is the last word on anything that has to do with formally catagorized musical information, and is now out in cheap paperback. Oh, by the way, *The New Grove Dictionary of Music and Musicians* (20 volumes), contains over 22-million words and 4,500 illustrations and is the largest special subject dictionary yet published.

STATION POINT ZERO —
THE ESTABLISHMENT OF THE TONIC NOTE

We already know that the frequency range of music is a huge, unbroken sweeping spectrum of sound frequencies, all with corresponding wavelengths. Somewhere along the line we have to stop at one point and say, "Here is the note upon which we will *start to build*. Here is the place from which all other notes will assume a relative position." We will use the note with the frequency 440 hz (A above middle C). The first note of a musical scale is called the *tonic, key note, root note,* or simply *the first.*

OCTAVES

What do you do after you established one note? You decide to enter the world of considering two notes, that's what. *With this territory* comes the consideration of the interval: the measured distance between two notes. The second most important musical note that I want you to consider is the tone which takes its position on the frequency scale *precisely one octave* above the tonic. The frequency of this new note is determined by *doubling the frequency* of the original tonic. So, if the tonic tone that we started with is A-440, then the next higher octave of this note is an A-880. The magical thing about the octave note is that, although it occupies a position considerably higher in frequency (2X) than the original tone, *the upper tone marks the establishment of a second tonic note.*

Doubling the frequency of any note produces the upper octave of the original note.

What happens when the two notes are sounded together in a harmonic relationship? Well it is hard to put into words, this aural sensation. When sounded simultaneously, the two notes seem mysteriously identical to the listener, yet each note takes its respective position on two different parts of the musical range, one above the other. How can a note be the same yet different? It is evident that the octave is some sort of musical boundary. It defines a musical realm, a performing arena, a closed domain, a provincial orbit, in which the musician travels. The doubling of the fundamental frequency of any note provides us with this basic musical measurement. You work in octaves, you play in octaves. The guitar can play four, the piano can reach seven and a third, the saxophone plays just over two and a half. Try to sing three octaves — don't strain.

Octaves of A

110   220   440   880

The whole secret behind being dangerous on rock guitar is knowing how you want to divide up any *one example octave*, at any given time, and apply the resulting interval pattern across all of the guitar's playable octaves (6 strings, 24 frets). Musicologists have always been at somewhat of a loss to actually explain why the ear hears octaves the way it does. We already sort of understand how. Double or half the frequency for starters, that always makes octaves happen. When I wrote Jimi Hendrix-Note for Note, I used a three-speed reel-to-reel recorder to slow down Jimi's music to half-speed. This resulted in Jimi's guitarwork coming out of the speakers one octave lower than the original recording, and at half the normal breakneck speed.

Successive octave E notes on the guitar take place on 6/0, 4/2, 1/0, 1/12, 1/24.

Just like clockwork, every time you double or half the frequency of a fixed tone, you arrive at an octave mark of the original note. I give no undue importance to the upper octave mark. The lower octave of 440 hz is 220 hz. The same rules apply to the lower realm. If you continue to double or half the frequency again and again, all of the acoustic octaves will manifest themselves. These specific divisions will be found to encompass the entire range of human hearing (10 octaves) and also that of the musical range (approximately 7 octaves). Picture it, the whole range divided into octaves. It is tempting to say octaves are strictly "identical" to each other. Thing is, each progressive octave covers twice as many frequency cycles in its range. There is an entire octave between 20 hz and 40 hz. There is also an octave between 10,000 hz and 20,000 hz. Hardly identical.

Octave

1	2	3	4	5	6	7	8	9	10	11
20	40	80	160	320	640	1280	2560	5120	10,240	20,480

Cycles per second   D-1-6

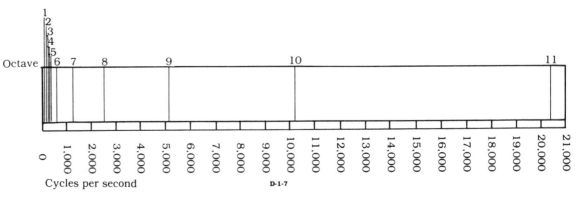

Cycles per second   D-1-7

If we know all this about how octaves work, why then are we not sure of why? The musical dictionary explains the octave to be "the most perfect consonance, so perfect indeed that it gives the impression of being a mere duplication of the original tone." Still no reason why. Oh well, just do what all musicians do — just take it for granted and go with it. The octave is the first interval, the next interval to be considered will be the first slice of the octave. All together now: *what do we know for sure?* WE KNOW that in order to arrive at the upper octave mark of a fundamental tone, the applicable formula is 2 X F, or simply 2 F.

Octaves will be shown to break down into proportionately "identical" divisions. These will provide for us equally comparable scale degrees for all octaves. The upper octaves of the piano are mapped out in twelve notes to the octave, measured in the same size piano keys that produce the scale degrees of the lower octaves. The six strings of the guitar, when considered open, carry the ball through two octaves from a low E string producing a frequency of 82.41 hz, all the way through to the thin high E string of 329.63 hz (double 82.41 hz twice). You can register two more octaves above this point by running your finger up the thin string over the progressively closer frets until you arrive at number 24. At this point you can produce a crowning E note of 1318.51 hz (double 329.63 twice). So we mark the passage of the octaves.

THE MONOCHORD

Way back in the Middle Ages, the Germans came up with this apparatus called a *monochord* which consisted of a single fixed string stretched over a long wooden box. The string was fixed over two bridges at either end of the box; but what made the instrument unique was that it had a *single moveable fret*. This simple little box allowed the music teacher to demonstrate *two equally important* principles to the student. First off, he could use the monochord to produce examples of harmonic overtones. By lightly touching the string at just the right spot (called a node), the fundamental vibration is damped out and the pitch of a chosen overtone is accented. Secondly, the teacher could use the movable fret to demonstrate the relationship between string length and frequency.

Let's look at the fundamental mode of vibration of the fixed string of a monochord (or stratocaster for that matter).

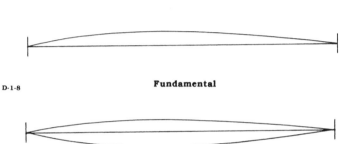

D-1-8   Fundamental

Now that we have that over with, and you understand that the fundamental is the identifiable pitch and measured in hertz, we will proceed to the string shaking in halfs. This is the way the string vibrates when it produces the *first overtone*. This book always uses the term *overtone*, because it directly refers to a tone somewhere "over" the fundamental. The term *harmonic* is also commonly used, but, wouldn't you know it, they call the fundamental the first harmonic, so the first overtone is the second harmonic. Shall we!!!

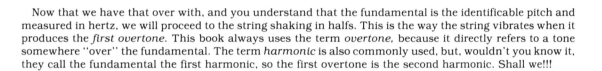

D-1-9   First Overtone

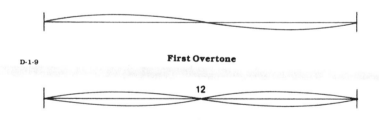

12

Don't forget all of the things that a tone has (frequency, intensity, envelope curve characteristics, etc.). When you study a single overtone, you do not consider timbre, because you are looking at one pure tone; it is a combination of overtones which determines timbre. The progressive frequencies of the overtone series are 2F, 3F, 4F, 5F, etc. If the fundamental is 440 hz, then the first overtone is 880 hz. Does this double business sound familiar? You know that IF YOU DOUBLE THE FREQUENCY, YOU GET THE OCTAVE!!! The first overtone produces a tone one octave above the fundamental.

Node time. A node is a divisional point along the string's length where the string seemingly stays still, that is, in the same line it would be in if the string were not sounded, while the regular up and down movement of the string takes place between nodal points. An anti-node is positioned halfway between nodes and represents the place where the string's vibrational movement is greatest. As you might suspect, the first overtone is so basic that it is the one and only overtone which has a single central node in its makeup. This, of course, is halfway along the string's length (over the twelfth fret to you). Look for the double dot at that twelfth fret and live it. Relish the fact that the simplest string division takes place at this point. As we get into this, you will find this point to be a very important crossroads for the guitar player. One which will never change.

If you pluck any one of the open strings of your guitar and touch the string lightly, not down to the fret, but enough to quiet the fundamental which reaches its *anti-node* at this particular point, you will find that your guitar will sound an octave note above the open string sound. WE'RE TALKING AN ACOUSTICALLY PERFECT OCTAVE HERE, AND HERE COMES THE MOST AMAZING MIRACLE FACT: ONE YOU DON'T HAVE TO TUNE.

The first overtone is one octave higher than the fundamental tone.

What happens if we move the fret to the point directly under the single node of the first overtone and bring the string down onto the fret and pluck the string? Take a look at the diagram below and check out how the string length is divided.

D-1-10

Fixed string fretted at the node of first overtone

Pretty direct stuff, huh? Can you see that cutting the string's length in half with the fret and plucking the string will result in the identical tone produced by the first overtone, and that this tone will be one octave above the fundamental? *Of course, they can see this!!! Hey, they aren't in first grade, Richard. I mean, THEY ALREADY KNOW THIS STUFF. They already know that doubling or halfing any string length will result in the production of a tone precisely one octave lower or higher than the original tone. They already know that when a string is fretted at the twelfth fret and plucked, that the fundamental vibration of the shortened string is identical in pitch and string length to either one of the first overtone's vibration cycles. They already know that the first overtone of a string fretted at the twelfth fret will be two octaves above the open string's fundamental note. THEY ALREADY KNOW ALL ABOUT IT.* Let us proceed to the second overtone where the string shakes in thirds.

THE DOMINANT

A single vibrating string provides us with a multitude of musical phenomena. These include the fundamental note (the tonic), the octave above the fundamental note (the first overtone), and as we are about to find out, the primary musical divisional tones of the octave, eventually providing us with the basic components of the major chord, and major scale. Think of *each* of the six strings of your guitar as capable of producing a *virtual chorus* of simultaneously sounding, inherently related notes.

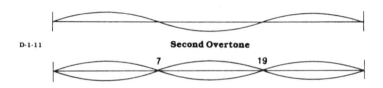

D-1-11

Second Overtone

7   19

Three is the recurring number associated with the second overtone. The string vibrates in thirds creating three complete vibratory lengths, each employing one-third the full string length of the fundamental, all with a frequency three times the fundamental (3F). Unlike the first overtone, which has only one central free node, the second overtone has two free nodes the same distance from each other as from either fixed end. This results in an "inner" vibratory cycle being defined only by nodes, free from either fixed end of the string. These two nodes provide us with *two independent places* from which to accent the second overtone. On the guitar, these two nodes appear over the 7th and 19th fret. The *same tone* is produced by lightly touching the singing string above *either of the two nodes.* At first glance, it seems to go against our learned experience to find that we can produce the same tone at two different places along a single string. But look at it closely, we are not talking about fretting the string here, only touching the string lightly to cancel the other modes of vibration. *Live with the facts:* the second overtone is produced over the 7th and 19th frets.

The frequency of the second overtone is three times that of the fundamental. This means if the fundamental is 100, the first overtone will be 200, and the second overtone will be 300. The overtone series provides us with consistently higher frequencies which produce tones *on or in* the octaves above the fundamental. The second overtone provides us with the second most basic scale degree of the major scale, the dominant tone. Here is our first peek at a major scale degree other than the tonic. Don't think that it is an accident that it is first to appear, or that it is called the DOMINANT. Just like the octave of the fundamental is provided by the first overtone, the tone and division of the octave provided by the second overtone is both acoustically perfect and naturally occurring. In order for us to understand how the dominant divides any and all octaves, just for kicks, lets establish the fundamental frequency of an open string at 100 hz. The first overtone octave will check in at 200 hz, and the second overtone dominant tone will divide the octave between 200 hz and 400 hz at precisely 300 hz. Here is how it breaks down:

The second overtone produces the dominant tone, one fifth above the octave of the fundamental sounded by the first overtone.

Vibratory Mode	Open String	First Overtone	Second Overtone	Third Overtone
	Full String	Halfs	Thirds	Fourths
Frequency	100 hz	200 hz	300 hz	400 hz
Tone	The Fundamental	1st Octave	Dominant	2nd Octave

I jumped ahead a little and presented you with the fact that the third overtone produces a note two octaves above the fundamental. This overtone, which vibrates the string length in fourths, will be studied in the section labeled Mediant. So you see, the dominant divides the second octave above the fundamental. Using the way this single octave was divided by nature, we can come up with a universal ratio figure that we can use to find the position of this particular scale degree *between any two octave frequencies*.

3/2

So, we get this wierd top heavy fraction. But the thing works every time. Just multiply it by an established tonic frequency, and you will get the upper fifth. It is simple as that. If the tonic note is 440 hz, (with an upper octave of 880 hz), the dominant between is going to be:

440 x 3/2 = 660 hz

And what Ludwig could do with a dominant note. He worked it against the tonic just right, boy, just like Led Zep. Truth is they both did. Both used, more than likely without conscious knowledge of doing so, this very simple ratio figure to determine an acousticly perfect specimen of the dominant type. Yea.

Let's dust off the monochord and see what happens if we move the fret to under the first node (the one on the left) and we'll see what happens. This will divide the working string length to 2/3 of the full fundamental length. To get two birds with one stone, we will also look at the fret moved to the position under the second node (the one on the bottom).

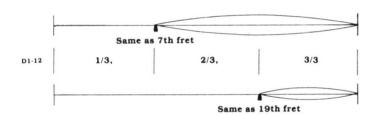

Same as 7th fret

D1-12 | 1/3, | 2/3, | 3/3

Same as 19th fret

The diagram on the top shows the fundamental mode of string vibration when a string is shortened by one-third of its total length with the use of a fret. This is the same thing as fretting a guitar string at the 7th fret. In this position, the fundamental string length of the fretted string is twice as long as any one of the three vibrating lengths of the second overtone. For this reason, the pitch of the tone produced from this fretted string will be a dominant tone one octave below that of the second overtone.

The diagram on the bottom shows how the fundamental works for the fretted string which cuts off two-thirds of the string's full length. In this case, which is the same as fretting a guitar string at the 19th fret, the fundamental of the vibrating string will be the same length as any one of the three vibrating lengths of the second overtone. For this reason (just like at the twelfth fret), the note you sound with the harmonic technique (lightly touching the singing string) over the 19th fret, will be the identical dominant note you would get if you were to fret and pluck.

Wait a minute, we keep talking about where the dominant is, and how it is derived, *but what is the dominant tone?* It is the first natural division of the octave. It occupies the most commanding position, next to the tonic, of all major scale degrees, of which it is the fifth. It plays against the tonic with determined relativity. There is a ying/yang relationship between these two most important scale degrees. When a melody line moves towards the dominant, it is said to be *resolved*. But after resolution, its usually right back to the tonic again. The harmonic relationship between the first (tonic) and the fifth (dominant) is the backbone of all rock's dynamic power chords, and as nature would have it, the base of the major chord. Even lead guitar is founded around the sounding of these two notes. When you hear the beginning of Johnny Be Goode, that little triplet opens it up, but then you get that double thin string repitition. It's just 5,1...5,1...5,1 again and again. That single chord that is repeatedly pounded through Whole Lotta Love, it's 1,5...1,5...on and on. The opening chord of Honky Tonk Woman — same thing. This note called the dominant — YOU LIVE WITH IT!!!

RING THE HARMONIC, OR FRET THE NOTE

What's shaking *naturally?* The fundamental (100 hz), the first overtone (octave of the fundamental, 200 hz), the second overtone (dominant tone above the first overtone, 300 hz), and the third overtone (string shakes in quarters producing the note two octaves above the fundamental, 400 hz).

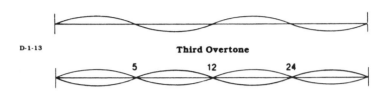

D-1-13　　　　　　　　　　　　**Third Overtone**

The third overtone, with a free node over the fifth fret, sounds the double octave of the fundamental produced by the full string length.

Here we go again. This time we have three free nodes with which to contend. These three nodes are positioned above the 5th, 12th and 24th frets (most strats have 21 frets). The common place to bring out this overtone is at the node over the fifth fret. As you may have noticed by looking at the harmonic overtone fretboard diagram on the wall poster (the fretboard that runs vertically on the right side of the poster), the twelfth fret is an intersection of overlapping nodes for several modes of string vibration. In a case like this, THE LOWER OVERTONE ALWAYS PREDOMINATES WHEN SOUNDED. Just like the fundamental hogs the scene when you just pluck the string open, the amplitude of the first harmonic will override all other common overtones having a node at the twelfth fret. This same thing happens wherever nodes overlap — the lower overtone takes the note. So much for the 12th fret.

The node over the 24th fret produces the *double octave* the same way as the node over the fifth fret. Trouble is, at the 24th fret, it is difficult to bring out the overtone if you touch the string and pluck it at the same time (immediately removing the finger). This is the most common way rock guitarists sound a chosen harmonic overtone. You can pluck the string open and *then* lightly touch the node with good results at this high position, but touching and plucking simultaneously is rough because you are setting only one quarter of the string's length into action.

What happens when you fret at the three nodal points of the third overtone? Well, things were simple back at the first overtone when the accented overtone produced the same note as the fretted string at the twelfth fret, but those idyllic days are gone. Fretting at the fifth fret, the site of the first node of the third overtone, will sound the fourth of the major scale above the fundamental — a tone not immediately relative to the third overtone. We already talked about what happens over and on the twelfth fret. The 24th fret, the third nodal position of the third overtone, is the last place on your guitar, along with the 12th and the 19th frets below, that you will be able to play either the accented overtone or the fretted string and produce the same pitch.

When a string is fretted, it immediately starts to shake in halves, thirds, fourths, etc., at the shortened length.

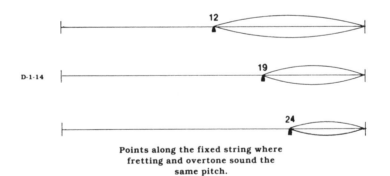

D-1-14

Points along the fixed string where
fretting and overtone sound the
same pitch.

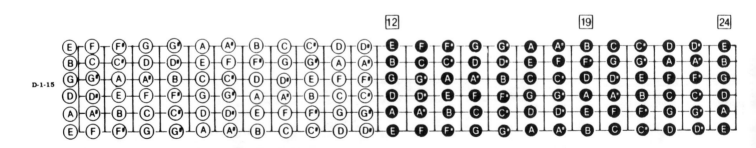

D-1-15

THE MEDIANT

We have been removing the veils from the mystery of the vibrating string *one by one.* Just like at the movies, in order to actually get to see the mummy walking around, you have to wait through an hour of eating popcorn and watching them get to the castle. Well, your hour is up! Now you will find out that the fourth overtone, produced when a fixed string shakes in fifths, will provide us with (in addition to the tonic and the dominant) a third vital component from which we can construct *all of the degrees* of the major scale — the basic vehicle of western music.

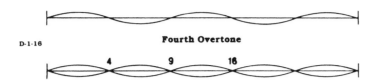

D-1-16

Fourth Overtone

4   9   16

As you can see, there are four nodal points along the length of the string. The number of free nodes always goes along with the numbered name of the overtone. For instance, the fourth overtone has four nodes, the fifth has five, etc. Simple but true. The more we study, the more complex the story gets. So if you can't take the heat, get out of the kitchen and I'll see you playing guitar for the Partridge Family in a few years, okay???

Now, if you set up the single string on a monochord to play 100 hz, the first overtone would be the first octave at 200 hz, and the 300 hz second overtone would be the dominant tone between the 200/400 octave, the upper figure being provided by the third overtone. So what is with 500 hz? Well, this is the frequency produced by the fourth overtone when the fundamental is 100 hz. Yes, five times the frequency of the whole string, with five separate cycles of up and down motion. The importance of this frequency is that it divides the octave between 400 hz and 800 hz (the second octave above the fundamental) in its own inimitable, inevitable, invincible, and individual way just like big brother dominant divided the octave between 200 hz and 400 hz. *Get the picture* — creak, shrink, clang, clank, out of the dark comes not the mummy but, but ... no, it can't be ... it's the MEDIANT, the THIRD. Oh noooooo.

Sorry, it's too late now. The components of the major chord are the tonic, the mediant, and the dominant, better known as the first, the third and the fifth. If the mediant is 500 hz, and the tonic frequency below this intraoctave division is 400 hz, then the universal ratio number to be multiplied against any tonic frequency is:

$$100 \text{ hz} / 100 \text{ hz} \div 500 \text{ hz} / 400 \text{ hz}$$

For instance, if the tonic note is 400 hz, the mediant note is:

$$400 \text{ hz} \times 5/4 = 500 \text{ hz}$$

If the tonic is 440 hz, the mediant will be:

$$440 \text{ hz} \times 5/4 = 550 \text{ hz}$$

Why do we call this elemental octave division the mediant? *Because* it divides the difference in frequency between the tonic and the dominant in half. If the tonic is established at 100 hz, with an upper octave of 200 hz, the dominant tone will check in at 150 hz (100 hz x 3/2 = 150 hz). This is half-way between the two octave marks. The mediant checks in at 125 hz (100 hz x 5/4 = 125 hz), half-way between the tonic and the dominant. This is easy to see on paper, but when we deal with a fixed string, we always have to deal with a sliding proportion of ever-decreasing measured space. Let's just say that it was up to you to place the guitar frets on an uncut fretboard. You have to do it right the first time without any mistakes. Well, the first rule to cut the string length in half produces the octave of the open string's tone, so you definitely put a fret under this half-way mark. Then you measure the distance from this fret to the bridge (half the string's length), and again divide this in half and place your second octave fret at this position. Even though you *can* further divide this interval again and again into halfs, things get entirely too tiny after the second octave fret. Besides, where could we put the big bad high output pickups if you went any further?

The fourth overtone produces the mediant tone, one third above the double octave of the fundamental produced by the third overtone.

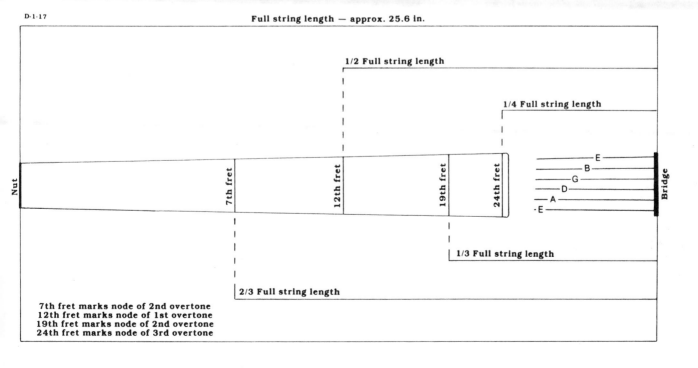

D-1-17

Full string length — approx. 25.6 in.

1/2 Full string length

1/4 Full string length

Nut

7th fret

12th fret

19th fret

24th fret

E
B
G
D
A
E

Bridge

1/3 Full string length

2/3 Full string length

7th fret marks node of 2nd overtone
12th fret marks node of 1st overtone
19th fret marks node of 2nd overtone
24th fret marks node of 3rd overtone

In order to establish the position of the lower dominant fret (7th fret), you measure the distance along the string between the nut and the half-way mark (12th fret) and divide that distance by 3/2; same thing goes for the mediant at 5/4. To divide the upper octave, you start with the distance between the 12th and 24th frets, or one quarter of the string's full length. You see, these universal ratio numbers are used for multiplication against any tonic frequency, but are also used to determine the physical placement of frets, and also, incidently, the length of organ pipes and valves in horns. Are you beginning to see The Big Picture?

JUST INTONATION

So what we got? By now, everybody already knows that the simple breakdown of a single string's vibration offers up to the musician the fundamental (1/1, and upper octaves 2/1, 4/1, 8/1), the mediant (5/4), and the dominant (3/2). If we already know the BIG THREE (the first, the third and the fifth), how do we arrive at the famous seven degree major scale. Well, the BIG THREE Just happen to be the components of the major triad or chord. The way it works out, the other four degrees which make up the major scale are multiples of the BIG THREE. The tonic is the first. The second of the major scale is actually a double fifth, obtained by taking the ratio of the dominant fifth (3/2) and multiplying it by itself (3/2 x 3/2 = 9/4). This figure of 9/4 represents a frequency in the octave above the tonic, so in order to bring the dude down an octave, we divide by 2 (9/4 ÷ 2/1 = 9/8) providing us with a universal ratio figure of 9/8 for the second or supertonic.

The third is spoken for. The fourth of the major scale is often misunderstood because of its name, the subdominant. You know, most people would think that the name comes from being the degree directly under the dominant. Truth is, this note earns its handle by being a dominant fifth *below* the tonic (2/1 ÷ 3/2 = 4/3). So the universal ratio number for the subdominant fourth is 4/3. The dominant fifth is also spoken for. So what about the sixth? Well, the sixth, also called the submediant or the superdominant, is derived by multiplying the ratio for the third (5/4) by the ratio of the fourth (4/3). By doing so (5/4 x 4/3 = 20/12 = 5/3), we arrive at the figure 5/3, the corresponding ratio for the sixth. How about the last and lonely seventh, the little major scale degree that went weeeee all the way home? Just take the dominant (3/2) and build an interval of a mediant (5/4) on top of it and we come up with (3/2 x 5/4 = 15/8) the figure 15/8 the ratio for the seventh, leading tone, or subtonic. Here is the bottom line:

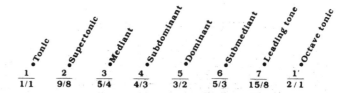

•Tonic	•Supertonic	•Mediant	•Subdominant	•Dominant	•Submediant	•Leading tone	•Octave tonic
1	2	3	4	5	6	7	1'
1/1	9/8	5/4	4/3	3/2	5/3	15/8	2/1

Look, here is another way of seeing it: all seven major scale degrees can be obtained from the building of three consecutive identical triads. Each of the three triads will be the major triad (1, 5/4, 3/2 = 4/4, 5/4, 6/4) taken from the overtone series of the guitar string. We start with the middle triad and build additional triads above and below the outer degrees (the first and fifth) of the center triad. Although not in numberical order, all seven scale degrees of the major scale can be derived in this fashion.

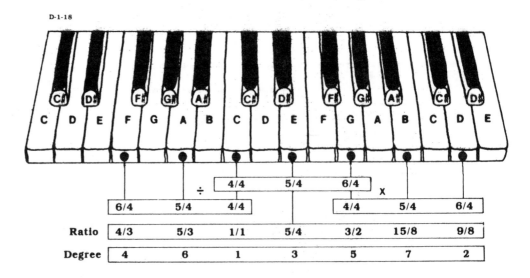

D-1-18

This method of deriving the major scale is called *just intonation* because of its "accoustically pure" intervals and tonal characteristics. After all is said and done, we can take the seven degrees, place them in order and study how the major scale degrees divide the octave. At this point, something very interesting first becomes evident. When we look at the distance between the major scale degrees we come up with THREE DIFFERENT SIZE INTERVALS.

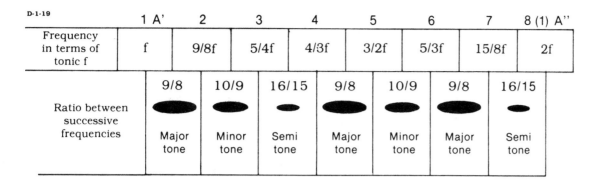

D-1-19

Frequency in terms of tonic f	f	9/8f	5/4f	4/3f	3/2f	5/3f	15/8f	2f
	1 A'	2	3	4	5	6	7	8 (1) A''

Ratio between successive frequencies	9/8 Major tone	10/9 Minor tone	16/15 Semi tone	9/8 Major tone	10/9 Minor tone	9/8 Major tone	16/15 Semi tone

1	Major	2	Minor	3	Semitone	4	Major	5	Minor	6	Major	7	Semitone	1
	204 cents		182		112		204		182		204		112	

1200 cents = 1 octave

For years and years all I ever heard from music teachers was that the major scale was built from either whole steps (2 frets) or half steps (1 fret). After checking the facts on my own, I dug up the truth, and was surprised that my teachers either overlooked pure intervals or were ignorant of them. I believe that it is important for all musicians to know the facts, if for no other reason than to know the difference between pure and adulterated tones. There is, however, a functional reason that I explain this phenomenon to the guitar student. And that is, that, for the rest of your life, you may understand the true difference inherent in *tuning the fixed fret six string guitar.* More shortly. For now, *witness below* the octave divided by the three intervals of just intonation. The measurement unit of "cents" has been used to equally divide the octave into 1200 equal tonal increments. The advantage of using cents is that, unlike units of frequency and linear string measurement, you can set the tonic to zero and not hassle with upper or lower octaves, or building in halfs. The veils are off, check out the difference in the length of the three pure intervals.

D-1-20

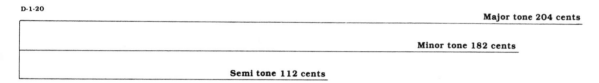

Major tone 204 cents

Minor tone 182 cents

Semi tone 112 cents

You see, the major and minor tones are practically, but not actually, the same size. The semitone is practically, but not actually, half the size of either of the larger tones. There are three. *It was from this system* that the present *half note/whole note* system evolved. You know, the invention of the musical scale took place well before its use in harmonic composition. Matter of fact, before the 11th century, linear melodic composition was the only musical form. You can get away with singing successive just intervals, and even build on secondary degrees, without adverse consequence because you simply "go to" the right note with the voice. The same ease of playing pure intervals is experienced by any "unfixed" instrument like the sliding trombone, etc. The earliest melodic interval was created, no doubt, by some guy "holding a note" of a line in progress, as another musician proceeded with the same melody. Still no problem. The wrench drops into the works when you fix an instrument to play with just intervals, and then try to build on degrees other than the tonic. Those two different whole note sizes create an unresolvably sticky wicket.

Try to use it for the fixed intervals of a guitar or piano and you quickly find all sorts of irregularities mounting up. What is perfect for dividing the octave up between two octave points is not perfect for the divisions themselves. Necessity really is the mother of invention. When the instrument designers ran up against this problem in the 17th century, the human mind went to work and came up with, what else — A CHEATER SYSTEM.

Tape Side	Window
1 A	1
1 B	1 cont. 2, 3
2 A	4, 5, 6
2 B	6 cont. 7, 8
3 A	8 cont. 9
3 B	9 cont. 10, 11, 12, 13
4 A	14, 15, 16, 17
4 B	18, 19, 20
5 A	20 cont. 21, 22
5 B	22 cont.
6 A	23, 24
6 B	24 cont.

EQUAL TEMPERAMENT

The word *intone* means true to the pure tone. The word *temper* means to adjust to the needs of a situation. *Equal temperament* is the process of slightly modifying the musical intervals of the pure scale to produce *a set of 12 equally spaced tones to the octave* which enable the fixed note instrument to play in all 12 possible keys. After fooling around with an inadequate system called meantone, which allowed the musician to play in a few basic keys, some guy named Andres Werkmeister invented the equal tempered system in 1690. This arrangement of tuning allowed for transposition (changing an entire piece to another key) and modulation (changing key within a piece) and was brought into popularity by Bach's <u>Well Tempered Clavichord</u> (1722).

Equal temperament represents the perfect marriage of the three different size intervals of the just system. The two larger intervals (204 and 182 cents) are brought together to form a single common interval of 200 cents. This makes the familiar WHOLE STEP. The semi tone from the just system (112 cents) was rounded off to the value of 100 cents. Here we have the establishment of the HALF STEP, the smallest common interval of western music.

D-1-21

Just Intonation

| | Semitone | | Minor tone | Major tone |

0 cents · **Equal Temperament** · 112 cents · 182 cents · 204 cents

Half-step · Whole-step

0 cents · 100 cents · 200 cents

| 1 | 2 | 3 | 4 | 5 | 6 | 7 | 1-8 |

0 cents 100 200 300 400 500 600 700 800 900 1000 1100 1200

D-1-22

Note	A	B	C	D	E	F	G	A
	Tonic	Supertonic	Mediant	Subdominant	Dominant	Submediant	Leading Tone	Tonic
Just Intonation								
Frequency, Hz	440	495	550	586	660	733	825	880
Frequency ratio	1/1	9/8	5/4	4/3	3/2	5/3	15/8	2/1
Interval, cents	0	204	386	498	702	884	1088	1200
Equal Temperament								
Frequency, Hz	440	493	554	587	659	734	830	880
Frequency, ratio	1.000	1.1225	1.2599	1.3348	1.4983	1.6818	1.8877	2.000
Interval, cents	0	200	400	500	700	900	1100	1200

Equal temperament paved the way for the twelve note chromatic scale which was ultimately applied to the fretboard of Jimi's strat. Beside taking care of all those nasty modulation and building problems, the equal tempered scale also provides an easy answer to the question of dividing the two larger steps of just intonation into half steps. Everything is even up. The chromatic scale is every successive note, twelve to an octave. Even though we have seen that the chromatic actually was derived from the pure major, IT IS THE CHROMATIC WHICH IS RECOGNIZED AS THE MASTER SCALE. All other scales, including the major, are a "selection" of certain notes from the twelve chromatic notes. So, if you consider the range of the electric guitar, four octaves divided into twelve equal intervals, you have 48 little friends to take onto the stage with you. Madison Square Garden, here we come!

Even though equal temperament is imperfect, you would never know it from playing today's electronic keyboards, which are fixed with the equal tempered chromatic scale. You see, although imperfect, the tempered scale allows endless building (triads, all intervals) on any of its twelve degrees. Below, please witness the big picture. Everything revolves around a 440 A note (A_4) and all A notes are multiples of this anchor note. Each column has two octaves, with eight octaves on the chart. The six strings of the guitar are represented, from low to high, by E_2, A_2, D_3, G_3, B_3, E_4. The figure C_4 represents middle C.

EQUAL TEMPERED CHROMATIC SCALE
$A_4 = 440$

D-1-23

American Standard pitch. Adopted by the American Standards Association in 1936

Note	Frequency	Note	Frequency	Note	Frequency	Note	Frequency
C_0	16.35	C_2	65.41	C_4	261.63	C_6	1046.50
$C\#_0$	17.32	$C\#_2$	69.30	$C\#_4$	277.18	$C\#_6$	1108.73
D_0	18.35	D_2	73.42	D_4	293.66	D_6	1174.66
$D\#_0$	19.45	$D\#_2$	77.78	$D\#_4$	311.13	$D\#_6$	1244.51
E_0	20.60	E_2	82.41	E_4	329.63	E_6	1318.51
F_0	21.83	F_2	87.31	F_4	349.23	F_6	1396.91
$F\#_0$	23.12	$F\#_2$	92.50	$F\#_4$	369.99	$F\#_6$	1479.98
G_0	24.50	G_2	98.00	G_4	392.00	G_6	1567.98
$G\#_0$	25.96	$G\#_2$	103.83	$G\#_4$	415.30	$G\#_6$	1661.22
A_0	27.50	A_2	110.00	A_4	440.00	A_6	1760.00
$A\#_0$	29.14	$A\#_2$	116.54	$A\#_4$	466.16	$A\#_6$	1864.66
B_0	30.87	B_2	123.47	B_4	493.88	B_6	1975.53
C_1	32.70	C_3	130.81	C_5	523.25	C_7	2093.00
$C\#_1$	34.65	$C\#_3$	138.59	$C\#_5$	554.37	$C\#_7$	2217.46
D_1	36.71	D_3	146.83	D_5	587.33	D_7	2349.32
$D\#_1$	38.89	$D\#_3$	155.56	$D\#_5$	622.25	$D\#_7$	2489.02
E_1	41.20	E_3	164.81	E_5	659.26	E_7	2637.02
F_1	43.65	F_3	174.61	F_5	698.46	F_7	2793.83
$F\#_1$	46.25	$F\#_3$	185.00	$F\#_5$	739.99	$F\#_7$	2959.96
G_1	49.00	G_3	196.00	G_5	783.99	G_7	3135.96
$G\#_1$	51.91	$G\#_3$	207.65	$G\#_5$	830.61	$G\#_7$	3322.44
A_1	55.00	A_3	220.00	A_5	880.00	A_7	3520.00
$A\#_1$	58.27	$A\#_3$	233.08	$A\#_5$	932.33	$A\#_7$	3729.31
B_1	61.74	B_3	246.94	B_5	987.77	B_7	3951.07
						C_8	4186.01

Multiply any frequency by 1.0595 and you will get the next higher half step frequency

OUR TUNING DILEMMA

The keyboard player does not worry about tuning, he just goes about his business. The rock guitarist, on the other hand, is left to struggle with his own device, a wickedly variable contrivance called *the electric guitar*. After playing the guitar for 18 years, the best news that I've got on tuning is: sometimes it seems to tune great, other times, with all efforts, it is impossible. The very characteristics that allow the guitar to be the incredibly warm and distinctively individual instrument that it is, are the same inherent qualities which make it a monster to consistently tune. There are three ways in which the frequency of a string can be varied: length, tension and mass. The fundamental frequency (F) of a fixed string of length (L) is given by the following equation where T is the tension of the string and ML is the mass per unit length of the string.

$$F = \frac{1}{L} \sqrt{\frac{T}{ML}}$$

A set of medium gauge strings (.010 - .045) creates a total tension of about 90 lbs. on the bridge/string holder. A very light set (.008 -.038) create a tension of about 65 lbs. It seems that everything affects the tension of the strings. The weather, handling the guitar, stage heat, string bending, and just common playing can change the note of the open string. Ironically, the tuning of any one string changes the frequency of other strings by slightly flexing the wooden neck of the guitar. When putting on new strings, don't waste time with exact tuning until all six are on and in the ballpark and had a few good bends, because they all affect each other. Be it ever so slight, the combined total of these factors can drive your axe right through the gates of SOUR NOTE CITY. Be aware and prepared for the worst.

Intonation, the process of minutely adjusting string length at the bridge is, needless to say, of ultimate importance to the rock guitarist. That string is stretched *over* those frets. It doesn't know they're down under there. It is up to you to get the intonation correct so that the frets can cut the string off at the proper equal tempered half step interval. If you don't already know about intonation, talk to the guy at the local guitar shop. For now, hit the twelfth fret harmonic (first overtone) and compare the tone to that which you get when you fret the string at the same position. If the fretted note is lower than the harmonic, then the bridge has to be adjusted closer to the fretboard. That is just one rough fact. Get to know about it. Understand it. If the bridge is too high, or the nut, or God forbid, the neck is somehow out of kilter, you will not be able to tune to any reasonable medium. So, you have to live with the weather and handling. But with intonation, you are either in or out, make up your mind.

Any and all of the above named conditions are working against you at any given time. There are, unfortunately, two more conditions that I want you to consider, because if you own a guitar, buddy, you already bought into the mess. The first is the matter of the fret.

Remember the monochord with its movable fret? Well, the way it works out, it would be better in theory if we could bring the fret up to the node point and let it fix the string at that particular point. Instead, we have to bring the string out of its straight line, and down to the fret, thereby messing with its length and tension. This distortion is particularly noticeable on the lower frets, by the nut. This makes the "open chords" particularly difficult to tune, one with the other. You can get the E chord right, but good luck with the A major chord. The second string is open for the E chord but fretted at the second fret for the A major. The first fret is the most difficult of all because when you pull the string down off the nut. Bar chords allow you a little more leeway because you are working one fretted chord against another, and you can always bend upward to correct frequency imperfections.

The final point I want to introduce on tuning is the natural inclination for the guitarist to tune the six strings of the instrument to "just" or pure intonation. If you strike a chord (usually an E) and tune the axe up to sound this one chord, you will, unless otherwise directed, tune those strings to the perfect interval of just intonation for that particular chord. The problem is, when you go to build a triad on any one of the other notes, you are going to get all of the problems associated with just intonation (two different size whole steps, etc.). In other words, you can get one chord to sound great, but try to make other related chords without retuning — quick drive to Sour Note City. Envy the keyboard player. At least his instrument is *fixed* out of tune slightly, so as to always be able to play in all keys. The guitarist is led into that perfect trap where just when it sounds really right at one spot, he gets burned because it doesn't work across the board. The solution: TEMPER YOUR TUNING. Compromise so that, like the equal tempered fret placements that you already have, the tuning of the open strings *relative to each other* allows for the sounding of a number of relative chords. This is the real reason that I bothered to tell you about the three different size intervals from the just scale — I wanted you to know how much you have to cheat in order to bring the bad boy into usable tuning.

Now, if you know that you have to play a certain song, try "running through" the necessary chords to the piece to see if you have any lemons before you start playing. If a particular chord (or part of a chord) is unacceptable, either slightly change the tuning, testing against the other chords for temperament, or hunt down a different voicing or position to make the bad chord. Sometimes this will get you off the hook. Scales, because of their linear nature, are not as much of a hassle to bring into usable focus.

How do we bother to tune? The first way that we all learned is by sounding the note on 6/5 (check out the roadmap for info on this call system) and tuning the fifth string to this note. This method of tuning the upper string to

String Gauges

Regular
.010
.013
.017
.026
.036
.046

Light
.009
.011
.016
.024
.032
.042

Extra Light
.008
.011
.014
.022
.030
.038

Hybrid
.009
.011
.016
.026
.036
.046 inch

the tone of the lower string fingered at the fifth fret (with the annoying exception of 3/4) is not a bad way to get your strings roughly in tune, keeping within the framework of Equal temperament. The question remains: can you play a variety of chords without dischord?

Tuning by harmonics has a little more flashy class, but there is the potential for trouble. The harmonic above 6/5 (double octave of the fundamental low E) can be tuned to the harmonic above 5/7 (the dominant fifth E above the A string fundamental). You can also tune the 5/7 harmonic to the one above 6/12. Tuning in this fashion usually provides you with a great relationship between the two strings in question, but the "pure" interval provided by the overtones are, as we already know, trouble makers. Look at the above chart which compares equal with just and see what is what. The problem of just intonation is real, especially when you tune "to the chord." If you simply finger the chord and tune accordingly, you will tune the chord to sound perfectly using the irregular just intervals. You will have trouble sounding other relative chords. One of the old rock tricks is to tune one of the studio guitars up to a perfect ringing E major chord and just bar the strings across with one finger (tap ons are fun, too!) in order to change chords. Limited approach admittedly — BUT ONE THAT WORKS GREAT TO GET THE RHYTHM TRACK IN PERFECT TUNE.

Here is the bottom line. First get a good electric, put new strings on it, then get the intonation perfect. At this point, proceed to tune each of the six open strings to an electronic guitar tuner (digital or meter). These tuners are set up in such a way that (set to 440 A) each open string tone has been equal tempered. This should allow you to successfully play families of related chords. If not, become a candlestick maker.

THE GREAT STAFF

The chromatic scale is every half step between any two octave points. It is important to know this, because the chromatic is truly the skeleton from which all of today's music is made. The major scale, however, is really the most basic musical *vehicle*. Unspecified generic musical references are always understood to refer to the major scale. For instance, a call to the *fifth* is a reference to the fifth degree of the major scale, never the chromatic. In the texts of most musical encyclopedias, the major scale is referred to simply as *the scale*. As you can see from the diagram below which runs the E chromatic scale up the low E string and the E major scale up the high string, there is indeed an unchanging relationship between the two scales.

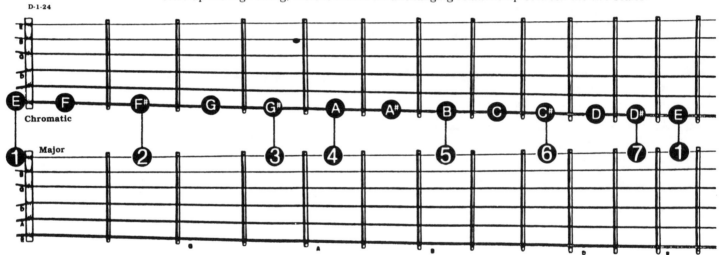

Although the chromatic scale is more fundamental, it is the major scale which is truly the BIG BOY. Please notice that for now, and for all time, there is a whole step between all successive degrees of the major scale except the 3rd and the 4th, and the 7th and the 1st. Nobody has ever been able to tell me *why* these two irregularities exist, but apparently, nature wasn't happy with the octave being regularly divided. For the sake of simplicity, the music world's basic means of transcription, the five line staff, overlooks the two varieties of intervals which make up the major scale (half step, whole step). A dot placed *on* or *between* each line of the staff represents a major scale degree.

The familiar example below shows both the treble (upper) and bass staff, which together comprise the Great Staff. Middle C falls on the single ledger line between the two staffs. Just as with the major scale, progressing seven steps above or below a point on the staff will lead to a higher or lower octave point. The boxed notes are the open strings of the guitar. The upper A note is the universal 440 A note. As you can see, the open strings of your guitar fall primarily into the bass range.

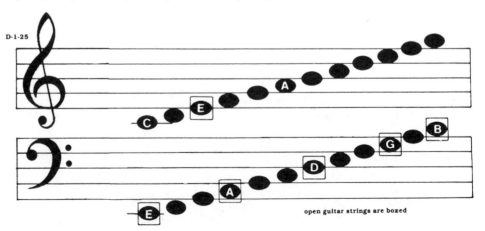

open guitar strings are boxed

INTERVALS

The half step, also known as the semitone or half tone, is the smallest common interval and is brought into use by the fixed frets on our fingerboard. One fret equals one half step; live with it. Somebody in the back inevitably brings up the fact that in some dusty corner of the globe the residents commonly use *enharmonic* or *microtonal* scales which involve less than a half step. Hey, good for them. Please send a postcard. *I don't know about them.*

The whole step is the most common musical interval and is, with two exceptions, the standard major scale interval represented by two guitar frets. A *melodic* interval occurs when two notes are sounded successively. A *harmonic* interval occurs when two notes are sounded simultaneously. What I call the *one word intervals* refer to the number of major scale steps between two major scale degrees, counting both steps in the process. Here they are: unison or prime (c-c), second (c-d), third (c-e), fourth (c-f), fifth (c-g), sixth (c-a), seventh (c-b), octave (c-c'), ninth (c-d'), tenth (c-e'), eleventh (c-f'), twelfth (c-g'). There you have it. A *simple* interval spans less than an octave whereas a *compound* interval is a single interval larger than an octave (e.g. a ninth). Now, if two different intervals add up to an octave, they are called the *complement* or *inversion* of each other. If an interval's motion is downward, then it is refered to as *lower*. For instance, G is the lower fourth of C'.

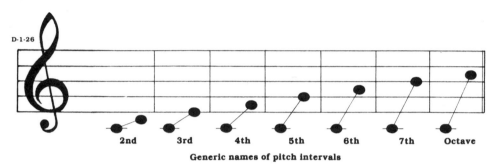

Generic names of pitch intervals

Intervals, of course, aren't just built above the tonic. The single word intervals are also used to describe distances above or below any major scale degree. Herein lies the rub. Because of the two half step irregularities in the make up of the major scale, a third between C and E (4 half steps) is different than a third between E and G (3 half steps). In order to specify the exact number of chromatic scale degrees (half steps) in any given interval we have the *two word intervals*. What this boils down to is giving a two word description to each of the twelve degrees of the chromatic scale. I usually just yell over at the guy next to me, "Go up three frets." It is all the same. Look see.

Number of Half Steps in Interval	Formal Name of Interval	Abbreviated Name or Symbol	Chromatic Scale Key of C	Major Scale Degree in Key of C
0	Unison or Prime	Octave	C	1
1	Minor Second	m2	C#	
2	Major Second	M2	D	2
3	Minor Third	m3	D#	
4	Major Third	M3	E	3
5	Perfect Fourth	P4	F	4
6	Diminished Fifth	Dim 5	F#	
7	Perfect Fifth	P5	G	5
8	Minor Sixth	m6	G#	
9	Major Sixth	M6	A	6
10	Minor Seventh	m7	A#	
11	Major Seventh	M7	B	7
12	Octave	0'	C'	8

CONSONANCE AND DISSONANCE

Down through the ages, musicologists have always tried (or at least been tempted) to place specific intervals into two "opposing camps": those that sound consonant or pleasing to the ear, and those bad boys that sound dissonant, unpleasant, somehow disturbing. Within the confines of a single octave, the chromatic scale offers twelve intervals, seven of which are major scale intervals. It is *generally* thought that all of the intervals inherent in the major triad (prime, a third, a fifth) and also a 4th and a 6th are, indeed, consonant. All other intervals, including a 2nd, a 7th, and those resulting from altered major intervals, fall into the dissonant catagory. This is a nice tight package. Problem is, the interaction and momentum provided by the melodic and harmonic interaction of a moving piece of music has been known to blow all of the catagories away. So it is hard, if not impossible, to be fully objective.

Just because you can't easily categorize sensations, it doesn't make them any less real. You *know for sure* when you hear and feel them. Consonance conveys to the listener a certain state of dignified calmness, repose, stability, you know, a feeling of "belonging there." On the other hand, dissonance creates a disturbing tension, a feeling of constriction, a sensation of leaning towards a resolution. Rock is absolutely full of wonderful, purposeful dissonance. The slightly sour seventh chord (1,3,5,-7) is a cornerstone of blues and rock structure. The pentatonic blues scale is the perfect animal to convey both sides of the story. And talk

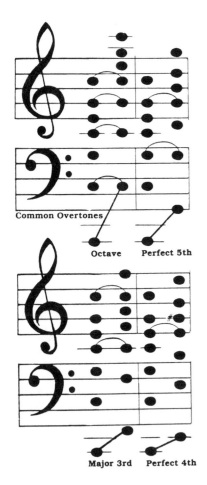

Common Overtones

Octave   Perfect 5th

Major 3rd   Perfect 4th

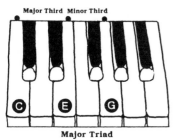

Major Triad

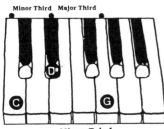

Minor Triad

Diminished Triad

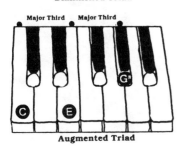

Augmented Triad

about sour, chords just don't come any more upsetting than rock's augmented 9th chord (1,3,5 -7,-3'). Jimi used it for that grating chord you hear just as he starts to sing the words <u>Purple Haze.</u> Remember that ugly choppa choppa chord Steppenwolf pounded into the ground on <u>Born To Be Wild?</u> Same chord. Demonstration later.

Searching for some kind of tangible reason for the cause of consonance and dissonance, a gentleman by the name of H.L.F. von Helmholtz theorized in his book, On The Sensations Of Tone (1836), that consonance is caused by the sharing of one or more common overtones between the two notes of an interval. For instance, the interval of a fifth, between the tonic or first (at an arbitrary 200 hz with overtones of 400 hz, 600 hz, 800 hz, 1000 hz, 1200 hz), will have a common overtone at 1200 hz. Furthermore, he proposed that dissonance is caused by an acoustic disturbance known as "beats" which occur between the overtones of two different notes. Beats are created when two tones (fundamental or overtone) are very close, but not identical, in frequency. If two tones of 440 hz and 442 hz are harmonically sounded, a beat of 2 hz will be in evidence.

The very same phenomena which causes beats is also responsible for the phantomlike occurance of *resultant tones*. A resultant tone, better known as Tartini's tone, is a singularly identifiable third tone which results from the difference in the frequency of two louder, higher pitched tones. By harmonically sounding the two tones of 600 hz and 800 hz, you will create a resultant tone of 200 hz.

One last thing I'll say about the sweet and sour controversy; what is acceptable seems to change with time and cultural tastes. The music composed by Wagner and Strauss was absolutely unbearable to many of the music critics of the time because of its "dissonance." I remember when I was shorter than the kitchen counter, looking up at the little plastic radio playing Jerry Lee Lewis' <u>Great Balls of Fire.</u> Man, I thought something was wrong with the radio - honestly. It sounded like ten things at once. Now when I hear it, well, it's only rock and roll.

TRIADS

We already know that the overtone series of the vibrating fixed string provides us with the basic elements of the major triad; the fundamental, its upper third, and its upper fifth. There are four types of triads, determined by the type of third (major or minor) used to build the two higher degrees. The triad chart below will fill you in on the four different types of triads.

D-1-28

Type of Triad	First Note	First Interval	Second Interval	Example in C
Major Triad	Fundamental Note	Major Third	Minor Third	C-E-G
Minor Triad	Fundamental Note	Minor Third	Major Third	C-D#-G
Diminished Triad	Fundamental Note	Minor Third	Minor Third	C-D#-F#
Augmented Triad	Fundamental Note	Major Third	Major Third	C-E-G#

The major triad, or chord (1,3,5), will always be the most important combination of tones to any musician, particularly the rock guitarist. There are only twelve major chords, one for each key. The minor triad (1,-3,5) is formed by simply lowering the third one-half step from its position in the major triad. The piano is the easiest way to see it happen. Check out all four species of triads on the old 88.

OTHER COMBINATIONS

The major triad is the most basic of all chords. Change it around a little and you come up with the minor, augmented, and diminished triad, so forget about the other three for just a second. 1,3,5. Let's write these three degrees in stone, shall we? Chip, Chip, Chip *Forever in Stone*.

Now, what do you add to that which is written in stone? The answer: whatever is left. Namely, the 7th, the 6th, the 2nd (usually called the 9th), throw in a 4th and the altered "chromatic" steps and ... that's it. Thing is, there are certain rules, regulations and specifics you need to know about how it goes down. First of all, the definition of a chord is "the simultaneous sounding of three or more tones." A triad fits this description, so triads are just basic chords. Two tones sounded together are called an interval. The major triad with the seventh major scale degree included (located one half step below the tonic) is called a major seventh chord. This is a nice silky chord which opens the jazz classic <u>Misty.</u> When rockers refer to the "seventh chord," they are talking about (know it or not) the major triad with the flatted seventh degree included. Now, chord names which contain numbers above seven in their names (9,11,13) contain degrees found in the upper octave from the one which the 1st (tonic), 3rd (mediant), and 5th (dominant) are originally found. The ninth chord contains the second from the upper octave, which is the same chromatic degree as the flatted 3rd from the upper octave.

Now get this, if the chord name is higher than seven, it includes the flatted seventh as the chord builds. For instance, a 9th chord consists of 1,3,5,-7,9. To get around this understanding, the plus sign (+), or the word add, is put after the name of the triad. For instance, the major add 9 chord (or major +9) is simply 1,3,5,9. The rules that apply to adding degrees to major chords also apply to minor chord names, except you flatten the third degree. Look at the minor 9th chord: 1,-3,5,-7,9. In the middle of all this, some bored musician came up with the idea of building in seconds (C,D,E,F) and then called them, of all things, *tone clusters*. Brilliant idea, buddy. Trouble is, tone clusters sound like somebody accidentally sat on the piano keys. Oh well, it's original.

Chord Name	Scale degrees of successive notes					
Major	1	3	5			
Minor	1	b3	5			
Dominant 7th or 7th	1	3	5	b7		
Major 7th (ma7)	1	3	5	7		
Minor 7th (m7)	1	b3	5	b7		
Augmented (+)	1	3	#5			
Diminished	1	b3	b5			
Major 6th	1	3	5	6		
Major 6th	1	3	5	6		
9th	1	3	5	b7	9	
11th	1	3	5	b7	9	11
Major add 9 (+ 9)	1	3	5	9		
Minor 9th (m9)	1	b3	5	b7	9	
Major 6/9th	1	3	5	6	9	

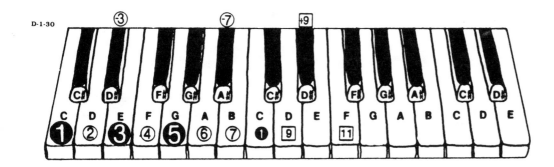

D-1-30

This is all bottom line stuff. We are *listing* the components of possible combinations. More times than not, though, musicians will use only part of a chord, or particularly on the guitar, octaves of component degrees. I already told you that the standard Chuck Berry/Elmore James staccato opening (played on 2/5, 1/5 for A) is actually the 1st and 5th from the major chord. Effective rock power chording (e.g. Whole Lotta Love) is actually just 1,5,1' on the bottom three strings. Look familiar? It's the fundamental with the first two overtones. How basic can you get? No more basic than rock, that is for sure. What makes great rock so great is shear invention with the basic blocks. On Foxey Lady, Jimi used the outside altered degrees of the augmented ninth chord (1,3,5,-7,+9) for that sour crunch that you hear. The bass ran back and forth over the notes in the triad while he pounded just the -7 and the +9 in one swipe. He isolated just THE MOST DISSONANT PART OF THE CHORD. That's rock.

INVERSION

When we studied intervals, we looked at how a single octave can be divided up. When we turned to chords we looked at some of the consequences of building intervals on one another. Every now and then it is good to take a step back and remind yourself that whatever happens in one octave holds true for all octaves throughout the musical range. Inversion is the process by which one of the twelve musical tones, either alone, in a simple interval, or in a chord, is transposed to an identical scale position in a higher or lower octave.

An interval (C,D) is inverted by replacing the lower tone with a tone precisely one octave higher (D,C'). The major triad (C,E,G) has two common numbered inversions. The first inversion takes the 2st (C) into the next higher octave. (E,G,C'). The second inversion starts with the first inversion and proceeds to move the third (G) into the upper octave (G,C'E'). Now you know about inversion in its simplest form on paper. The subject of inversion, on the six string guitar, is pretty deep water. To a certain degree, the study of the guitar is the study of inversion. The six strings, tuned a major fourth away from each other, will always provide you with a universe of octave matching possibilites. It doesn't come clear all at once, but slowly with use. Take a bite right now just by forcing yourself to think about it.

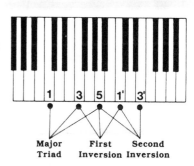

Major | First | Second
Triad | Inversion | Inversion

The piano is designed so that one hand can reasonably play the major triad with an octave note of the first on the top (1,3,5,1'). The guitar starts turning octaves on a bar chord after three strings, with two full octaves across the open strings. Consequently, the components of chords crop up in a jumbled sequence which makes for a tremendous variety of choices for the guitarist. Thing is, you have to know what's there in order to choose and this comes from acquired knowledge (the wall poster should help). Now, a simple E chord at the nut (6/0, 5/2, 4/2, 3/1, 2/0, 1/0) offers us this snarled inversion of the 1,3,5 major triad — with the low string first — 1,5,1',3',5',1". On the guitar, there is always something interesting going on right next to the string you are playing.

As I once wrote in The Heavy Guitar Bible, after a while of listening to rock records, *the use* of chords and scales seem to blend into one giant blurring whole called *good electric guitar*. My job is to hold back those chomping at the bit and say, "Hey, look. Someday when it is all quiet, you will see that, no matter how fast or hard, THE METAL is still music. And although it does away with all rules, all restrictions, it is still within, not the constrictions, but the definable boundries of musical limits."

RANGE

Every instrument operates within frequency limits known as its range. On the guitar, middle C is found on 2/1, with the C below appearing on 5/3 and 6/8, and the C above on 1/8 and 2/13. So you have an octave above and below middle C, that's a good start. The electric guitar has a four octave range defined by these five E notes; 6/0, 4/2, 1/0, 1/12, 1/24.

Everyone has his/her own singing range which is usually about two octaves. Formally, the various ranges of the voice are classified into six types: bass, baritone, tenor, contralto, mezzo, and soprano. You can usually work out the vocal line of a song on the guitar between 3/0 and 1/5.

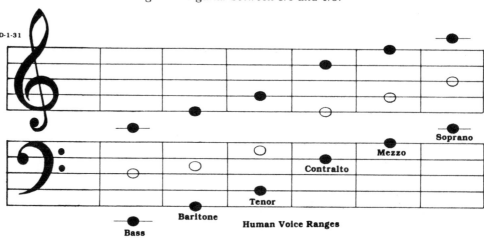

Human Voice Ranges

TIME

The *beat* is the regular pulse of the music. *Tempo* is a word that indicates the speed of the beat. Even though beats are points in time which occur at regular time intervals, they are gathered, by accent and "feel," into groups called *measures*. A measure is defined by vertical lines which run through the five line staff. A *time signature,* which appears as a fraction at the beginning of each work, indicates the grouping and type of beat. For instance, 3/4 meter (or time) tells you that there are three beats to the measure (upper figure), and that each of those beats is a quarter note (lower figure). The quarter note is not standardized to any exact time interval, but is understood to be a regular, usable beat interval from which to judge all others. The first beat of each measure is usually accented, but this is not a rule by any means.

As far as I'm concerned, 4/4 time is all that is necessary. Anything else I can handle in stride. 4/4 time is standard for rock and roll, and that's good enough for me. Besides, when you play, you don't think about it anyway. At any rate, for the record, below you will find the table of time signatures and other examples that pertain to beat and measure. The compound meters are derived by multiplying the common meters by three.

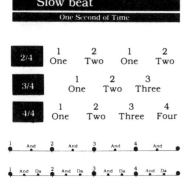

Common meters
Duple (2/2, 2/4, 2/8)
Triple (3/2, 3/4, 3/8)
Quadruple (4/2, 4/4, 4/8)

Compound meters
Compound duple (6/2, 6/4, 6/8)
Compound triple (9/4, 9/8)
Compound quadruple (12/4, 12/8, 12/16)

FORM

What form does it take, Rock and Roll? The answer is on the records. And what records we have in our archives. Plenty, plenty, plenty of albums. They are stacked by the hundreds in the corner of every living room and dorm from coast to coast and beyond. The various incarnations of rock that fill these albums form a seemingly endless ocean which is getting deeper everyday. Hey, enough overwhelming numbers, what stays the same in all of this variety? Where is our anchor? It is those FIXED FRETS, and those SIX STRINGS held over so firmly at that familiar, determined distance from each other by the bridge.

We are living during the evolution of rock, so it is hard to be objective. Charlie Christian played the electric guitar in the late thirties. and at the time, he looked back twenty years to the delta, to guitarists like Charlie Patton. Robert Johnson (who made Crossroads famous), Elmore James and Muddy Waters all worked the blues form as examples for Chuck Berry, Elvis, The Beatles, The Stones, Hendrix, and Zepplin.The groups from the late sixties and early seventies forged the renaissance period of rock. Everything was new. The proportions of the blues form could be streched, extended, and endlessly explored. The promise of the "new birth" was in our hands, eyes, hearts and minds. The eclipse was happening and everybody knew it and lived it. By the time Van Halen and the new school of fire breathers came on, rock guitar had entered its baroque period, characterized by the exaggerated elaboration of the original pure form. These guys throw the form around with carefree abandon. Speed, sustained power plays, harmonic overdrive and, of course, eating the guitar itself became common place.

At first, I doubted the value of studying the standard definitions relating to musical form because most of the descriptions pertained to classical stuff. The rock experience is so enthralling, so singular, so seemingly disconnected, that it was hard for me to see that rock had anything to do with previously figured musical catagories. If you can remove yourself from the "magnet to the moment" effect that great rock has, you will eventually see the underlying thread that runs through all of the faces of rock. Yeah, after consideration, I concluded that rock is not absolutely different from other types of music. It is about the ability to convey one's ideas musically, and dominance over the instrument, which has endlessly filled the conversations of aspirants throughout musical history.

A-B-A
A standard structural pattern based on the statement of a theme, departure to a new idea, and return to the original theme.

CADENCE
A melodic or harmonic inflection at the end of a musical phrase that gives the effect of rest or conclusion.

DEVELOPMENT
The basic technique of composition in which musical themes are "worked out" and thereby subject to a process of growth and transformation by being broken into fragments or motives. This does not occur by the addition of new themes, but by the combination and fragmentation of existing themes. May include changes in melody, harmony, rhythm, meter, dynamics, register, timbre, instrument, imitation, augmentation, inversion of theme line, etc.

DYNAMICS
Pertaining to the volume of performed music: its loudness or softness.

FIGURE
A melodic rhythmic fragment used in building a composition.

HARMONIC ANALYSIS
The study of a piece of music by the examination of its harmonies and tonal functions. Each chord (or interval) is broken down as to its structure (triad, seventh, etc.), and the inversion of the chord (where it takes place in the range).

IMITATION
A proceedure in which a riff is restated in close succession in a different part of the instrument's range. Imitation may include modification by inversion, augmentation, dimunition, etc.

OSTINATO
A melodic or rhythmic figure which is regularly repeated by one instrument, while others are free to improvise as they "play off" of the repeated figure.

REGISTER
A portion of the range of an instrument or voice (high, middle, low).

TEXTURE
Harmony and melody together represent the *horizontal* and *vertical* elements of musical texture. By studying how the melody line works with the chords, the "weave" of the music's texture is discovered.

VARIATION
The process of altering a musical theme through modification. The original theme is subject to changes by invention, improvisation, modulation, combinations with other themes, etc.

WINDOW #2

Axe of Ages

Primary Objective Statement

To present the chromatic set-up and fingering principles of the six string electric guitar

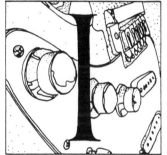

I don't believe anybody really knows where the first precursor of the guitar came from. I have read that small representations of stringed instruments have been found carved into the walls of ancient Egyptian temples. Some say that stringed models were brought across Asia to the Mediterranean area from the Orient. It is a pretty good bet that the lute (derived from the Arabic *al'ud)* was introduced to Europe through Spain by the Arabs after a trip across the sands of north Africa. By the 1600's, the lute, with its half pear shaped body, was *the dominant instrument throughout Europe* enjoying the position that the piano holds today. At this time, Spanish aristocrats were playing the *vihuela* which had the flat back "waisted" body of the guitar with the size and tuning of the lute. From this instrument, it is proposed, the spanish folk instrument known as the guitar was born.

Think of it! GUITAR HISTORY. The same six strings, tuned the same way you know them, in the hands of Ferdinand Sor (1780-1839), known as the father of modern guitar technique. The desire to be dangerous on guitar is nothing new. We have a proud heritage. The size of the human hand, which determined all critical dimensions of the guitar (longest fret interval, distance between strings, etc.), has not changed. The moves have been known for a long time, but it took the electric guitar to make them come alive. It was the year 1940, when at the age of 20, Charlie Christian became famous with the Benny Goodman orchestra playing the first real production electric guitar: the hollow body Gibson ES-150. With this axe, Charlie could compete with a line of horns and play single note lead breaks like a saxaphone. You see, it was the invention of the electro-magnetic pickup that made it all possible.

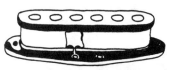

polepieces
wire wrappings

Double coil

Single coil

THE ELECTRO MAGNETIC PICKUP

When you put a string on a guitar, you use the muscles in your hand to turn the tuning machine head until the string comes under tension. And that is the way that it stays. It is this potential energy, held in the string, that allows a singing string to transmit its vibration through the bridge to the body of the guitar. Unlike the clarinet reed, the singing fixed string does not itself move enough air to set up a significant sound wave. The string vibrates at 440 hz, the guitar top vibrates at 440, and the air pressure waves move away from the guitar at 440 hz.

The electric guitar pickup is nothing more complicated than a bar magnet wound extensively with superfine copper wire and placed about 1/8 of an inch under all six strings, placing them in the "field" of the magnet's pull. When the string is still, all remains the same. The electric current starts to flow as soon as the string is plucked. The *Biot-Savart law* of physics, which relates magnetic flux to electric current, applies to our axe. Yes, it seems that the vibration of the string is transfered, through the mystery of magnetism, into a corresponding electric pulse in the wire out of the guitar.

OUR CHROMATIC SITUATION

The guitar is set up chromatically. Every finger can play a chromatic degree. The piano is also set up chromatically with every ascending key (black and white) being the next higher note in the *equal tempered* chromatic scale. The piano, with its 88 consecutive half steps, gives a clear visual example of how the chromatic scale works because all successive octaves (all divided into twelve degrees) all have the same size playing keys. The *guitarist* deals with thinner strings and shorter fret intervals as he moves up in range. This characteristic, coupled with the *cross string* (open string) interval of a major fourth between any two strings (except the major third between 2nd and 3rd string), make the guitar unique. It is not an accident that in the history of music, it was THE GUITAR which was the instrument upon which rock was built. It is easy to play the guitar, really. The best stuff is simple one finger crossover moves with catchy rhythms. There are six strings about which to know. Each has its own special range of two octaves (24 frets) with all six together spanning four consecutive octaves. Maybe a look see at the next diagram will help you see how the various string ranges compare.

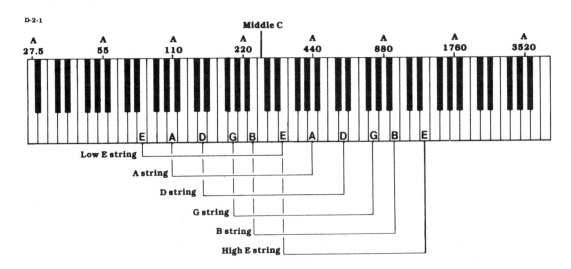

The six strings of the guitar are not, of course, staggered, but run across the nut and bridge side by side. The open strings sound the notes E,A,D,G',B',E''. Now look at the diagram below which shows every note on the board. What do you see? Well, the notes that run above 6/5 are the same notes that run above 5/0. And, the notes on the high and low E strings are identical in name but pitched two octaves apart. But what I really want you to notice is that the notes across the twelfth fret and twenty-fourth fret are the *same* notes. This brings us to a very basic concept. And that is: THE CHROMATIC SCALE, AND THEREFORE ALL SCALES AND RESULTING CHORD PATTERNS, IS CONTAINED IN A PATTERN TWELVE FRETS LONG AND SIX STRINGS WIDE. AMEN. After twelve frets the pattern repeats. This is precisely the principle behind the *Universal Diagram Series* which appear on the wall poster. The chromatic example is below. All twelve frets of the repeating pattern are shown, along with three frets *above and below* the BIG TWELVE to allow the basic fingering principle to manifest itself.

The Universal Chromatic Diagram

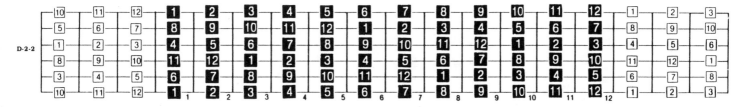

Every note on the board

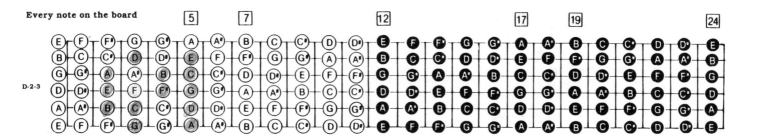

Every note on the first twelve frets

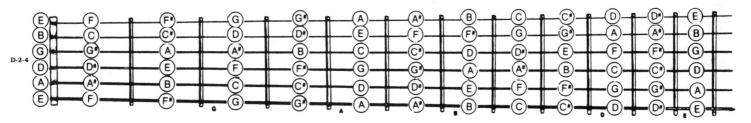

Next, every chromatic step in the octave below middle C is shown in dark circles, with the octave above middle C outlined in lighter notes. The transcription demonstrates a passage through these two octaves, with middle C on 2/1.

C Chromatic

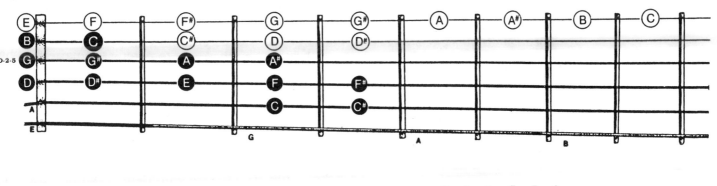

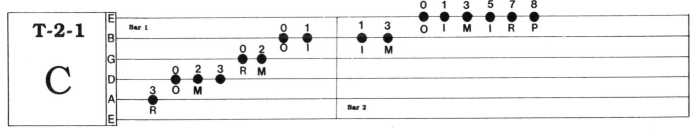

For starters, we will run through the first octave of the guitar, between 6/0 and 4/2, with a few basic scales. First the chromatic, then the major, then the minor, then the blues scale. Just for starters, O.K.?

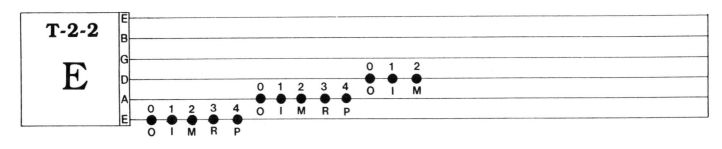

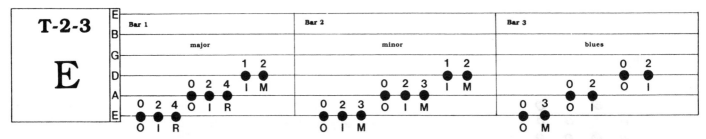

FINGERING PRINCIPLES

The human hand is the measure of all things, if you consider the fretboard to be everything. You know, the axe is set up to play ONE FINGER FOR EACH FRET. This is all so profound that I hope it sets you back to looking at your fretboard in hard terms. Every fret gets a finger. Even the longest fret interval between the nut and the first fret is naturally workable. The board is JUST RIGHT FOR THE HAND. It took the early guitar/lute makers a few years to get it right, so don't just take it for granted. Next we will work on the most basic of all fingering schemes. Play all notes across the first fret with the index, adding another fret for each finger above the first finger.

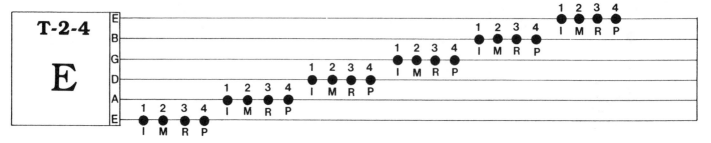

The above example provides us with "classical" or "typical" fingering proportions. From this example, we can plainly see that the largest common interval that the hand can reach on a single string is four frets (a minor third). You can push it to five frets by assigning an additional half step to the pinky, but you better wait until you are above the 7th fret where the fret intervals are no longer large. The other way to extend the pattern is by allowing the index finger to play one fret lower (where position allows), but this is considered breaking formation, because the other three fingers always follow the index. Yes, as a rule, index sets the box.

I don't hold strictly to any fingering rule. The common box is only for outline reference. Now and again, a question will pop up — is this the right way or the wrong way? The strict music teacher will set the question against the common box and figure out the logical answer. I don't. If you can pull the lick off smoothly THEN DO IT THAT WAY. Personally, I do everything against the standard. I play the two low strings with my thumb if I feel like it. Another thing, I'll sometimes play the minor third between, say, 1/5 and 1/8, with my index and ring (instead of my pinky). It doesn't really matter, as long as you can play to your own liking. Now check out this neat way to play *every note* in the chromatic.

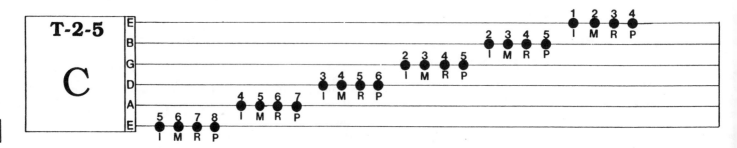

WINDOW #3

The Scale

Primary Objective Statement

To study the major scale throughout its repeating pattern

The maple neck Stratocaster is my favorite electric guitar. The "fretboard" in which the metal frets are laid is the same single piece of blonde maple wood from which the neck itself is fashioned. The playing surface is coated with clear polyurethane and inset with black marking dots. If you've ever seen the cover of the "Derek and the Dominoes" album by Eric Clapton and Duane Allman, that is a picture of a maple neck strat with the polyurethane finish worn through from playing. The Strat has a slightly longer fixed string length than the Les Paul, and is outfitted with three single coil pickups to the Les Paul's two double coil humbuckers. As soon as the drummer shows up and the talking stops, after a few minutes of playing, I inevitably end up playing the maple neck Strat with only the treble pickup on. That's just the way it goes.

Now, as I stated before in WINDOW 1 (The Big Picture), it is a common practice for musical reference books to refer to the major scale simply as the scale. What I want to do right now is present to you the Universal Major Scale Diagram. This is the entire twelve fret repeating pattern which encompasses the major scale. It is set up with numbers representing each of the major scale degrees. As with all Universal Diagrams, the number 1 from any of the diagrams can be assigned to any one of the twelve "letter named" degrees of the chromatic thus making the diagrams universal to any of the twelve musical keys. More important than adaptability is the fact that the Universal Major Scale Diagram presents All TWELVE FRETS OF THE REPEATING SCALE PATTERN. The nut brings the fretboard to an abrupt end, and with it the end of "seeing" the pattern as continuous. THINK BIG. There is, despite the limited field of the guitar, only ONE universal chromatic pattern, and because of this, there is only ONE twelve fret repeating major scale pattern. Study this guy up and down and across, and for the time being, don't think about keys. Think ONE BIG PATTERN. You will live with it, if you are to Be Dangerous On Rock Guitar.

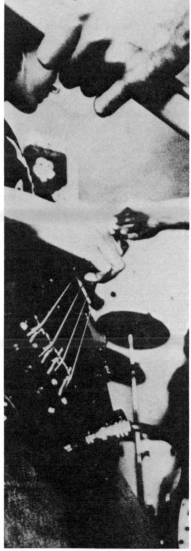

Universal Major Scale Diagram

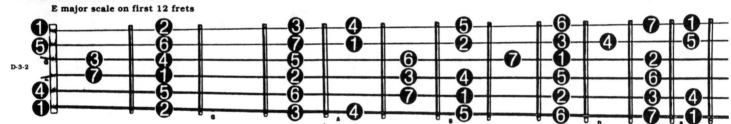

D-3-1

THE E MAJOR SCALE

Next, we will look at how the major scale manifests itself in the key of E over the first twelve frets of the guitar. Notice that the open strings in the diagram below represent the first fret from the Universal Major Scale Diagram. In order to set up in the key of E, we simply assign the E note, the lowest note on the guitar, to the number 1 in the universal diagram. The transcriptions below represent a few ways in which the hand can subdivide the twelve fret major scale pattern into workable boxes. Each transcription begins and ends on a tonic note, and includes every successive ascending major scale degree. Both the boxes and the fingerings are suggested possible models and are not meant to be all inclusive. Don't sit and look. PLAY, PLAY, PLAY.

E major scale on first 12 frets

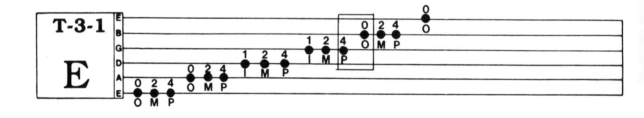

D-3-2

①	E
②	F#
③	G#
④	A
⑤	B
⑥	C#
⑦	D#

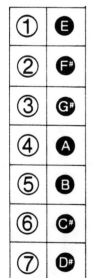

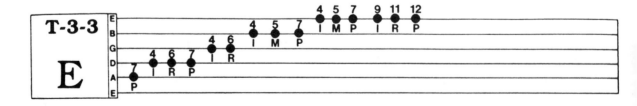

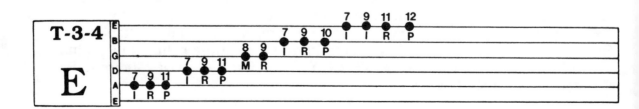

30

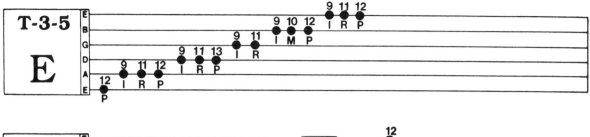

Tape Side	Window
1 A	1
1 B	1 cont. 2, 3
2 A	4, 5, 6
2 B	6 cont. 7, 8
3 A	8 cont. 9
3 B	9 cont. 10, 11, 12, 13
4 A	14, 15, 16, 17
4 B	18, 19, 20
5 A	20 cont. 21, 22
5 B	22 cont.
6 A	23, 24
6 B	24 cont.

THE A MAJOR SCALE

Okay, so now we know how the *Universal,* twelve fret, major scale pattern applies to the first twelve frets for the key of E. What do we do now? Well, we move what we already know up five frets and we have the major scale pattern as it applies to the key of A. Yep, what you just went through for E between the open strings and the 12th fret, will now take place for A major between the 5th and the 17th fret. Now you can witness firsthand how transposing moves but does not change, the universal pattern. One thing about the key of A: because the first fret of the twelve fret repeating major scale pattern is now at the fifth fret, you will have access to the four frets and the open strings under the starting mark, unlike the key of E where the pattern starts on the open strings. Here is how the major scale unfolds for the key of A on the first 17 frets of the guitar. Transcriptions will light the way through the tangled pattern.

A major scale on first 17 frets

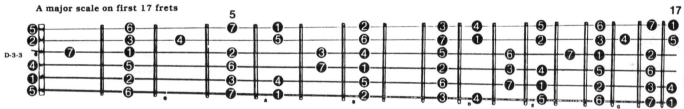

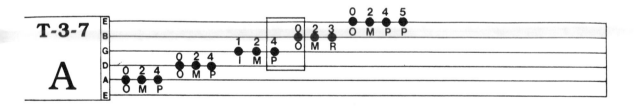

①	Ⓐ
②	Ⓑ
③	Ⓒ#
④	Ⓓ
⑤	Ⓔ
⑥	Ⓕ#
⑦	Ⓖ#

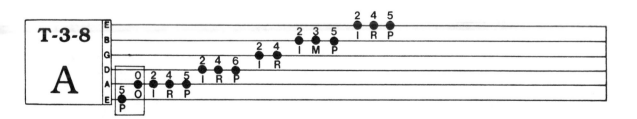

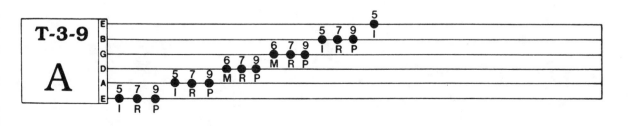

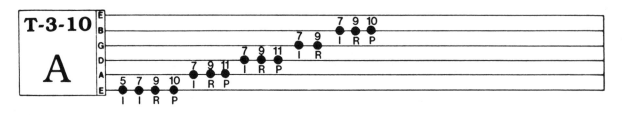

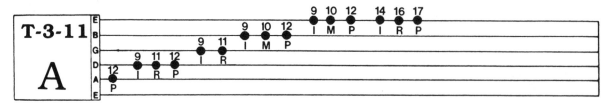

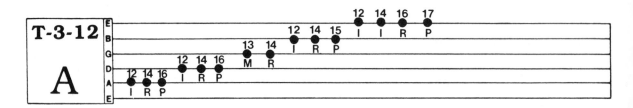

TWO FULL CYCLES

The major scale remains the same. Both the whole step between the 1st and the 2nd, and between the 2nd and the 3rd are built above the tonic. That first half step interval between the 3rd and the 4th is like an oasis before the long haul; that being the three whole steps in a row dividing the 4th and the 5th, the 5th and the 6th, and the 6th and the 7th. One final short step between the 7th and the 1st, and the wheel turns on and on.

It is easy to see the rundown on one string, so just imagine six independent strings fixed beside each other and you have the story of the guitar. Because each string has a range of two octaves, it makes good sense that the 12 fret Universal Chromatic Scale Diagram will unfold twice on a 24 fret guitar. That is two full cycles. Now, in order to adjust any scale pattern to a chosen key, simply set the number 1 from a universal diagram to the chosen key note as it is found on the low (or high) E string and everything will fall in place. Because the low E string spans two octaves, there will always be two "key" or starter frets for any scale in any key. E is the single exception with three positions on the open strings, the 12th and 24th frets. For the key of A we have the 5th and the 17th frets. For G, look to the 3rd and the 15th frets. It's all right there on the wall poster, plain as day, every note on the board, lifesize, spelled out from top to bottom.

WINDOW #4

The Chords

Primary Objective Statement

To introduce the major triad in all inversions, and all common chords

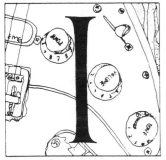

In the beginning, there was the fundamental. Then along came the *fifth* (emitted by the second overtone), and the *third* (from the fourth overtone), and the *major triad* was born. Everything else musical came from these three notes. The intervals inherent in the major triad were extrapolated, and the seven note major scale, which divides each and every octave in the same way, was brought into existence. The chromatic scale is nothing more than the major scale with all five of its larger steps divided into two smaller half steps, with all twelve half steps tempered to the same size. From the chromatic, all scales are subsequently derived. But after all is said and done, you still have those three natural notes — 1, 3, and 5. Don't forget it. Every time you pluck a fixed string, you inevitably sound all three.

The matter of *key* is only one of starting point. Where do you, the performer, decide the starting point to be when you build an interval, chord or scale? Start formulating your thought by accepting the fact that there are twelve divisional points which equally divide the octave (eleven actual divisions and the octave point itself). Now, for the sake of understanding scale and chord construction, forget about just intonation or the possibility of arbitrarily establishing a point anywhere along a sweeping frequency spectrum. Just pretend that these realities are a far away dream, and resign yourself to the adjusted musical universe in which we live. Here are the facts: 440 hz is A, 880 hz is the A above, and 220 hz is the A below. The tonal range between these points is divided into eleven equally tempered chromatic scale degrees. The word building refers to "going above" any chosen note by a certain interval. We already know about building the major triad: you just go up a major third and then an additional minor third above a determined "tonic" degree. Thus, by having done this, we turn a letter named note into a cluster of tones we call a letter named chord.

Tonic A ● 880 hz

Dominant E ◄ 660 (just)
659 hz (equal)

Mediant C# ◄ 550 hz (just)
554 hz (equal)

Tonic A ●– 440 hz

Dominant E ◄ 330 hz (just)
329 hz (equal)

Mediant C# ◄ 277 hz (equal)
275 hz (just)

Tonic A ●–220 hz

A major triads

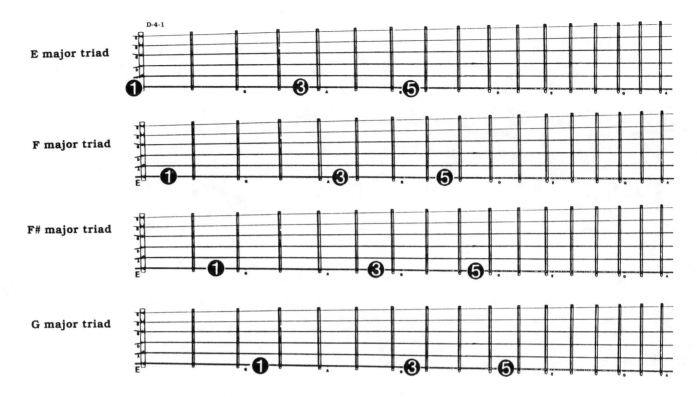

E major triad

F major triad

F# major triad

G major triad

The musician is always up against two different things. First, he has to see the picture of how a particular scale or chord works in the framework of one model octave. Secondly, he has to see the picture of how things work out on his instrument, giving consideration to key, position and range. This is why both the Universal Diagram Series and full size fretboard representations are given on the wall poster. I figured that as long as you have to deal with both worlds, you might as well have master outlines for both.

If we look at the components of the major triad for the key of E on the low string, we find the 1st (E) on 6/0 and 6/12, the 3rd (G#) on 6/4, and the 5th (B) on 6/7. If we go up each of the other five strings marking them for the 1st, 3rd and 5th in this key, we get the diagram below which shows E chord inversion. After the first twelve frets, the pattern starts to repeat itself on higher frets.

E major chord inversion on first 12 frets

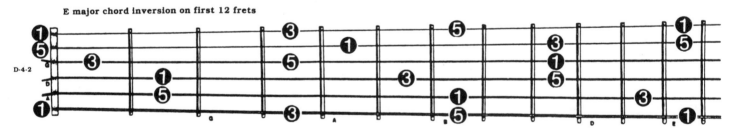

At this time I would like to make one thing perfectly clear: all of the chord configurations that you see in the above diagram are *inversions of the E major chord* when played in the position shown. The tonic (1), mediant (3), and dominant (5) stay the same. What changes is the respective sequence and position of the major chord's elements. The most basic form of the E major chord is found at the bottom of the board in the open string position. Notice that the degrees of the chord across the open strings are the same as those across the twelfth fret. Next I will introduce the Universal Major Chord Diagram which spells out the same information as the above diagram for E major inversion, but can be equally applied to any of the other eleven keys. The first fret of the repeating twelve fret Universal diagram (marked by a small number 1) corresponds to the open strings from the above E inversion diagram.

Universal Major Chord Diagram

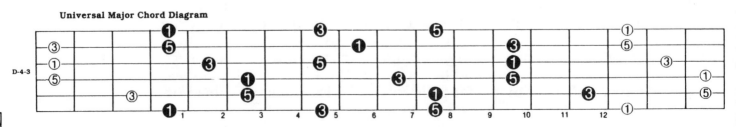

Here is the deal: all of the chords that we first learned to play by letter name in the "open" position down at the nut (E chord, A chord, D chord, G chord, C chord) are contained in the twelve fret/six string makeup of the Universal Major Chord Diagram. Yes, each configuration is just a different form taken by the three degrees of the major triad. There are only twelve major chords in all of music, and all twelve take on all chord forms shown in the above Universal diagram once they are individually centered for key. Why is it then, that certain configurations got "branded" with certain letter chord names? Well, for each of the twelve different musical keys, the first fret of the Universal Major Scale Diagram has to be adjusted to a different guitar fret. As the Universal diagram is transposed to different keys, the various chord configurations found in the pattern "pass over" the fretboard area on and above the open strings. Like the signs of the zodiac, each workable chord figure eclipes this area.

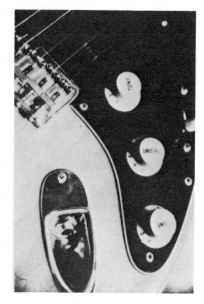

For example, if the Universal pattern is centered to the key of D (with its first fret across the tenth fret of the guitar fretboard), the pattern falls in such a way that the familiar "D chord" configuration aligns itself with the open string position. You know, the folk guitar D chord. The diagram below (taken from The Heavy Guitar Bible) outlines all of the various E chord inversions, but identifies each box by its familiar letter name. Even though all of the boxed configurations are E chords, it is only the open string position which is commonly called an E chord.

E chord inversion with generic named chords

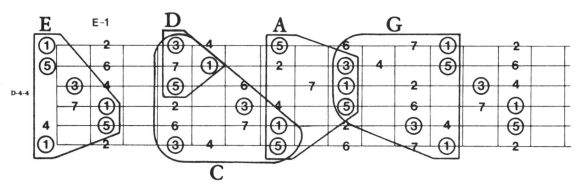

Now you can see what's really going on. Talk about interrelated! Look how the D chord is found in the C chord, and check out how the A chord and G chord relate. Notice how the notes of the G chord on the high and low E strings are actually the notes that you know and love from the open strings of the E chord. There is a lot to look at here, so let's get started. Each independent Universal Chord Figure will now be studied, of which there are five — E, A, D, G and C. From these five configurations, the other common major chord inversions are produced by bar techniques. The F chord is only the E chord moved up a fret. The B chord is the A chord moved up two frets. Now, we will look at the most basic rock guitar chord — the Universal E Chord Figure.

Universal E chord

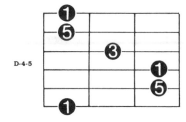

Here is the big guy. Wow, what a great chord! It fits the hand so well. It has just got to be the reason that the blues is so easy. The bottom three strings of this figure, which have the degrees 1, 5, 1', are the primary box for rock chording. Notice how the 3rd doesn't come into the picture until the third string, and look how the top two strings play 1 and 5 in the same way as the fourth and fifth strings. Across the six strings, from low to high, the major scale degrees occur in this sequence: 1, 5, 1, 3, 5, 1. That makes for three tonics, two dominant notes, and a single mediant degree.

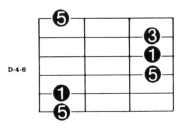

Universal A chord

Next, sister A chord. This chord is the major triad built on the fourth of the major E scale. This is, of course, the same interval used to tune the guitar strings to each other. As there is an E string, so there is an E chord. Same with A; there are both string and chord. You see the pattern created on the fifth, fourth and third strings? It is the same power chord pattern that we were just talking about that appears on the lower three strings of the E pattern. Look at both chords, for Jimi's sake. The A would be identical to the E chord, but moved up one string, if it were not for that damn tuning irregularity between the 2nd and 3rd string. The 3rd in the A chord appears on 2/2, but in the E chord it is 3/1. This will be of consequence when in a latter WINDOW we will study adding on the fourth of the scale (sus 4), which is a half step above the third. The note E is the fifth in the key of A. For this reason, you see the 5th degree appear on the sixth string of the Universal A Chord Figure. The sequence of major scale components across the six strings, from low to high, reads like this: 5, 1, 5, 1, 3, 5. That makes for three 5th, two tonics, and a 3rd to boot.

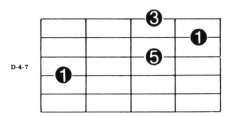

Universal D chord

What have we got here with the D chord? Looks like the same deal that went down when we moved the E chord over on string to make the A chord, except now we are moving the A chord over one string. This happens again because the open D string is a major fourth above the open A string, just like the open A string is a major fourth above the open E string. The basic interval between the first and the fifth that we know from the 6th and 5th strings of the Universal E Chord Figure, now appears on the 4th and 3rd strings of the Universal D Chord Figure. The D chord is sort of like an A chord that popped up in the middle, owing to the tuning irregularity between the 3rd and 2nd string. The D chord is known as a "fourth string root" chord, because the tonic falls on this named string. The A chord is a "fifth string root" chord, and the E chord is a "sixth string root." So now we know that the pattern of the major scale degrees across the open strings set by the Universal E Chord Figure (1, 5, 1, 3, 5, 1) is moved to the fifth string by the A chord, and to the fourth string by the D chord. They are, after all, the same chord in different keys. The intervals and degrees of the major triad don't change. Patterns do.

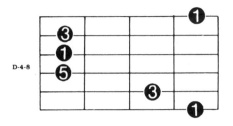

Universal G chord

Here is an example of a "sixth string root" chord which uses the same degrees as the E chord on the sixth and first strings. These degrees are common to both chords, but the E chord works the area above, whereas the G chord works the area below this key fret. The three degrees that you see straight across the 4th, 3rd, and 2nd strings are also common to the A chord. In a later WINDOW we will take another look at this chord.

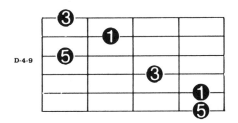

Universal C chord

The Universal C Chord Figure is a "fifth string root" chord which combines the top three strings of the D chord with the bottom two strings from the A chord. The C chord figure is useful in the open string position, but is of limited use for bar chords.

COMPLEX CHORDS

The major triad is the most basic chord. To this fundamental chord form we can add other notes, either major or altered, to form complex chords. The rules for chord building are spelled out in WINDOW 1. What we are going to do now is check out how added degrees figure into the triad picture presented by the *Universal Major Chord Diagram*. When we first looked at the major triad, we laid it out only on one string, then we proceeded to show the pattern across all six strings. Well, the same procedure can be followed for complex chords. For instance, the diagram below shows the components of the E 7th chord on the first twelve frets of the open low E string.

E 7th chord on low E string

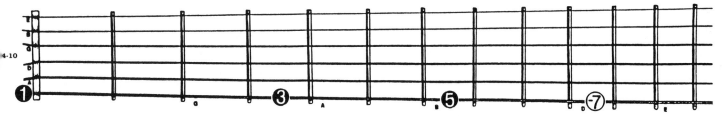

This is the major triad with the flatted seventh added. This new "added" degree is always found a whole step below the tonic, so as we extrapolate this pattern across all six strings, you will see how the seventh chord is formed for each of our five *Universal Chord Figures.*

E 7th chord inversion on first 12 frets

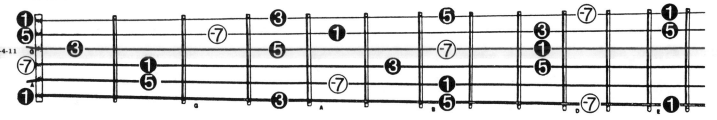

You can do the same thing for any complex chord. Sus 4, 9th, flatted 3rd, 6th, you name it, it will play out every time *right across the board.* Next, I want you to see the *Universal Figure It Out Pattern.* This pattern relates every note on the board to a major scale degree. It is the same as the *Universal Major Scale Diagram* with all of the altered degrees shown with a minus sign. From this bad dude we can figure out everything but eclipses of the sun.

Universal Figure It Out Diagram

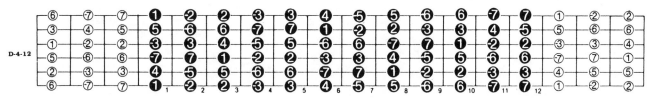

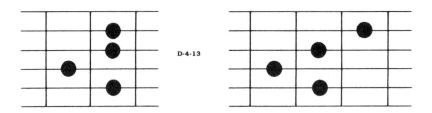

Let us just say that you figure out these two chords and you want to know what they really are. You know that they are fifth string root, but you are not sure about much else. Well, you just set the tonic note to the number 1 and dig in.

Universal Figure It Out Diagram

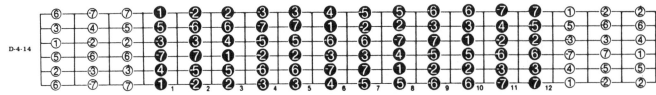

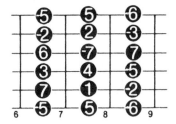

Augmented 9th chord

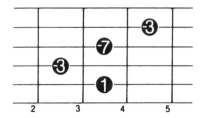

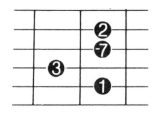

By working in this way with the *Universal Figure It Out Pattern,* you can reckon any chord, scale, or passage about which you have a question. Just throw your game at the pattern, and the degrees you are using will become evident. The following chord chart was taken from my book Blues Guitar—Inside and Out. Don't skim — study, look and learn.

Chord Chart

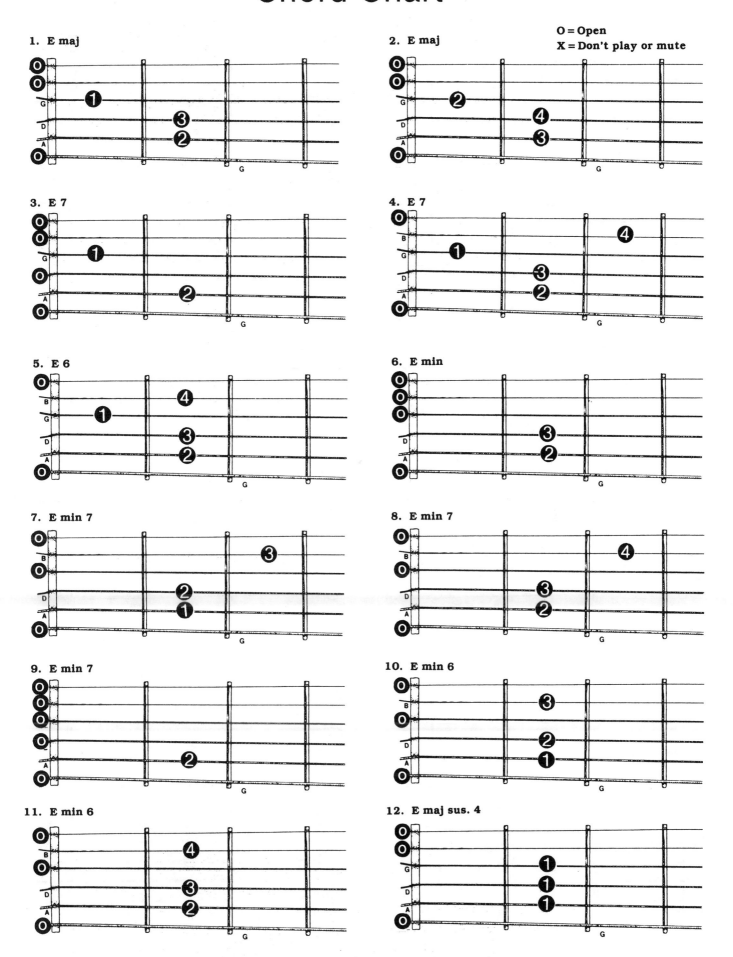

13. E maj sus. 4

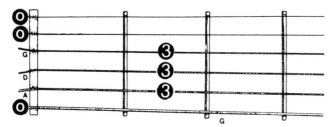

14. E 7 sus. 4

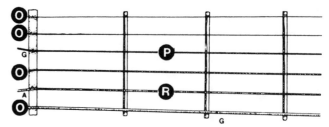

15. E 7 sus. 4

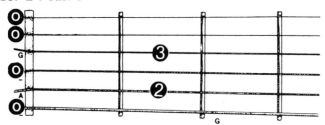

16. E 9

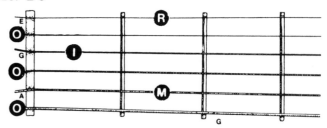

17. E aug 9

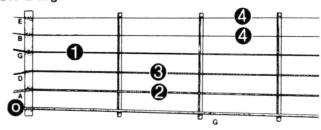

18. A maj

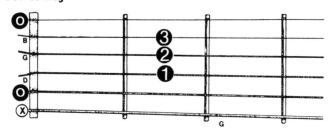

19. A maj

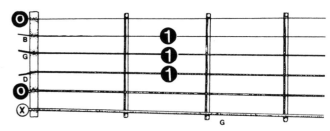

20. A maj

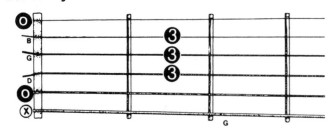

21. A 7

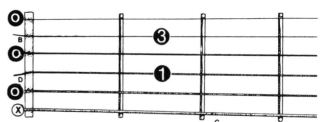

22. A 7

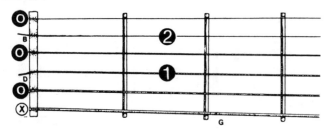

23. A 7

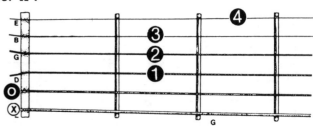

24. A 7

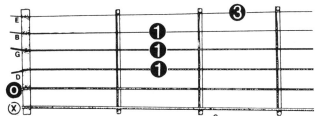

25. A 6

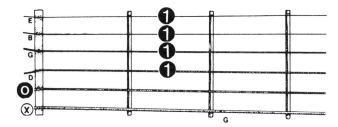

26. A min

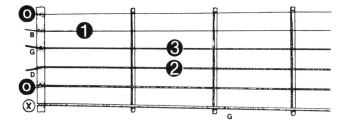

27. A min

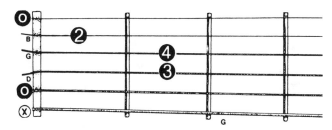

28. A min 7

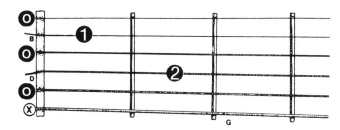

29. A min 7

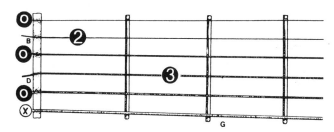

30. A min 7

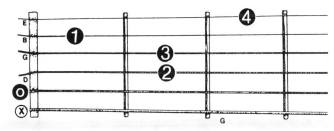

31. A min 6

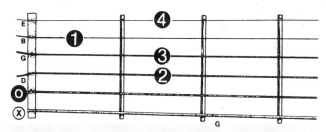

32. A maj sus 4

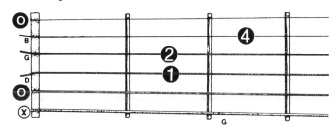

33. A maj sus 4

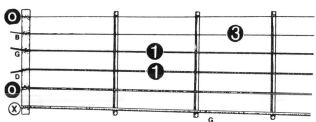

34. A 7 sus 4

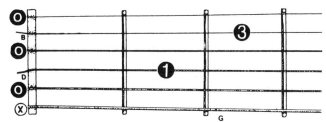

35. A maj 7

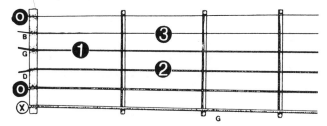

36. B maj

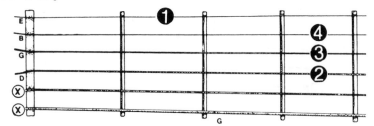

37. B 7

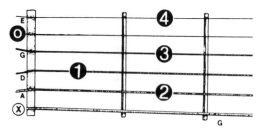

38. B min

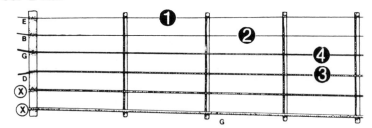

39. B 9

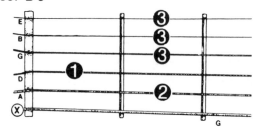

40. D maj

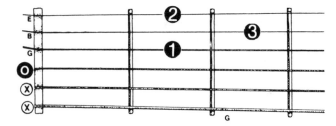

41. D maj

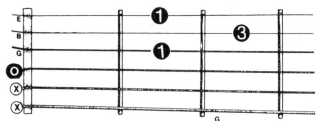

42. D 7

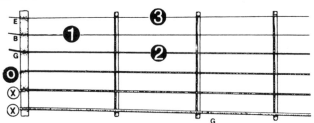

43. D 6

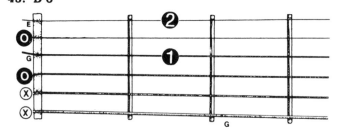

44. D min

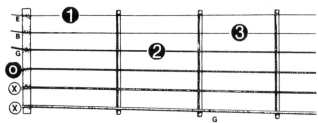

45. D min 7

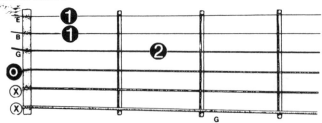

46. D min 6

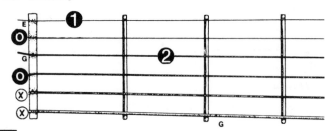

47. D maj 7

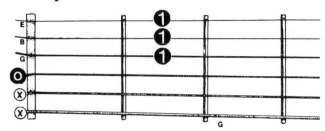

48. C maj

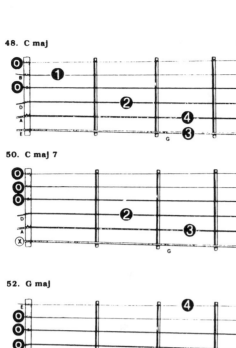

49. C 7

50. C maj 7

51. C 9

52. G maj

53. G maj

54. G 7

55. G min 7

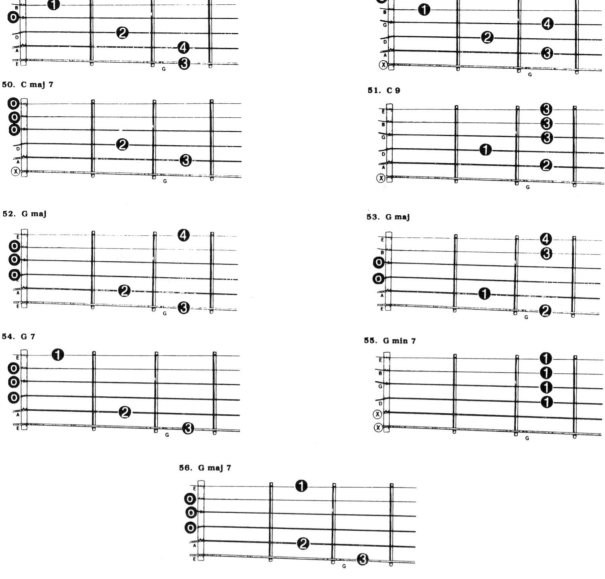

56. G maj 7

E bar chords at fifth fret -- Sixth string root.

57. A maj

58. A 7

59. A 7

60. A 6

61. A min

62. A min 7

63. A min 7

64. A min 6

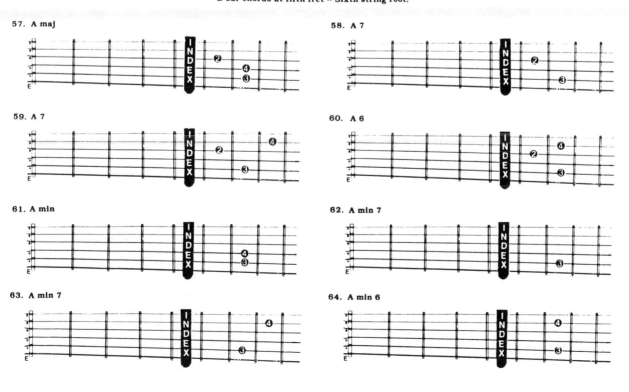

43

65. A maj sus. 4

66. A 7 sus. 4

A bar chords at the fifth fret -- Fifth string root.

67. D maj

68. D 7

69. D 7

70. D 6

71. D min

72. D min 7

73. D min 7

74. D min 6

75. D maj sus. 4

76. D 7 sus. 4

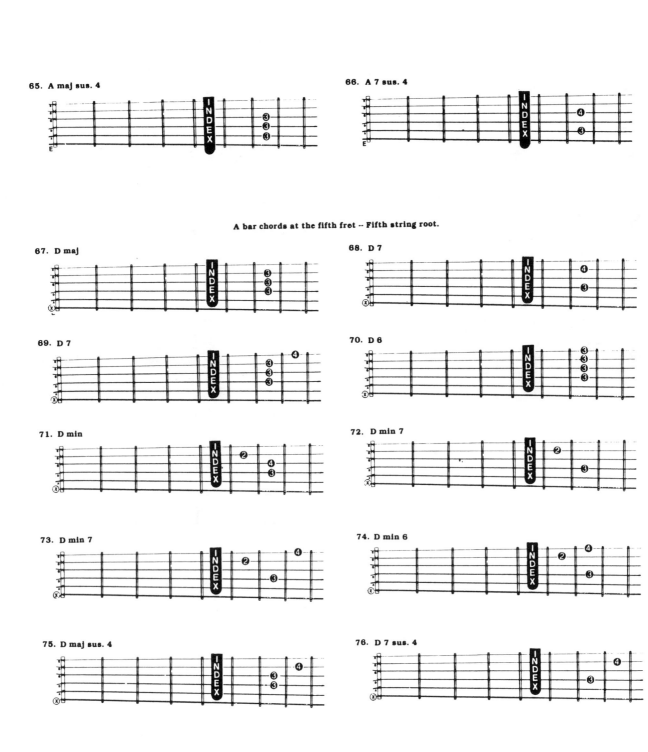

77. Movable 7th Sixth string root.

78. Movable 7th Sixth string root.

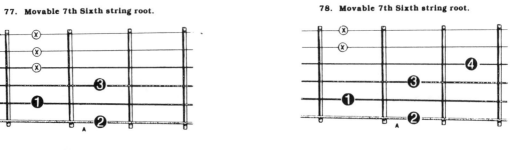

79. Movable 7th Fifth string root.

80. Movable 9th Fifth string root.

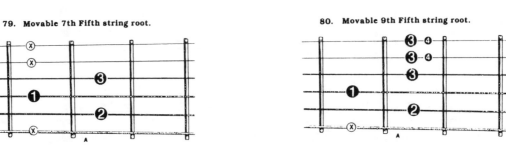

WINDOW #5

Rock Structure

Primary Objective Statement

To present the framework of rock song structure

Rock grew from the blues. Because it did, rock has always had the advantage of building on an already developed base. The blues is known as a distinct musical form with rigid inner boundries of unyielding count and predictable chord sequence. It is this fixed inner backbone which allows for the expansive, unreserved outer boundries of the blues form. Unlike the centuries old classical form, with its stuffy melodic considerations, the blues ticks off song time like a universal clock upon which the performer can depend, play against, throw riffs, scream over or simply let pass. No matter what you do over the top, the beat continues and the chord wheel turns, turns, turns on.

Rock and blues have always had a lot in common. Back in the forties when blues started to make it onto the radio in a big way, it blew away all of the other staid musical formats which the listeners took for granted. The blues did not bother with convention, formulas or calculation. It was the people's music, and it caught on. The unstated message of the blues has always been that music can be *informal,* it can be *something that really relates to your life,* it can immediately *change the way you feel,* and, if not lift your spirits, at least make you *feel real.* Rock exploded out of the top of the blues tradition and played it looser still. To this day, the same basic intervals, chord moves, and five note scale remain common to both rock and blues. Thing is, rock would just not sit still for the perpetual time wheel which the blues form represents. By the mid-fifties, Leo Fender was pushing electrics off the assembly line and Chuck Berry's <u>Maybellene</u> won the Billboard Triple Award for total sales, radio play and jukebox sales. Berry's <u>Johnny Be Goode</u> remains for all time the perfect example of generic rock. It is simply geared up blues.

Although it is no secret that the Beatles and the Stones were spoon-fed American blues in the early sixties, it was not until the late sixties that rock guitarists picked up the blues elements and *went free form.* No need for me to strain an explanation, just put on Jimi Hendrix's first album <u>Are You Experienced</u> and listen to the title cut. The depth of the picture is expressed on that single recording. When I first heard it, I realized that rock is a force that was not purposely invented, but came into existence of its own accord.

THE 4/4 BEAT

I feel obliged to mention the most obvious musical element which rock inherited from the blues: namely, the relentless use of 4/4 meter. Listen to the opening bars of Van Halen's <u>Running With The Devil</u>, or Foreigner's <u>Hotblooded</u>, and you will hear the most basic of all musical figures: the thumping of the tonic note on the regular quarter note beat. Amen. Get it, feel it, trust it, use it.

THE INEVITABLE ONE, FOUR, FIVE RELATIONSHIP

It comes as no big suprise that the triad built on the tonic is rock music's big guy. The triad built on the dominant or fifth tone, as you might suspect, is also a base element. The twist is the triad built on the fourth, a major scale degree which we have only mentioned to this point. The relationship of the *triads* built on the 1st, 4th, and 5th of the major scale form a POWERFUL INTERRELATED TRIO in much the same way as the 1st, 3rd, and 5th *degrees* of the major scale forge the major triad. As far as rock goes, the chord built on 3rd (G# major in the key of E) is not fundamental. Let's outline the situation presented by the interplay of the three most important stationpoints of rock chording: the triad built on the 1st, 4th, and 5th.

*****The relationship between the tonic chord and the fourth chord is the most COMMON chord relationship in rock. The fourth stands as a "complimentary" position upon which chords, riffs, or melodic statements can be built which repeat (or reflect) those originally played over the tonic position. The suspended 4th chord, which adds the fourth degree to the major triad, is also essential to rock form.

*****The relationship between the tonic chord and the fifth chord is the most FUNDAMENTAL chord relationship in rock. The fifth represents the point of resolution for all chord progressions and melody lines.

*****The mutual relationship involving the tonic chord, fourth chord and fifth chord binds together the THREE BASIC ROCK CHORD POSITIONS. These three chords are used in the standard twelve bar blues, the skelton from which the blues/rock form takes its dimensions. Below you will find an alternative twelve bar arrangement along with an eight bar blues example.

Basic 12 bar blues arrangement

1	2	3	4	5	6	7	8	9	10	11	12
E	E	E	E	A	A	E	E	B	A	E	B
1 2 3 4	1 2 3 4	1 2 3 4	1 2 3 4	1 2 3 4	1 2 3 4	1 2 3 4	1 2 3 4	1 2 3 4	1 2 3 4	1 2 3 4	1 2 3 4

Variation on 12 bar blues arrangement

1	2	3	4	5	6	7	8	9	10	11	12
E	A	E	E	A	A	E	E	B	B	E	E
1 2 3 4	1 2 3 4	1 2 3 4	1 2 3 4	1 2 3 4	1 2 3 4	1 2 3 4	1 2 3 4	1 2 3 4	1 2 3 4	1 2 3 4	1 2 3 4

8 bar blues arrangement

1	2	3	4	5	6	7	8
E E E E	B B B B	E E E E	A A A A	E E E E	B B B B	E E A A	E E B B
1 2 3 4	1 2 3 4	1 2 3 4	1 2 3 4	1 2 3 4	1 2 3 4	1 2 3 4	1 2 3 4

Now, let's take a look at the intervals inherent in the 1,4,5 relationship.

The 1,4,5 relationship in the key of E

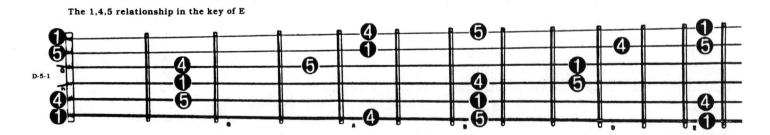

D-5-1

WHOLE STEP DOWN FROM 1, 4, 5

The building centers located on the first, fourth and fifth are stationpoints upon which other commonly used rock chords are relatively placed. One of these positions takes place a WHOLE STEP BELOW (two frets) each of the three primary centers we already have established. Yea, the whole step move is indeed one of rock's old standbys, proving itself to be an extremely versatile vehicle. So, let's identify the three positions a whole step below 2, 4, and 5. Below you see it spelled out three different ways: universally, for the key of E, and for the key of A.

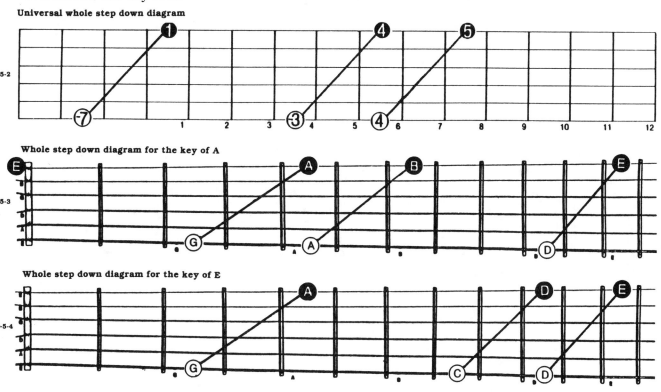

Universal whole step down diagram

Whole step down diagram for the key of A

Whole step down diagram for the key of E

Each of the three primary positions (1, 4, 5) has its own relative "whole step below" position, but it so happens to be that the whole step below the fifth is the fourth, a degree center already accounted for. So, what we have is two new chord centers. In the key of E, the 1st, 4th and 5th are E, A and B. So, the two new chords two frets below the 1st and 4th are D and G respectively. In the key of A, the 1st, 4th and 5th are A, D and E, so the two new chords will be G below A, and C below D. The fourth degree of the major scale has been identified as a center upon which musical statements are reiterated after they are first played over the tonic center. Well, the "whole step down" center is not really independent like the fourth center, but is usually directly incorporated into a chord move of riff with the primary center a whole step above.

The chord built on the whole step below the tonic (flatted 7th) has been used throughout the history of rock as an easy knock-about chord to batter back and forth off the tonic center. The examples go on and on. Remember <u>Tobacco Road</u> wherein the march-like rhythm used those two chord, the lower sliding into the upper? Or, the drawn-out opening of Van Halen's <u>Everybody Wants Some</u> which hangs on the lower chord before slamming to the upper? How about the Yardbirds old hit <u>Shapes</u>, or the Kinks double chord move in <u>You Really Got Me</u>, or the distinctive two-chord motif which sets off Hendrix's <u>If Six Was Nine</u>? ALL OF THESE use the tonic chord, with the "whole step below" chord to form the goods. Often the riff established in this position is taken to the fourth degree center (along with the whole step below) for repetition. A great example of this is the rock classic <u>Sunshine Of Your Love</u> by Cream. Recorded in D, the opening bars pound out D, D, C, D before the blues wheel turns to G, G, F, G.

What about the whole step move between the fifth and fourth two frets below? This whole step interval can be used in the same way as the other two whole step intervals built below the tonic and the fourth. Have you ever noticed that some of the songs on old blues records take the final four bars of the 12 bar blues form, where the resolution to the fifth occurs, and place them at the beginning of a song as an introduction? Well, this method of using a resolution as an intro was used by the Fab Four for the opening bars of <u>I Want To Hold Your Hand</u>. Remember those two chords that started the song off? That was the fourth being slid up a whole step to the fifth. YEAH, YEAH, YEAH.

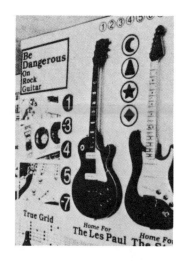

So far, we have talked about five major chords that are common to rock form: the major triads built on the 1st, 4th, and 5th, and also the triads built on the whole steps below the 1st (the flatted 7th) and the 4th (the flatted 3rd). These are the RAW ELEMENTS OF ROCK STRUCTURE. Interplay can be established in any number of ways. The blues standard Spoonful is a marriage of the tonic chord with the chord built a whole step below the 4th, so you see, there are no real rules — only parameters. The reason I am telling you all of this is so that when we get to the WINDOW called Copy Any Riff, Off Any Record, Note For Note, you will know what chords to look for. The transcriptions below will present you with a multitude of different ways to play the following intervals: THE WHOLE STEP, A MINOR THIRD, A FOURTH, A FIFTH, AND COMBINATIONS OF 1, 4, 5. All of these intervals (with the help of the whole step below the fourth) are surely found inherently in the proportions of the 1, 4, 5 relationship. Have a guitar lesson.

Wholestep

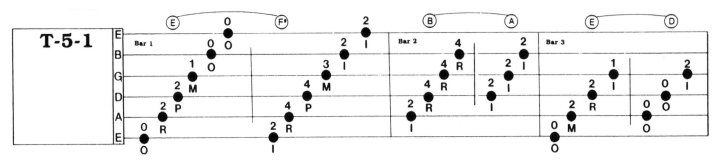

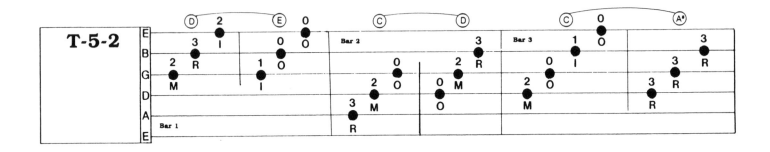

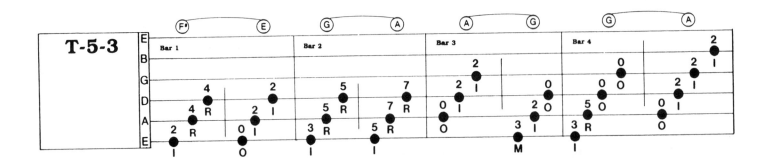

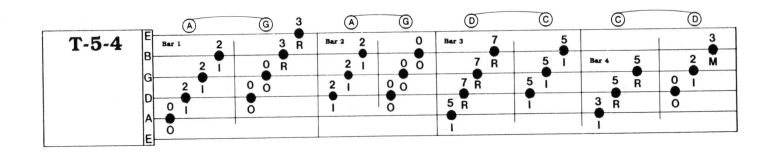

Minor third

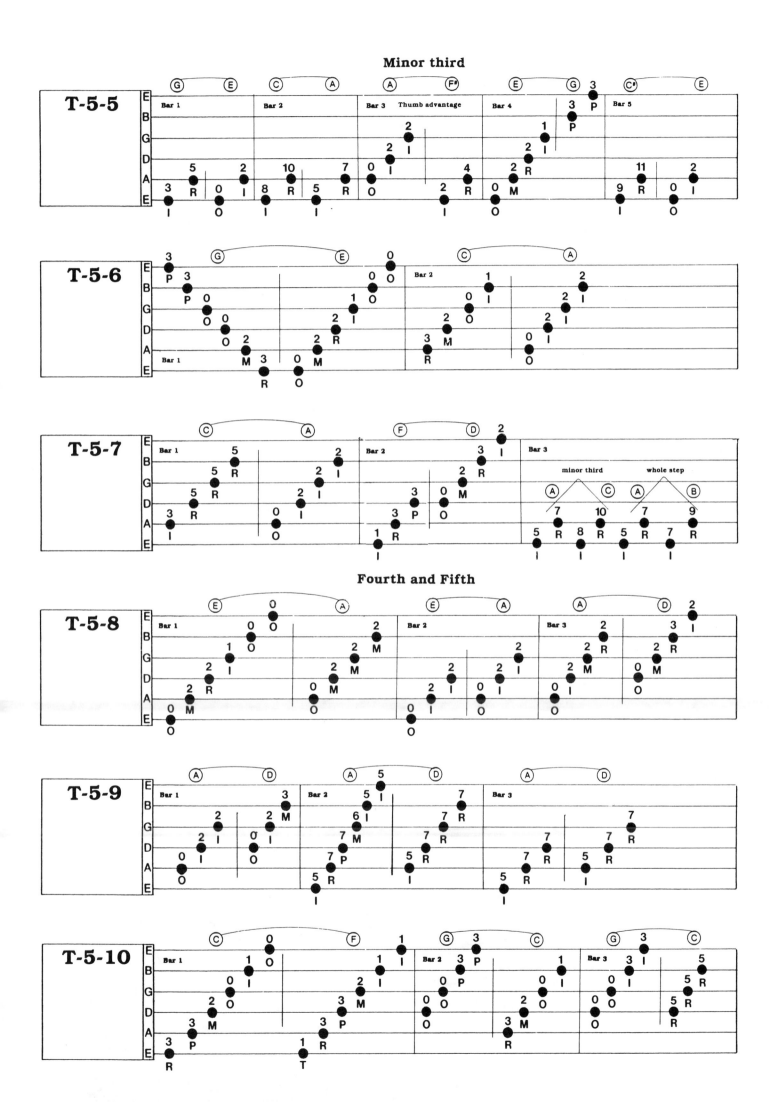

Fourth and Fifth

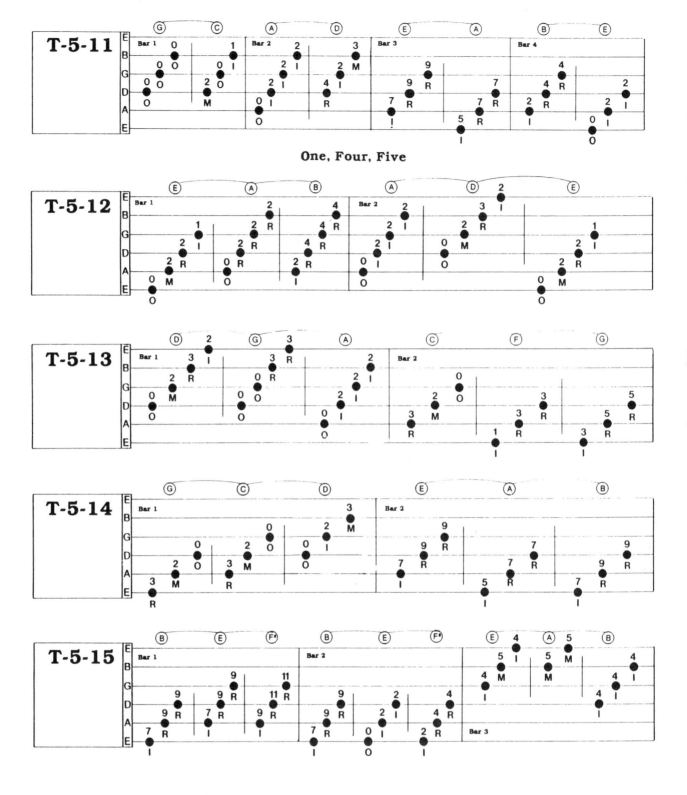

One, Four, Five

THE RELATIVE MINOR POSITIONS

Oh, I forgot to tell you — each of the twelve major chords has a corresponding relative minor chord which takes its place THREE FRETS BELOW THE MAJOR TRIAD POSITION IN THE FORM OF A MINOR TRIAD. What could be more mysterious than a *Relative Position?* Sort of like a hidden jungle city of gold that goes with each major chord.

Now, forget about twelve keys. Just think of the 1, 4 and 5 relationship. This means that with three primary degrees in the blues/rock scheme, we will now have three corresponding relative minor chords. First we will look at the situation for the key of A. The first is built on the fifth fret center, the fourth (D) is across the tenth fret, and the fifth across the twelfth fret. The relative minor positions, being three below the three primary positions, will take their places on the 2nd, 7th, and 9th frets. A major goes with F# minor. D major goes with a B minor. E major goes with C# minor. The fretboard diagram below does not show chords but relates notes on the two E strings.

Relative minor positions for key of A

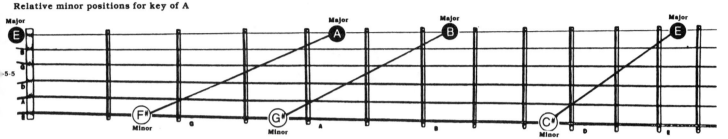

Now for the key of E. We can't very well play a note three frets from the twelfth fret position, the next E position above the open strings. This will put the relative minor to E at the 9th fret position (C# minor). Yes, C# minor is the relative minor to E major, F# minor is the relative minor to A major, and G# minor is the relative minor to B major. Now you know.

Relative minor positions for key of E

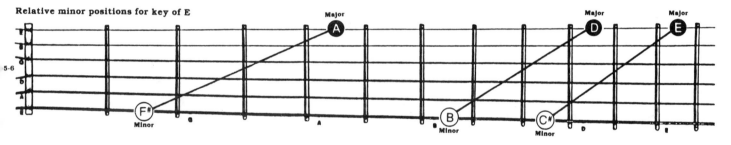

EIGHT IN ALL

The chords of rock are: the major triad built on the 1st, 4th, 5th, the whole step below the 1st, the whole step below the 4th, and the three corresponding relative minor chords, built on the 6th, 2nd, and 3rd of the major scale. Respectively in the key of E we have these chords: E, A, B, D, G, C# minor, F# minor, G# minor. And for the key of A it looks like this: A, D, E, G, C, F# minor, B minor, and C# minor. Of course, these eight chords are just a start because you can build any additional steps that you want, but, FOR STARTERS, HOW ABOUT UNDERSTANDING THESE EIGHT.

RIFF GOLD

Remember Whole Lotta Love? How could you forget with me reminding you all of the time, right? What Metal! What a great riff off the E chord. Really pure, really, well, something, I don't even know what. It is just a riff, like the one Keith used for Satisfaction. But that is what I am getting at. It is just a riff. What makes it so great? Well, what makes it so great is that rock is not embarrassed. It is, at its best, not KNOWING. Rock holds up its simple form for all to hear. The old school still thinks that music has to be something removed. You know, they have a little catagory called music, and it is something that is all complex, and fraught with difficulty, and just must be laborously fussed over, layed out on silly lines with dots, march all in a line with your tuba and all that schlock. I mean, just give it up. The boys in the back say, FORGET IT AND JUST POUND OUT THE RIFF FOR THE RIFF'S SAKE. THAT WORLD WHEN THE RIFF IS BEING PLAYED IS ENOUGH TO SUSTAIN THE DRIVER. One day, rock walked right up to the face of traditional methods and said LIKE IT OR NOT, YOU DON'T HAVE ANYTHING TO DO WITH ME. I STAND ALONE, AND YOUR RULES DO NOT APPLY TO ME. IF YOU DON'T LIKE THE FACT THAT WE PLAY ONE LICK OVER AND OVER AGAIN, LOUD AND DISTORTED, THAT IS TOUGH LUCK. I AIN'T GOING TO STOP JUST BECAUSE YOU DON'T LIKE IT.

Tape Side	Window
1 A	1
1 B	1 cont. 2, 3
2 A	4 , 5, 6
2 B	6 cont. 7, 8
3 A	8 cont. 9
3 B	9 cont. 10, 11, 12, 13
4 A	14, 15, 16, 17
4 B	18, 19, 20
5 A	20 cont. 21, 22
5 B	22 cont.
6 A	23, 24
6 B	24 cont.

THE TURNAROUND

Any series of chords or melodic structure that returns to its starting point in regular cycles falls into this broad catagory. Gloria by Shadows of the Night pops into mind right off the bat. In the key of E, the three chords that make up the song are E, D, and A. Easy stuff, I know, but IN THERE anyway. Same chords as the primary riff in AC/DC's Back in Black. Then you have stuff like Puff The Magic Dragon. Nice turnaround on that one. In the course of things, the relative minor to the tonic appears a little more than the relative minor to the 4th and the 5th, but you see all three if you pick apart a few Beatles songs. And furthermore, they don't have to be minor chords. That's right. You can go to the "relative" position three frets below the primary position, and just build the 1st and the 5th above. Just forget about the third and you will get the guts of the major chord. That makes a power chord. So, when you see the "three frets below" relative centers take on big, fat sounding chords, you know what is going on.

Next, you will find the circle of fifths (where you choose a letter name note and find the 5th to the immediate right, and the 4th to the immediate left) and the common chord chart for the key of E, A, D, G, B. These charts were first published in the beloved Heavy Guitar Bible.

Circle of fifths

A E B F# C# G# D# A# F C G D A E B etc.

Common Chord Chart

CHORD	KEY	E	A	D	G	B
1st Basic root or tonic		E	A	D	G	B
2nd Basic five frets above root		A	D	G	C	E
3rd Basic seven frets above root		B	E	A	D	F#
Relative minor to 1st Basic		C# minor	F# minor	B minor	E minor	G# minor
Relative minor to 2nd Basic		F# minor	B minor	E minor	A minor	C# minor
Relative minor to 3rd Basic		G# minor	C# minor	F# minor	B minor	D# minor
Relative 2 frets below root		D	G	C	F	A
Relative 2 frets below Fourth		G	C	F	A#	D

Let's see, in the key of E the fourth is A, and the D is a whole step below E, and G is a whole step below A....

WINDOW #6

The Blues Scale

Primary Objective Statement

To present the five note scale used for rock lead guitar

hat the *major scale* is to the classical violinist, the *blues scale* is to the rock guitarist. We have come a long way through the woods since WINDOW 1, wading through accounts of octave structure, tales of temperament, rantings about ratio numbers, all things musical which pertain to the guitar. But now is the time to get down to rock guitar. Because the guitar is first and foremost an instrument, I found it necessary to explain a lot of preliminary groundwork which I thought should be included in any good guitar instruction method, despite the particular style of interest. After all, the harmonic overtone series and the major scale work out on the classical guitar in the same way as they do on the jazz, blues or rock guitar. Sure, WINDOW 1 took me a few all-nighters, but I think it was worth it for the perspective provided.

The major scale is the big wheel. *The scale* is sort of a logical family, a series of seven notes which can be considered as a relative line. For instance, if you are just working the major scale down *one string,* you play either a whole step or a half step. When you are riding, you watch for the two half-step positions to "set off" a chosen spot. You know, *centering.* After going through twelve steps, you repeat your intervals in another octave. Carve the interval pattern of the major scale (W,W,H,W,W,W,H), along with the numbers (1,2,3,4,5,6,7) into your guitar, but leave plenty of room for even bigger numbers because the blues scale is on deck. Here, once more, the keystone of western music, set on the six string grid, is the *Universal Major Scale Diagram,* applicable in all twelve keys. Also find the keys of E major and A major on the first five frets of the axe.

Universal Major Scale Diagram

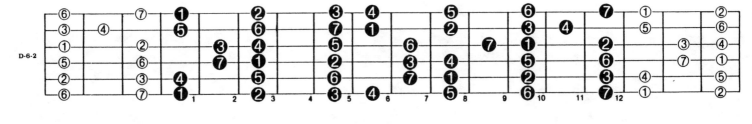

Universal Major Scale Diagram

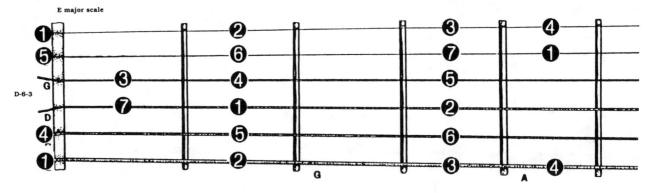

E major scale

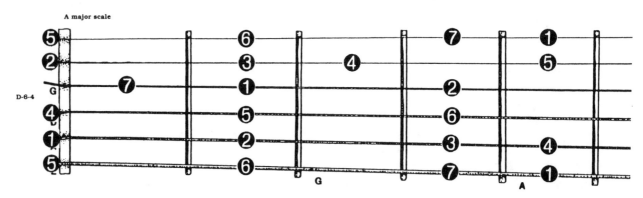

A major scale

The major is right here to look at. What, then, is the blues scale? How is it made up? What is its interval pattern? Where are the best boxes? Why is it used for rock? How does it work against the major chords built on the 1,4,5 degrees - I will proceed to tell you: THE BLUES SCALE IS DERIVED FROM THE MAJOR SCALE BY LOWERING THE 3RD A HALF STEP AND ELIMINATING THE 2ND, AND LOWERING THE 7TH A HALF STEP AND ELIMINATING THE 6TH. The blues scale is the sweet little guy. Yes, the blues scale is really a shorter *minor* version of the major, known as a pentatonic scale, which contains these five degrees; 1,-3,4,5,-7. Simple, *just like rock.* The tonic is the first, of course. The flatted 3rd is the same degree we came across in the makeup of the minor triad. The 4th and 5th are in the blues triangle with the 1st. The flatted 7th is the same "seventh" (actually flatted seventh) used on top of the major triad to make the "seventh chord." The pattern left by a five note scale is considerably easier to work with and study than a seven note "diatonic" scale. Check out how the blues came out of the major by studying the diagram below, which works off two different E strings.

Upper board E major - lower board E blues

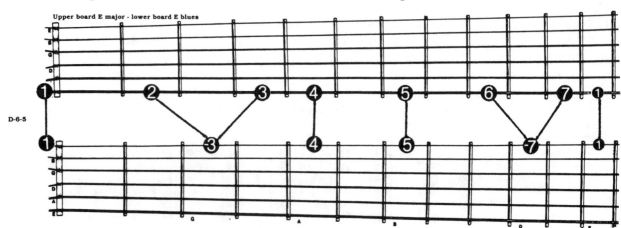

The interval pattern of the blues scale is: minor third, whole step, whole step, minor third, whole step. Right off the bat we encounter "the big guy," namely the minor third between the tonic and the flatted third, an interval unheard of in pure, successive, major scale study. That is what makes the blues scale unique. Known as a "gapped scale" because of it's larger intervals, the blues scale fits the hand a lot "tighter" than the major. The blues allows for simple, open boxes which you can "walk" across the board. Unlike the major, the blues scale has no half steps which cause you to run up the string.

Although the blues scale is a minor scale, derived from a more completely refined, seven note major scale, I never really thought of it as related to the major scale when I wrote about it in the first draft of The Heavy Guitar Bible in 1976. To me it was just five black dots which, taken together, all of the rock riffs worked out in. There was more discovery than this, of course, but if you go back and look at the Bible, the diagrams are basically layed out in just black dots without any clue as to how they relate to the major scale. The tonic degree was pointed out as prominant, but when it came right down to it, it was just *box city*. Now, I take great pride in telling everybody about how ROCK NOTES HAVE NAMES. Each of those faceless little dots which fill those patterns have their own little personal identities which have numbers and stuff. They sound different from each other, that's for sure.

The fourth and the fifth are common to both the blues and the major scale. After the initial minor third interval, there are two running whole steps between the -3rd, 4th, and 5th before you get to that big minor third again between the 5th and the -7th. The step between the last blues scale degree (-7th) and the tonic (1) is a whole step. Do you recognize the five degrees of the blues scale (1,-3,4,5,-7) to be those same tonal centers upon which we built to make the common rock chords? Yes, they are the same five points. You remember the rap I kept repeating in the chord WINDOW don't you: *the triads built on the 1st, 4th, and 5th, along with the triads built on the whole step below the 1st, and 4th.* Now it is the same rap, but we are talking FIVE BLUES SCALE DEGREES.

So, the blues elements can be derived in a number of ways. It is a great circle that has many seemingly different faces. But really, there is only ONE BLUES CIRCLE. And only those special degrees which have been awarded BLUES CLEARANCE are allowed to dance in the circle. Put triads on these special degrees and you have *the basic rock chords*. The classical form, with its endless major scale studies, was figured out on the guitar by 1800. The major derived styles work out nicely on the six string guitar; but it is the blues scale to which the guitar lends itself *inherently*. The major scale, fraught with half steps and intervals of a major third (two whole steps) on one string, does not sit across the guitar neck as "sweet" as the blues scale. Look, I'll show you. We will start by looking closely at the *Universal Blues Scale Diagram*, the master rock scale layout.

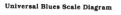

Universal Blues Scale Diagram

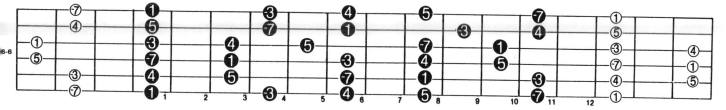

Would you please look at the first fret of the repeating twelve frets? IT HAS SCALE DEGREES STRAIGHT ACROSS ALL SIX STRINGS ON THIS UNIQUE FRET. None of the other eleven frets have this particular quality. Of the twelve frets in the repeating *Universal Blues Scale Diagram*, only this one earns the name ROOT NOTE FRET. The box built above this fret is a master box. Not really more important than others, just easier to work in. It is a natural spot; easy to "see" because the tonic notes take their position on the 1st and 6th string, easy to finger because the index finger can run a straight across "bar" or, EASIER YET, IN THE KEY OF E, PLAY EVERY STRING OPEN. It was no accident that the guitar was the instrument from which rock was born. I'm telling you, it wasn't Elvis or the Beatles, IT WAS THE ROOT NOTE FRET!!! The old blues records tell. Some of those guys were so laid back that there was no way in the world they were going to go out of their way for some complex interval pattern. Drink beer and hit it was the attitude. Easy guitar.

To put a red cherry on top, the E major and A major chord float over the six playable open strings in E like whip cream on chocolate pudding. No problem. The major scale has three frets from the twelve fret repeating Universal pattern which have "playable" scale degrees across all six strings, but oddly enough, none of them fall across the single fret where the tonic notes are on the two E strings. It took the blues scale, the simple "altered" scale to make the instrument "easy" for rock. The fact that rock uses the interval of a fourth in its chord structure makes the magic for chord building on rock guitar. Everything just added up and fell into place. The deal is all for you to see in the two diagrams below which chart the blues scale for the key of E and A on the first twelve frets of the guitar. You will find these two diagrams again (but extended to 24 frets) on the Be Dangerous On Rock Guitar Wall Poster. Behold for all time, THE ROCK SCALE.

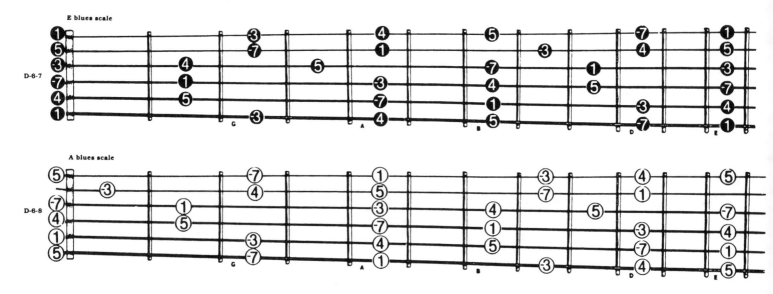

The root note fret is directly across the open strings and the twelfth fret for the key of E, and across the fifth fret for the key of A. You can see how the ROOT NOTE FRET is a logical place to start building. You know, right off the bat, there are two ways you can look at any twelve fret repeating pattern, and the blues scale is no different. You can look *up and down* the running length of the string, or you can study the pattern *across* each of the twelve frets. Like the weaving of an area of fabric, these two dimensions are used to frame "boxes" which accomodate our limited human hand. The ROOT NOTE FRET offers a terrific anchor for the centering of tons of rock guitar moves. Other boxes are marked in reference above or below this EASY MARK. Another thing about the root note fret: because the fretboards on the wall poster have 24 frets, that means any twelve fret pattern will repeat itself twice. This means that the root note fret will appear TWICE for each key (except E which has the open strings, the 12th fret, and the 24th fret). So wherever you find it once, just count up (or down) twelve frets and you find an entire other root note fret. So, now you know the whole picture from the *Universal Blues Scale Diagram*, and you know that the regions *on and above* the special root note fret are a portion of the whole repeating pattern. Can you tell that I am trying to pound this into your head? I AM. IT IS CRUCIAL THAT YOU CLEARLY UNDERSTAND THIS PHENOMENON IF YOU ARE TO EVER ATTAIN THE DREADED STATUS OF DANGEROUS! Now, as keys change, so does the position of the root note fret. The diagram below shows you the root note frets for E, G, A, B and D. Know them for future attack strategy.

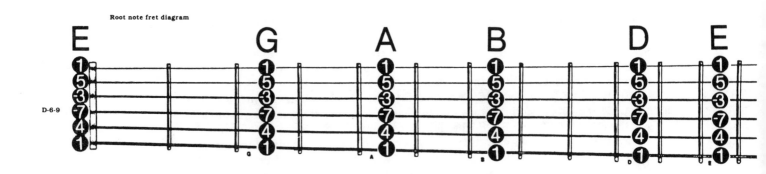

Where did the *root note fret* come from? Well, only the blues scale has the root note fret, but the blues scale is derived from the major, right? So take a look at the first two frets of the *Universal Major Scale Diagram*, and compare them to the first two frets of the *Universal Blues Scale Diagram*, and you will see how the root note fret came to be.

Evolution of the blues root note fret

UNIVERSAL BLUES BOXES

Our next goal is to get you to BECOME FAMILIAR WITH THE ENTIRE TWELVE FRET REPEATING PATTERN presented by the *Universal Blues Scale Diagram*. Once this noble goal is accomplished, you will be able to play the blues scale all over the board in any key. Needless to say, THIS DEED IS PARAMOUNT TO BEING DANGEROUS ON ROCK GUITAR!

Now I am going to subdivide the *Universal Blues Scale Diagram* into smaller *Universal Blues Boxes*, with each box noted by the letter U and a number (e.g. box U 3). Of course, each *Universal Blues Box* can be equally applied to all twelve keys. When a *Universal Blues Box* is applied to a particular key, the box will take on the letter of the key. For example, box U 3, will become box E 3, when the Universal Box is centered to the key of E (E = 1). Same thing with the key of A. The all encompassing chart study below will provide you with the *Universal Blues Box* in the left column, the E Blues Box in the center column, and the A Blues Box in the right column. Take a closer look and you will see that the *Universal Blues Box* will tell you the actual scale degree involved.

Come on, let's run. All the other stuff, just let it pass on. Just get into this one thing for now. Run and Run and Run. Just run until you can't run anymore.

More than anything else, the reason that I created the *Universal Blues Boxes* was just to break everything down. After that, you build everything up, to the point of a complete song, and you're on your way. The *Universal Running Boxes* are actually a little more to the point. In them, well, *you run*. Leave the FM radio on all night once and just listen to it. I am not saying that it is necessary for you to do this for your enjoyment, but before you get schooled in *anything, you have to bite the bullet*. Hear them run, run, and run. I have. And it seems to never stop with MTV and all that. I am happy really, because I have always loved rock, and I am glad to see it really become a true part of the American culture.

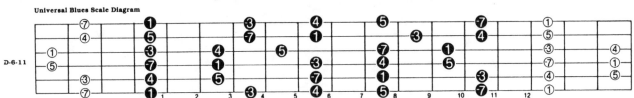

Universal Blues Scale Diagram

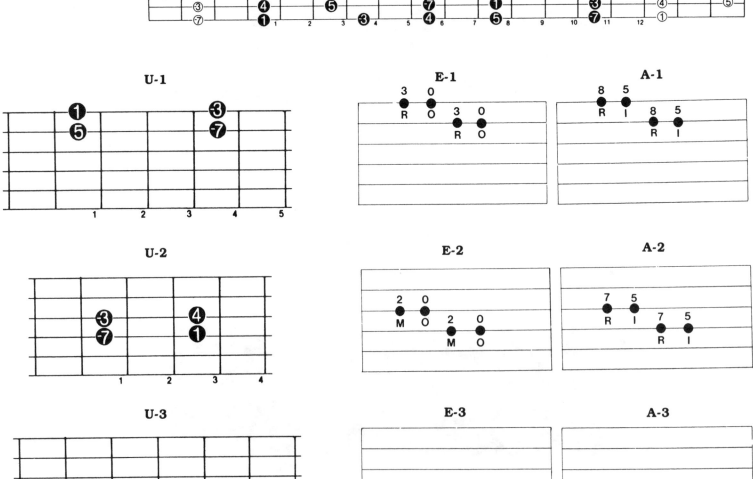

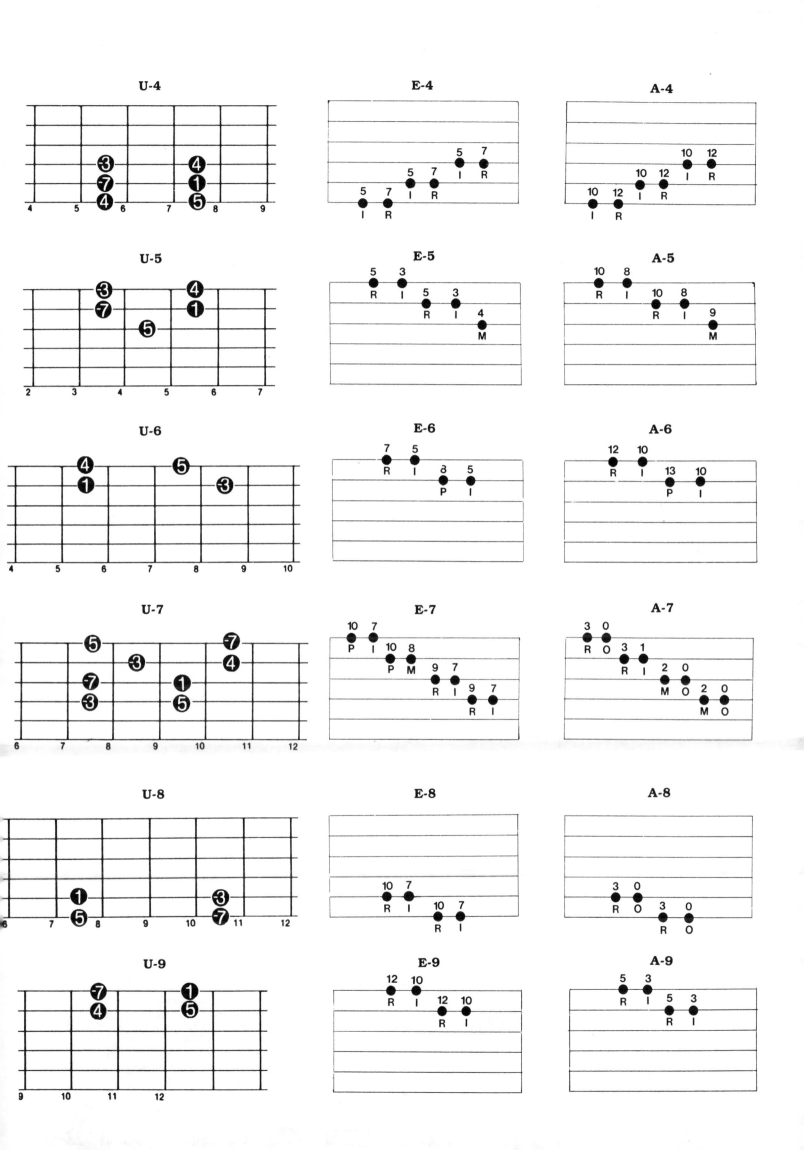

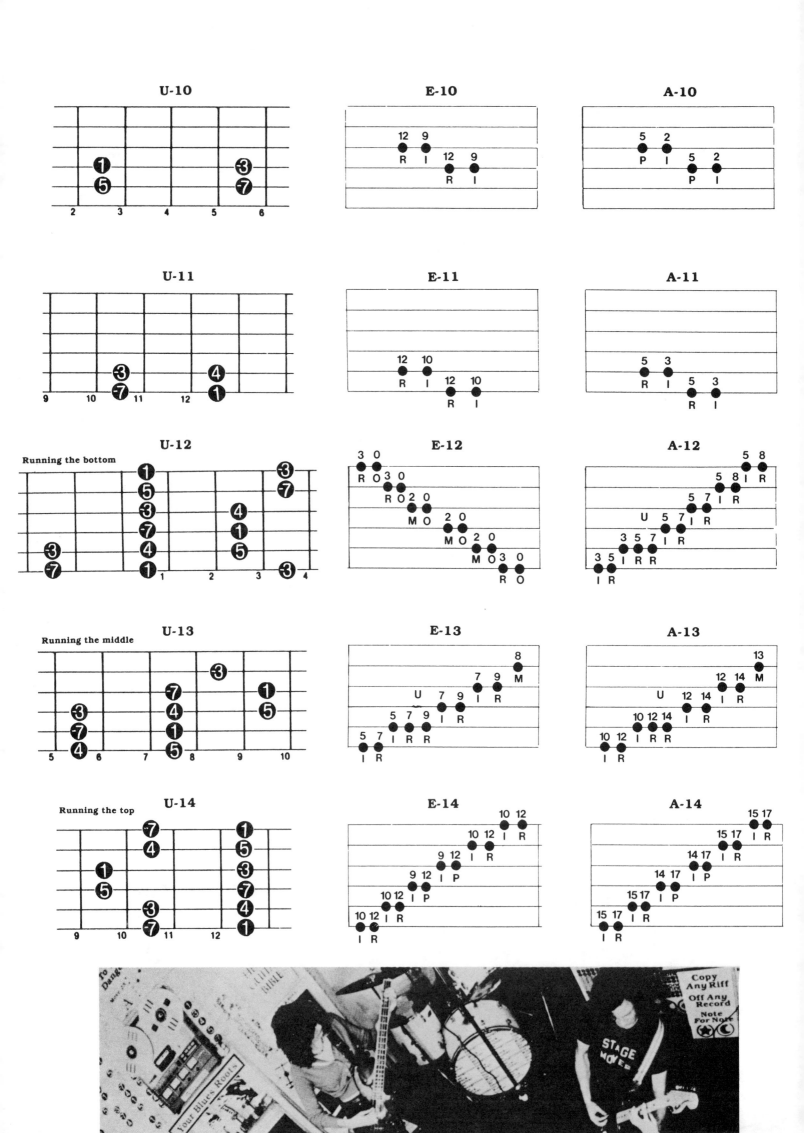

HAND BOXES FOR E AND A

So you have been through the mill once, right? Well, you're not getting off that easy! Don't forget, you don't know the forest's true nature by going through it once. So we will now march on. Yes accept this, HAND BOXES, what the hell will they think of next? These things fit your hand like a glove, each fret gets assigned a functional finger, you know, according to the little rule book of the official "crack your knuckles" school of half step pinky overdrives. I entertained the value of calling them *generic* boxes, you know, how many pieces of pizza are left? At any rate, they are there, right on the paper for you to see and learn from. These hand boxes will allow you to successfully understand both the *running area* of the 12 fret *Universal* pattern, and the *fingering sequence* of the run. Please take your time and slowly pass through each hand box for both the keys of E and A. These transcriptions were first published in my third guitar book <u>Blues Guitar - Inside and Out.</u>

Anytime you examine something closely under a bright critical light, as we have done with the blues scale pattern, you are bound to lose any flash and glory associated with the material's use. It's OK. Don't worry about it. The more cold facts that you know about the blues scale, the more hot performances you can turn out. It takes both worlds to get it: quiet study, hot action.

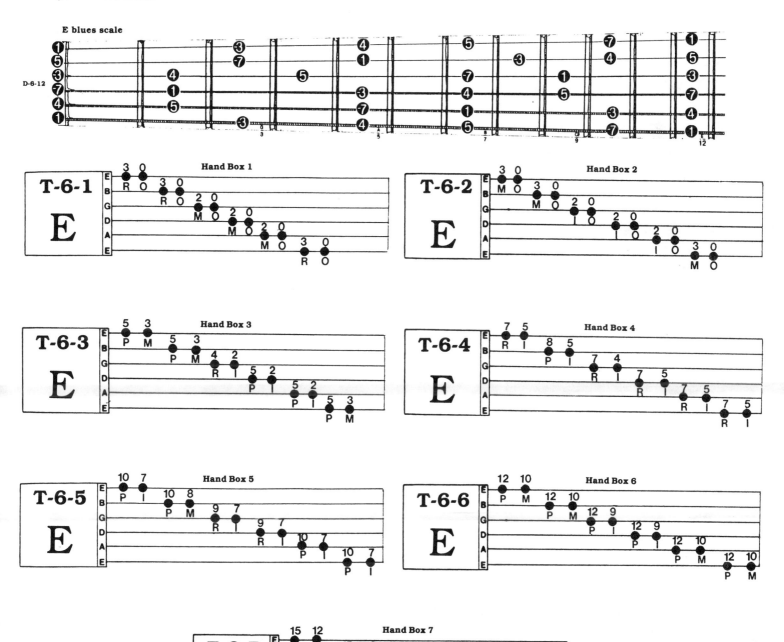

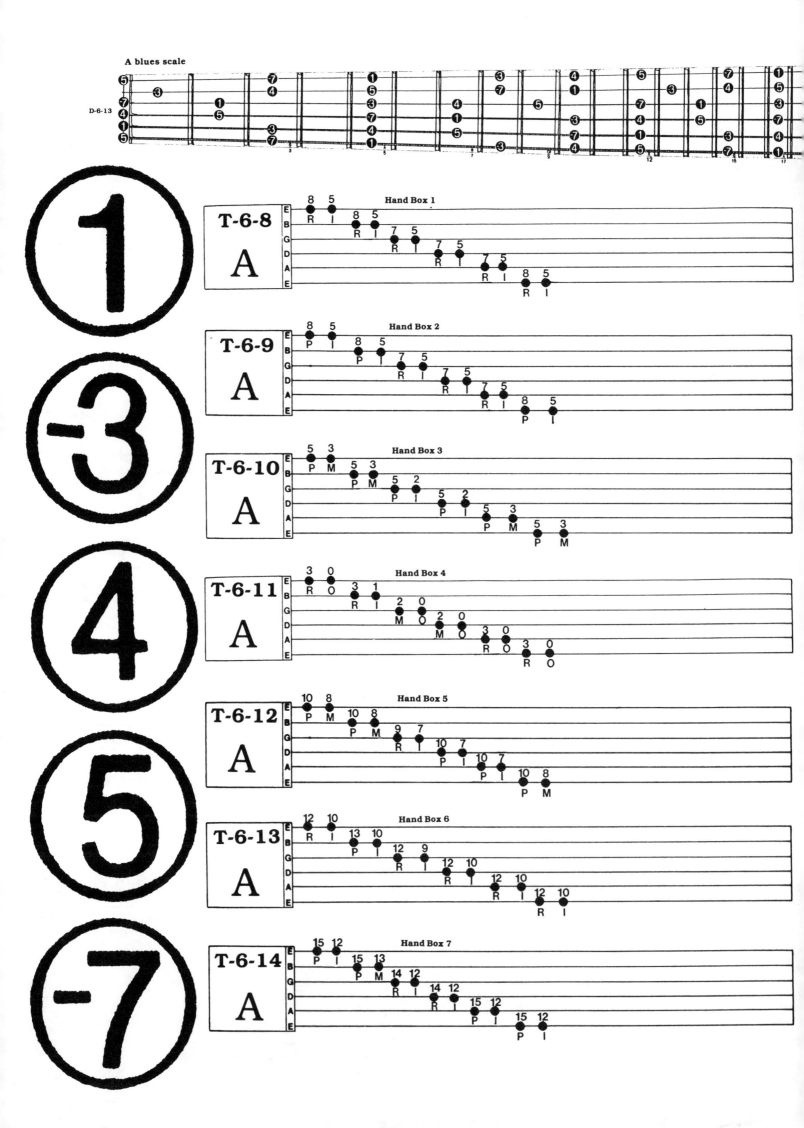

WINDOW #7

Octaves on the Guitar

Primary Objective Statement

To present the relationship of octave notes on the fretboard

What do the four Universal Diagrams, all featured below, have in common? For starters, they all represent twelve fret repeating patterns which reach across six tonally staggered fixed strings. We also know that each of the *Universal Diagrams* provides us with a "keyless" standard model which we can apply to any musical key. Each of the seventy-two black dots that you can see on the *Universal Chromatic Scale Diagram* represent one of the chromatic scale degrees. The dots which you see on the *Universal Major Scale Diagram* depict the seven major scale degrees, which leave behind the world famous, tried and true interval pattern of W,W,H,W,W,W,H. The *Universal Major Chord Inversion Diagram,* a subset of the previously mentioned diagram, presents us with the constellation of major chord figures which uniformly manifest themselves for all twelve major chords. *The Universal Blues Scale Diagram* portrays the scale pattern handed down to rock guitarists by blues artists for use in their frenzied art.

Note	Frequency
A_3	220.00
$A\#_3$	233.08
B_3	246.94
C_4	261.63
$C\#_4$	277.18
D_4	293.66
$D\#_4$	311.13
E_4	329.63
F_4	349.23
$F\#_4$	369.99
G_4	392.00
$G\#_4$	415.30
A_4	440.00
$A\#_4$	466.16
B_4	493.88
C_5	523.25
$C\#_5$	554.37
D_5	587.33
$D\#_5$	622.25
E_5	659.26
F_5	698.46
$F\#_5$	739.99
G_5	783.99
$G\#_5$	830.61
A_5	880.00

Two Octaves of A

D-7-1

Universal Chromatic

Universal Major

Universal Major Chord Inversion

Universal Blues

The number 1 remains the same on all four Universal Diagrams

The question remains: *What do all of these Universal Diagrams have in common?* The answer is: THE NUMBER ONE, the numerical representation of the tonic note. All of the Universal Diagrams carry the same tonic notes in the same cookie cutter pattern. Below, witness the universal element of the *Universal Diagrams, The Universal Tonic Diagram.*

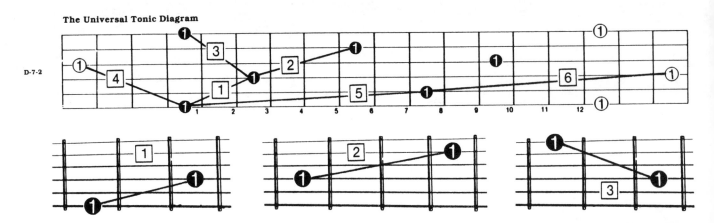

Any two tonic notes form either an *octave relationship,* or a *unison relationship.* I have spotlighted the three octave positions used most often by rock and jazz guitarists by isolating them from the Universal diagram for singular consideration. These three "fit" the hand pretty easily with the #1 and #3 octave span appearing naturally in the open E position, with the #2 span contained integrally in the open G chord. The half step tuning irregularity between the 2nd and 3rd string is responsible for the half-step difference between octave span #1 and #2, and also #3 and #4. Along with the octave positions used for lead and chord work, you should also be familiar with those that don't fit the hand, such as 5 and 6, I did not want to chop up the octave diagram with *too many* lines, so I stopped at six. If you take a minute to look, you can spot many more.

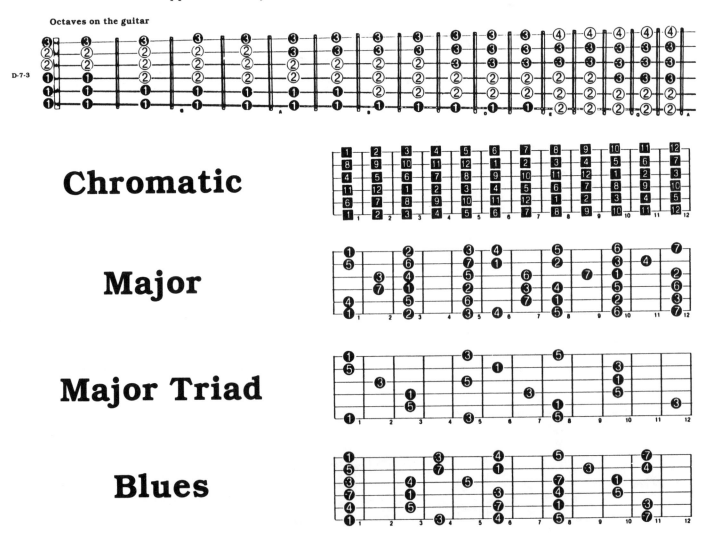

WINDOW #8

Single and Double String Technique with common boxes

Primary Objective Statement

To present an overview of string technique

Placing the tip of the finger on the string represents the most sensitive aspect of a guitarist's performance. The fingering of the string, along with all subsequent physical interaction, can be considered as *the point of art*. So fine is the distinction between the boundaries of catagorized technique, that after a certain degree of reflection, you must rely on a *native understanding* which springs from simply knowing basic procedural techniques. This will allow you to *identify* the string technique used by simply listening to a recording once. Although the search for control over the string's action can be an enjoyable lifelong search, after a short period of intense study you will notice a circle around the game and the string's sound won't fool you anymore. Everything after this point is an exercise in raw expression, purposeful exploration, of trancendental rock and roll fun.

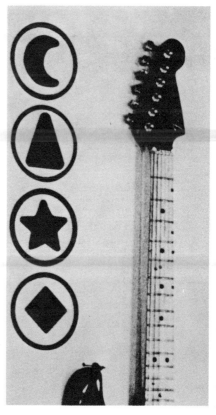

Here is the bottom line: any action of the finger on the fixed string results in a variation of tonal quality. This is a fact that guitarists cannot get away from no matter how hard they may try. Gaspar Sanz (1640-1710) wrote in his book on guitar technique: "Its faults or its perfections lie in whoever plays it, and not in the guitar itself, for I have seen some people accomplish things on one string for which others would need the range of an organ." Yes, it takes real-life *effort* to pull off expressive riffs; not neccessarily hard work, just concentrated attention to the elements of your own style. You really put yourself on the line when you play the guitar. There is no way to fake it. If you have a good touch, then it is immediately evident. If you don't, same deal. The archer has his bow, the pool shark has his cue, and the guitarist has his set of sensitive strings. What can you do? It comes with the territory.

I truly believe that sometimes things are better left unsaid, or better still, clearly recorded. So, with the technique catagories below, you get a brief description and a list of features you will hear demonstrated on the tape.

BENDING

Bending is the art of pushing the string *onto* and *across* the fretboard in the direction perpendicular to the string's length. Bending increases the tension of the string, and thereby increases the frequency of the resulting pitch. The harder you push, the higher the frequency will extend above the commonly fretted note. A little is a little, a half step is easy, a whole step is getting there, and a step and a half is pushing very hard. Any fretted note can be bent, excluding open strings and their harmonic overtones.

    A. Half Step
    B. Whole Step
    C. Towards Thick Strings
    D. Towards Thin Strings
    E. Bend and Bend Again
    F. Bend, Then Pluck, Then Relax
    G. Double Note Bend
    H. Subtle Texture -Slight Bend

PULLING

Pulling is the act of *snapping the finger off the fretted string* in a forceful manner which slightly bends the string before its release, and afterward leaves the string in motion to sound another lower note. In other words, you bend the string slightly before you pull it off, and when you do, you leave it ringing.

HAMMERING

Hammering is the act of bringing a finger down on a singing string to sound a higher note. Both the hammer (especially the repeated hammer) and the pull off technique are essential to *fast lead work*.

    A. Bring the finger down on a string that is already sounding
          a lower note.
    B. Repeat Hammer
    C. Repeat Hammer Pull Off

SLIDE

Sliding is the smooth movement of a finger along the running length of a string while holding the string to the board. When you slide up or down over a fret, the string's vibration is conserved for the sounding of a higher or lower note.

    A. Slide up
    B. Slide down
    C. Parts of chords

VIBRATO

Like I said, any movement of the finger on the singing string affects the tonal quality of the note. Vibrato is a broad "catch all" catagory for all of the various ways you can "rock your finger" on the string.

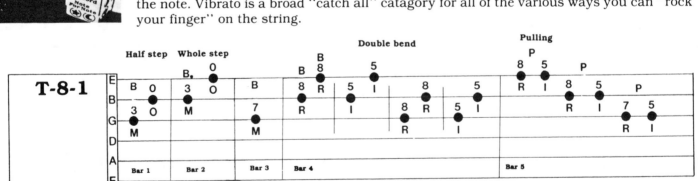

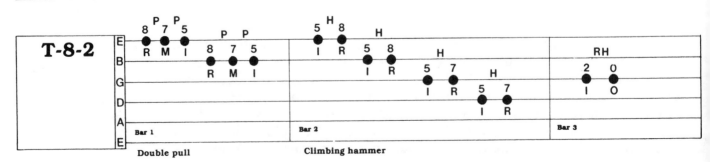

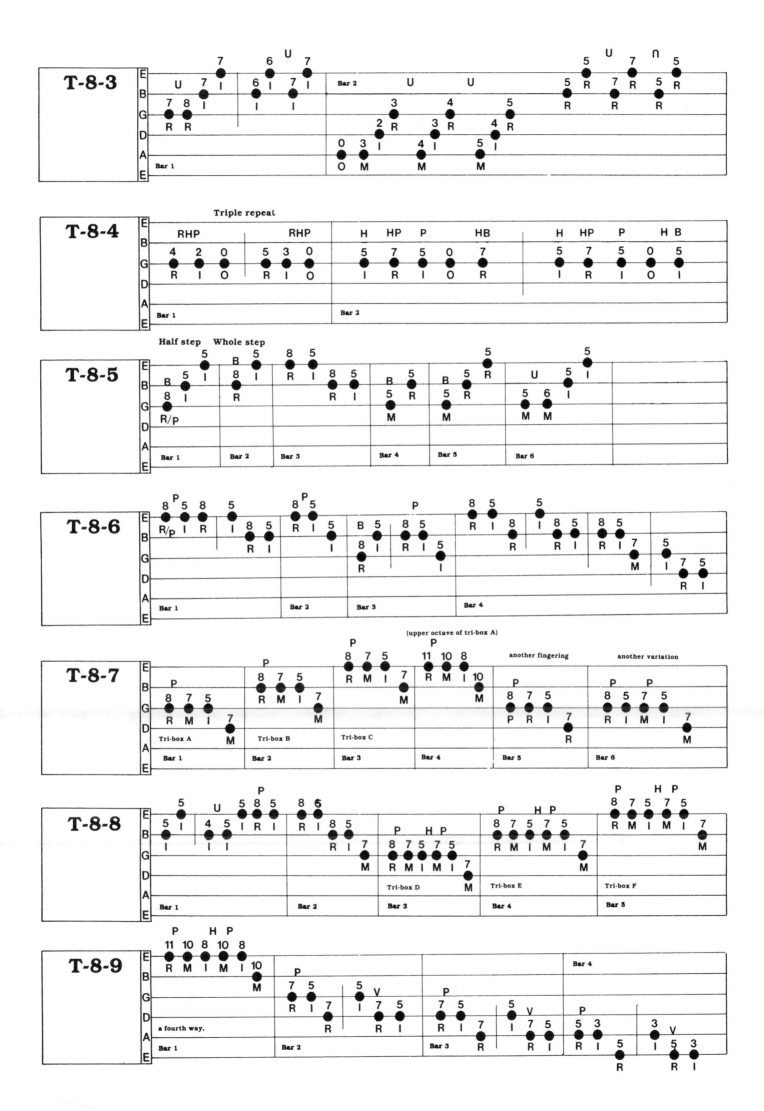

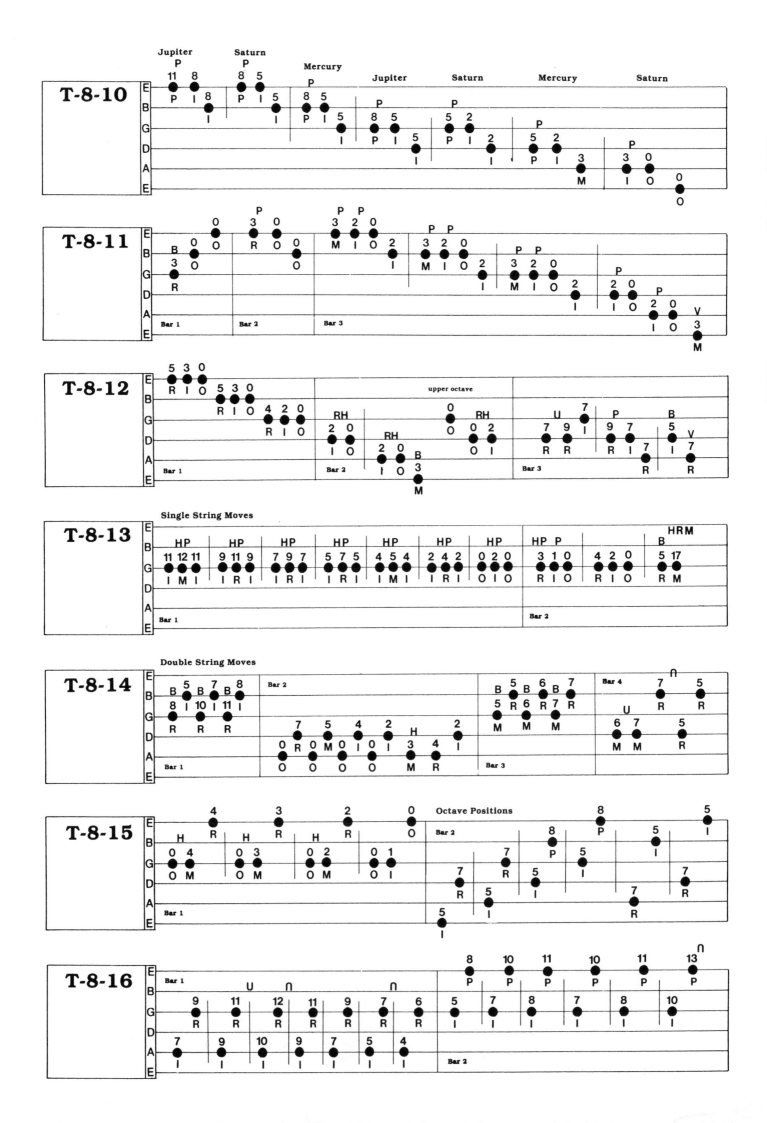

WINDOW #9

The Relative Scale

Primary Objective Statement

To study rock's "other" five note scale

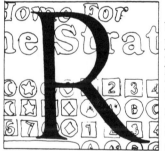

un the blues scale up and down your fretboard until you can do it in your sleep. Play each box through until you are absolutely certain where you are in the twelve fret repeating pattern at any one time. Start with getting to know the primary lead box located on and immediately above the root note fret. This miraculously simple flat bottomed box is a blind gift from the guitar's original designer to all of those who, centuries later, would travel the blues/rock crossroads. This unmistakable box covers four of the twelve frets, which leaves you with eight more frets across six strings with which to become familiar. After you actually play the pattern through the wheel for the first time, the old head lights start to come on. Sorry people, THAT'S JUST NOT GOOD ENOUGH. You have to devour the pattern, gobble the boxes, pushing yourself until you reduce the *Universal Blues* pattern to insignificantness, SWALLOWING IT WHOLE AT WILL.

Now, what is the relative scale all about? Here is the deal in a nutshell: the relative scale is a five note scale which is IDENTICAL TO THE BLUES SCALE IN EVERY WAY WITH THE EXCEPTION OF ITS POSITION. The pattern of the relative scale takes its place on the fretboard exactly THREE FRETS BELOW THE BLUES SCALE PATTERN. You might want to read the last two sentences a few times because of their importance. You see the relative scale is in the same key signature as the blues scale, it has the same shape, same boxes, same "root note fret" configuration, *same everything* except position. The reason that you don't see a *Universal Relative Scale Diagram* is because it would be identical in its configuration to the *Universal Blues Scale Diagram.* You just pick up the cookie cutter pattern of the blues scale and move it down three frets, simple as that. Let's take a look at the deal in the key of A. Diagrams are from <u>The Heavy Guitar Bible</u>.

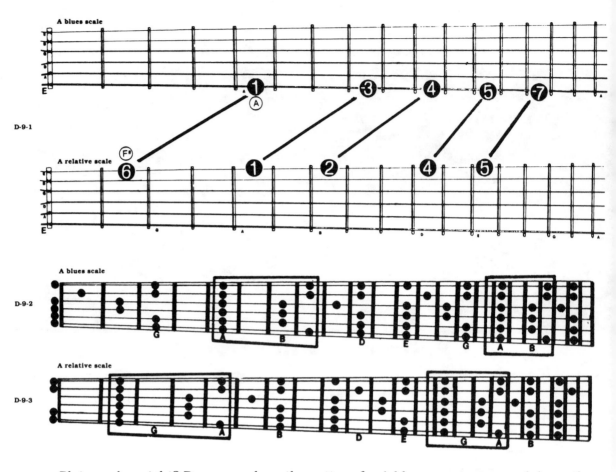

D-9-1

D-9-2

D-9-3

Plain as day, right? Do you see how the pattern for A blues was just moved down three frets to get the A relative position? Do you see that the relative scale in the key of A is the same as the blues scale in the key of F#? One and the same. Here is the blues/relative lowdown for the key of E. Notice how the "relative root note fret" now moves three frets down from the twelfth fret to the ninth.

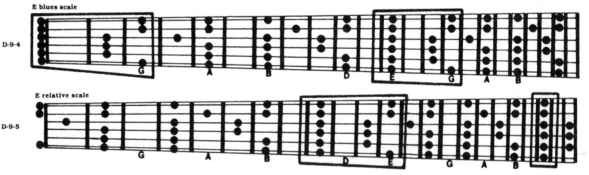

D-9-4

D-9-5

I always put the term "relative root note fret" in quotes because this special fret in the relative scale pattern is identical in nature to the root note fret found in the blues scale pattern, but the "relative root note fret" position does not actually carry the root notes on the two E strings like the blues root note fret. The most important concept to grasp is that we now have a *second center* that we can use to plan our lead work.

THE RELATIVE SCALE SOUND

Why the relative scale? What is it? What are its tonal characteristics? For years I have tried to put it into words, but I have come to know that some things musical defy description, and for the sake of quick understanding, are better simply *accepted as real.* The blues scale is real. The relative scale is real. The blues scale has a hard, cutting edge and is used for those up-front, direct, knock-over riffs. On the other hand, passages which use the relative scale exclusively have a very melodic, smokey, far away feel to them which sounds mellow when played against blues scale riffs. As a matter of fact, that is the best way to get a feel for the difference between these two important scales; play a riff in the blues scale, then move it down three frets and *listen to* the mellow difference. Both of these rock scales are used independently, and mixed and matched, to form a hybrid lead rock scale.

Both the relative scale and the relative minor chord use the same interval of a *lower minor third* (three frets down) to establish themselves below the primary centers of the blues scale and the major chord respectively. It is this "lower" positioning which establishes their musical relativity.

THREE PART CIRCLE: MAJOR, BLUES, RELATIVE

Tape Side	Window
1 A	1
1 B	1 cont. 2, 3
2 A	4, 5, 6
2 B	6 cont. 7, 8
3 A	8 cont. 9
3 B	9 cont. 10, 11, 12, 13
4 A	14, 15, 16, 17
4 B	18, 19, 20
5 A	20 cont. 21, 22
5 B	22 cont.
6 A	23, 24
6 B	24 cont.

The consequence of taking the twelve fret long, six string wide repeating Universal Blues Scale Diagram, and moving it down three frets to make the relative, is complex. The fact that the relative scale is functional does not in any way change the existence of the blues scale. So you are dealing with two independent scales.

When you take the lead, you can play with "eyes" just for the blues scale, or with "eyes" just for the relative scale. This would amount to playing entirely within the framework of one or the other scale. We will soon learn how to mix and match these two scales in a variety of ways. Now understand this: there are TWO BLUES SCALE DEGREES WHICH ARE ALSO RELATIVE SCALE DEGREES. The two degrees which both of these scales have in common are, not suprisingly, THE FIRST AND THE FIFTH FROM THE MAJOR SCALE. These are the two most common musical notes, and can be found as base degrees in all common scales. So let's take into account what we have here: two different five note scales with the blues scale consisting of 1, -3, 4, 5, -7, with the 1st and 5th common to both the blues and relative.

The twist to the story, the fact which starts to turn the findings toward a great circle, is that the other three "relative" notes are the 2nd, 3rd, and 6th of the major scale. In other words, the relative scale is the major scale with two degrees omitted. *The relative scale is a subset of the major scale.* What are the implications of this? Well, if the blues pattern is the same as the relative, and the relative "fits" into the major scale pattern, then the architecture of the blues/relative scale is found "in" the major scale pattern. This is not to say that the degrees of the blues scale are found in the major scale, only the configuration of its interval pattern. Look, let's take this thing piece by piece. Below you see five diagrams. The first pair show the blues scale (1, -3, 4, 5, -7) and the relative scale (1, 2, 3, 5, 6) for the key of E, then another pair shows the same deal for the key of A. The final diagram is the Universal Major Scale Diagram. If you see it on the blues scale diagrams, just move it down three frets and find it on the relative scale diagram. See you on the other side.

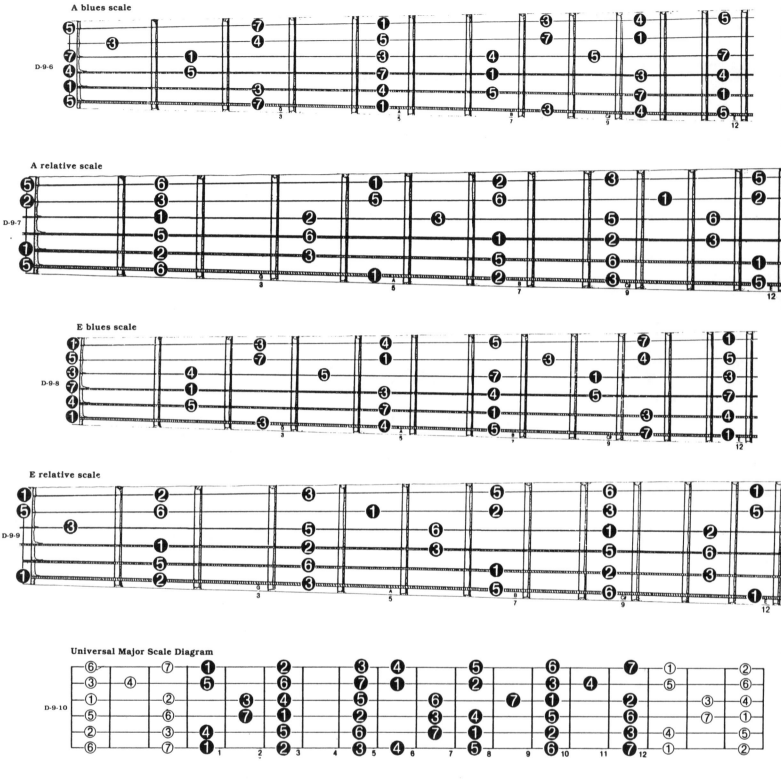

A blues scale

A relative scale

E blues scale

E relative scale

Universal Major Scale Diagram

The fretboard diagrams show only the first twelve frets of the guitar, but can be witnessed all the way up to the 24th fret on the wall poster. To play using the relative scale is, in effect, playing in the major scale. The "relative root note fret" found on the 9th fret for the E relative scale, and the 2nd fret for the A relative scale can also be found on the 10th fret of the Universal Major Scale Diagram. See what I'm saying?

Now, if the blues and relative share the 1st and the 5th, then the three other notes of the relative (2, 3, 6) fall where they may over the previously established BLUES SCALE PATTERN (refer to the *Universal Blues Scale Diagram*). Please note that the blues scale is shown in solid black dots, the relative scale by single line circles, with the two degrees common to both scales (the first and the fifth) shown as black dots with circles around them. The critical area above and below the root note fret will be shown for the key of A with only the first four frets of the same two scales shown for the key of E. Study har This is the game.

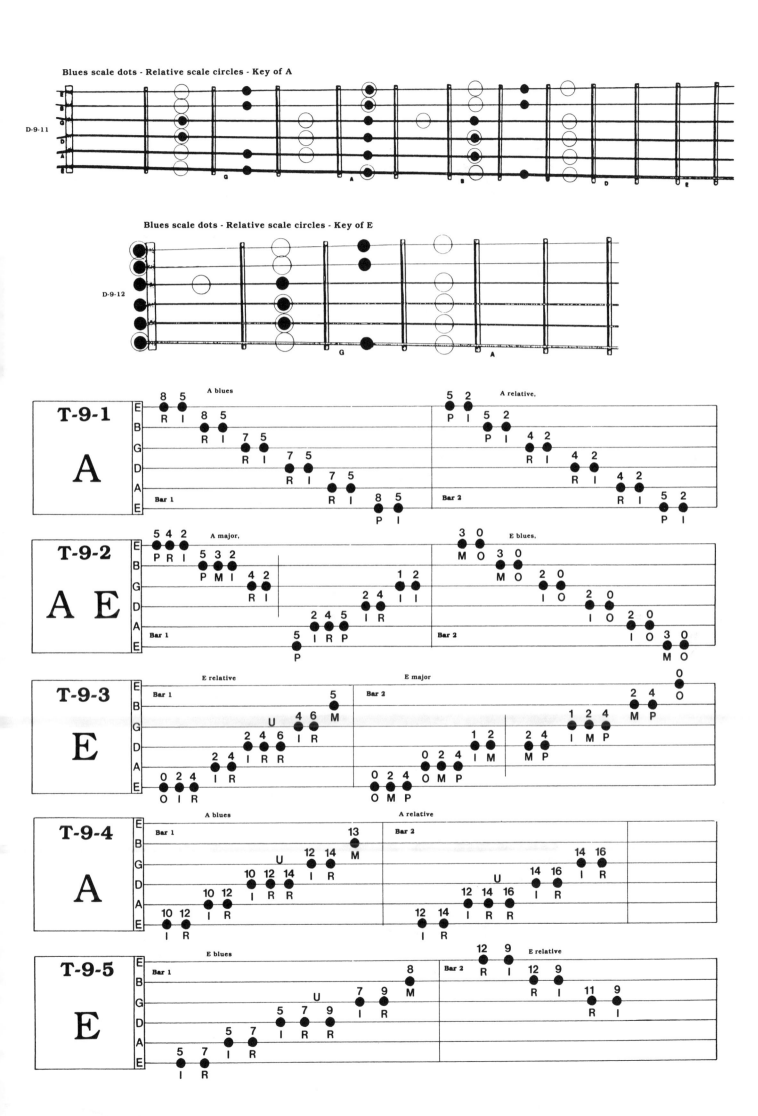

Blues scale dots - Relative scale circles - Key of A

D-9-11

Blues scale dots - Relative scale circles - Key of E

D-9-12

It seems that no matter what you do, you end up coming back to the blues scale, at least for reference. The blues scale has two "out" degrees (-3 and -7) but still holds on to the 1st, 4th and 5th. The relative scale, formally called the pentatonic scale (although the word can be used to describe any five note scale), is nothing more than the major with the 7th and the 4th lifted. Since the relative and blues scale share the same pattern, this ties the blues pattern in with the major. For instance if you play the G major scale 1/3, 1/2, 1/0, 2/3, 2/1, 2/0, 3/2, 3/2, the relative scale for G will be found to be the same as the blues scale for E: 1/3, 1/0, 2/3, 2/0, 3/2, 3/0. Sometimes it all seems so complex. The thing to do when it all starts to get you down, is to pick up a simple element of what we are dealing with, and just concentrate on that one thing. Take the Helpful Fretboard Dots and set up the box described above for just G. SPEND SOME TIME JUST CHECKING IT OUT. Look at it, play it, study it, commit it to your memory, then move on to another part of the picture. Believe me, the circles of musical interrelationship are there right now, waiting for you to see them.

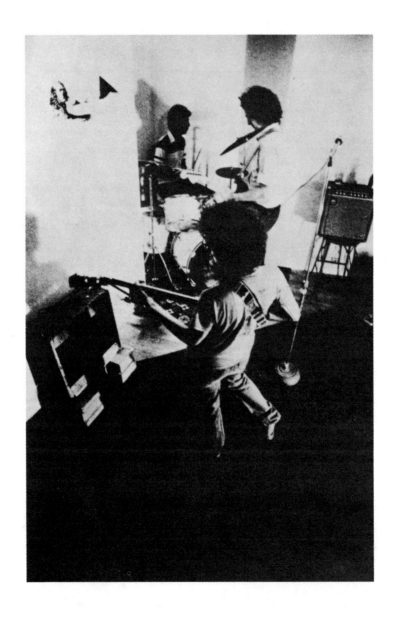

WINDOW #10

Ancient Symbols

Found in Rock

Primary Objective Statement

To study the common filler notes outside of the blues scale

hy do these five mysterious symbols keep popping up all over the globe? Recently found under layers of Beatle's graffiti, these five symbols were uncovered from the back wall of the famous Cavern Club in Liverpool, England. At the same time, across the Atlantic, these identical symbols were also discovered carved in the wall of a New York subway station directly under the site of Jimi Hendrix's Electric Lady studio on Eighth Avenue. On top of all this, they have been found etched into the ceiling of the king's chamber inside the Great Pyramid of Cheops, painted onto the elevator shaft of the Washington monument, and scratched into the underside of the pickguard of Frank Zappa's Custom SG. Yeah, and if you play Stairway to Heaven backwards on 78 you can *clearly* hear Robert Plant murmering something about stars, triangles and half-moons. What goes on here? Are these the signs of a lost musical cult, brought again to life by an unknown force? Do these figures represent spheres of influence which could someday affect the destiny of music, or maybe mankind itself? Not really, I know, FOR THEIR PURPOSE HAS BEEN REVEALED TO ME IN A VISION. A SPECTACULAR VISION OF A 500 FOOT TALL GOLDEN WINGED STRATOCASTER SPOKE TO ME IN MELODIC TONES SAYING, "RICHARD, THESE FIVE SYMBOLS REPRESENT THE THREE EXTRA RELATIVE NOTES NOT FOUND IN THE BLUES SCALE, AND TWO OTHER COMMON FILLER NOTES, WHICH TAKEN TOGETHER WITH THE FIVE NOTE BLUES SCALE, COMPRISE THE MUSICAL ELEMENTS USED TO CREATE HEAVY DUTY ROCK RIFFS." Uh, would you believe I made them up myself to make things easy to understand?

Rock guitarists are bred to look at the guitar with "blues scale eyes." I think we have all met a guitarist that says, "I don't know what scale or position it is, I just play by feeling." Next time you see the guy, take a close look at what he's doing and you will probably see his lead work out in one of the blues scale boxes. This does not mean that rock guitarists do not use the major scale, because they do. I am only saying that the blues scale is the scale of choice. It provides that sweet and sour feel that is just right for rock. The 1st, 4th, and 5th keep things basic, while the flatted 3rd and flatted 7th provide the tonal twists.

Once you know how the blues scale works and can play it in any position in any key, you are well on your way. What I want to do in this WINDOW is secure and expand your present blues scale outlook by introducing the common ''filler'' notes that rock guitarists use to supplement their blues scale usage. Keep your ''blues scale eyes'' working just like they do now. The information you will be presented with will not change the blues boxes. You will, however, be called on to understand how certain musical degrees ''outside'' of the blues scale find their way into and around the repeating blues scale pattern.

The diagram below will provide you with a basic outline of where the five symbols (star, half moon, triangle, diamond, square) fall in relation to the five notes of the blues scale through the first octave of the guitar on the low E string. As you can see, ten of the possible twelve chromatic scale degrees will be accounted for. The two degrees that are not commonly used (the half steps above the 1st and 5th) are just too close for comfort to the most basic of all musical degrees: the tonic and the dominant.

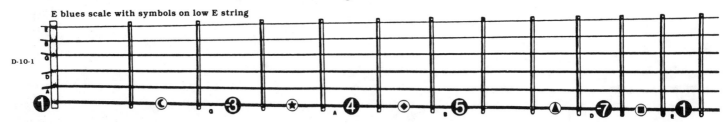

E blues scale with symbols on low E string

D-10-1

We will start by taking a close look at the three extra relative scale degrees which are not common to the blues scale. Remember, the 1st and the 5th are common to both the blues and relative scale, while the 2nd, 3rd and 6th of the relative scale lay outside the blues scale.

THE STAR

The *star* will be assigned to the 3rd of the major scale. This note is, along with the 1st and the 5th, one of the three degrees which make up the major triad. It will always be found one half-step above the flatted 3rd in the blues scale. Let's take a look at how it fits into the scheme of things by checking out its position in the *Universal Blues Scale Diagram* and immediately above and below the root note fret position at the fifth fret in the key of A.

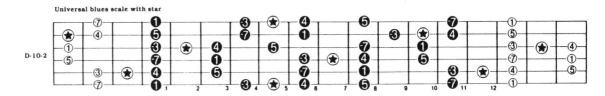

Universal blues scale with star

D-10-2

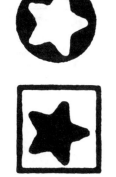

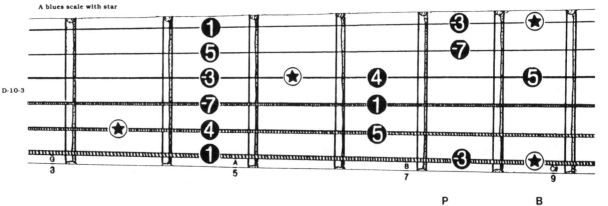

A blues scale with star

D-10-3

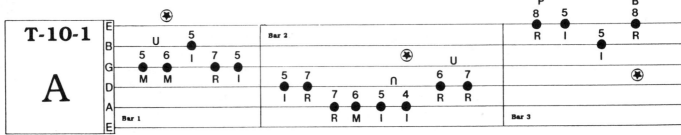

T-10-1

A

THE HALF MOON

The *half moon* will be appointed to the 2nd of the major scale. Located a whole step above the tonic, this little fellow is the same note which is used to make the 9th chord. It will forever be located immediately below the flatted 3rd. Notice the four positions that it takes around the root note fret.

Universal Blues Scale with half moon

A blues scale with half moon

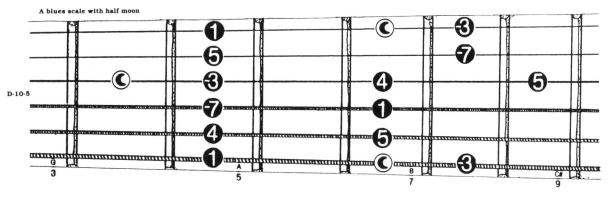

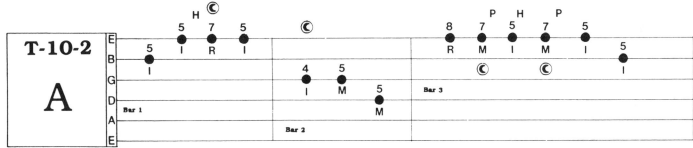

THE TRIANGLE

The *triangle* is actually the 6th of the major scale and takes its place a whole step above the fifth, and a half step below the flatted 7th. The star, half moon and triangle are all major scale degrees, and will prove to be wonderfully melodic tones which you can use to add "nice touches" to passages played primarily in the five note "minor" blues scale.

Universal Blues Scale with triangle

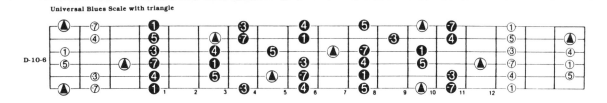

A blues scale with triangle

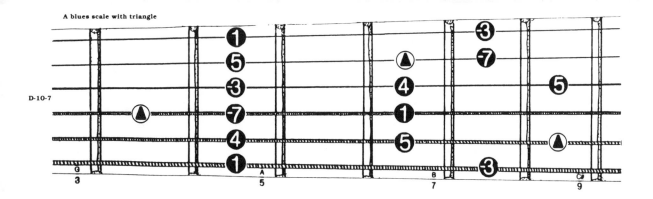

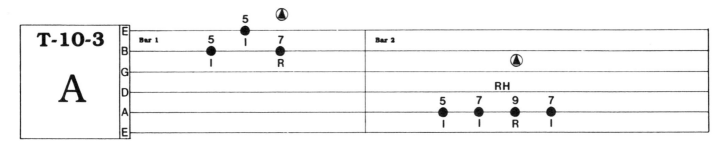

Taken together, the star, half moon and triangle (the three extra relative notes) form three convenient "clusters" around the root note fret that you have to know about. The grouping on the low three strings is a *unison* position for the cluster found on the third, fourth and fifth strings. The most commonly used of all three clusters, however, is found snugged under the flatted 3rd, flatted 7th and 4th degrees from the blues scale played on the first, second and third string respectively.

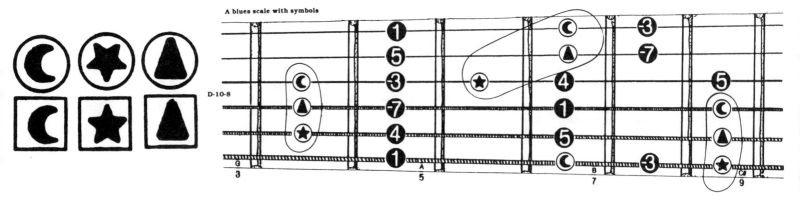

A blues scale with symbols

Refer to the <u>Be Dangerous On Rock Guitar</u> wall poster, which shows the star, half moon and triangle as they appear over the whole 24 fret board in both E and A, if you want to know more about where these three symbols appear in the blues scale pattern.

THE DIAMOND

The *diamond* will be used to represent the chromatic "filler" note located between the 4th and the 5th of the blues scale. Because of its use as a lead-in to the dominant tone, this "passing note" is very common in blues lead passages. Look at where the diamond appears on the second, third and fifth strings, and get ready to bend these notes up one half-step to sound the fifth.

Universal Blues Scale with diamond

A blues scale with diamond

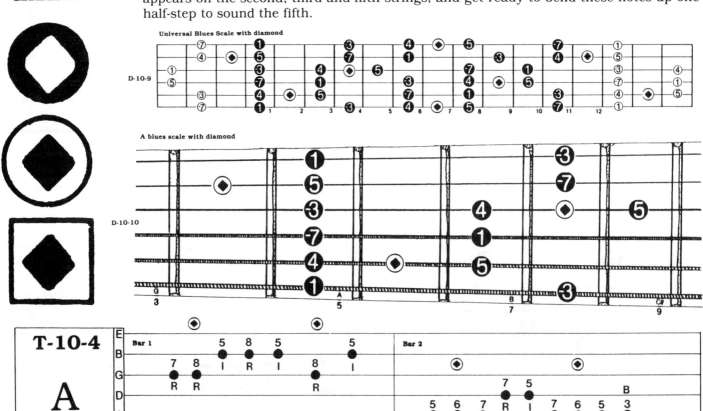

THE SQUARE

The *square* will represent the seventh of the major scale. Named the leading tone by the music encyclopedia, this guy is sometimes used to pass from the flatted 7th to the tonic.

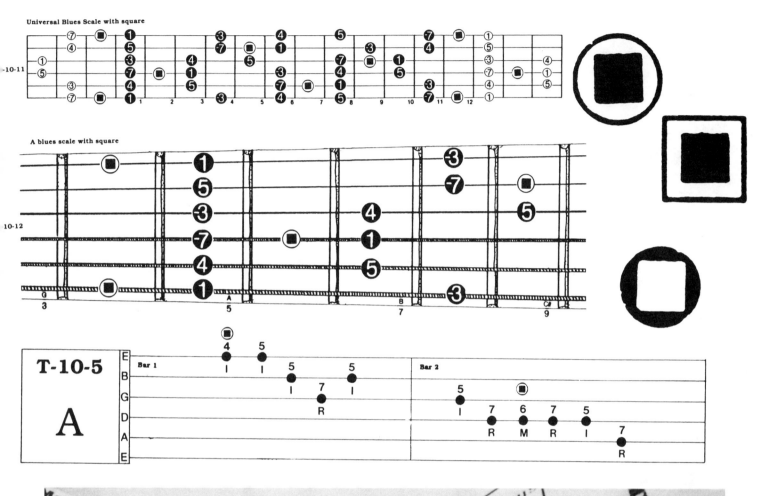

THE TWO SCALE RELATIONSHIP

The chromatic scale contains all twelve musical tones one after the other. The major scale is a selection of seven of these twelve tones. The blues scale keeps three of these major scale degrees (1, 4, 5) and flattens two more (3, 7). The relative scale (a subset of the major scale) has the same pattern as the blues scale and two of the same notes (1, 5). The three notes from the relative scale which do not appear in the blues scale (2, 3, 6) are the star, half moon and triangle.

The rock/blues guitarist's style is based on the use of the blues and relative scale. When you break down the leads to classic rock songs, you will usually find one of three things happening between the blues and relative scale. First off, the guitarist will be found to use only the blues scale exclusively. Secondly, you will hear the relative scale used exclusively. Thirdly, you will find the guitarist mix and match relative notes with the notes in the blues scale pattern.

If you take all of the components of the blues scale, and mix in the three extra relative notes, you come up with a hybrid eight note scale which looks like this.

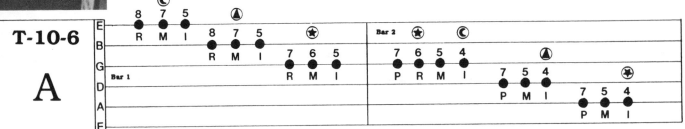

A more commonly used version of this scale is the blues scale with the half moon (2nd) and triangle (6th) added on. This results in a seven note scale, commonly found in rock, which has the same pattern as the major scale in an adjacent key. Here is how it works for the key of A. First you center your blues scale across the fifth fret, then you add the 2nd and 6th immediately under the flatted 3rd and flatted 7th. This is actually the same scale pattern as the major scale in the key of G. It is just the blues scale with two notes added on, no big deal.

Universal Blues Scale Diagram with symbols

A blues scale with symbols

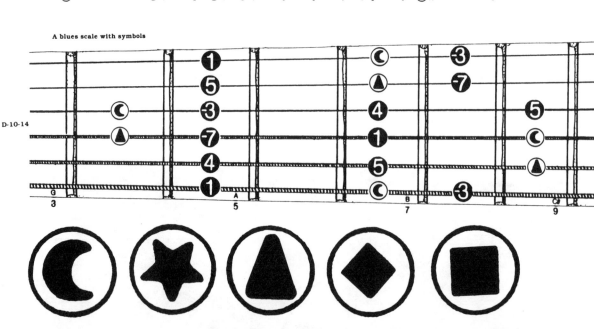

WINDOW #11

Mister Big

Primary Objective Statement

To study rock guitar's primary lead box

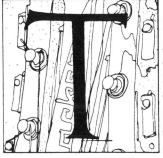

The root note fret is a wonderwork for which all rock guitarists should be eternally grateful. It is along and above this fret, more than anywhere else in the 12 fret repeating pattern, that all of the elements of lead guitar come to an eclipse. All five of the blues scale degrees (with two tonics on the E strings) appear *straight across the neck,* with all other blues and relative scale degrees easily accessible for total fingering. Mister Big is a very special five fret section of a very special pattern. Use it to study the positions of the guitar's blues scale degrees, the relationship between the blues and relative scale, the range of the octave, or the endless variety of rock moves which take place in, on and through this one position. This is the rock guitarist's primary lead box.

A blues scale at fifth fret with symbols

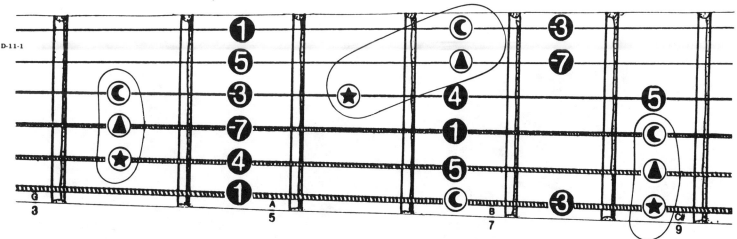

Little brothers - E and A to the twelfth fret

Blues scale with three extra relative degrees - Key of E
D-11-2

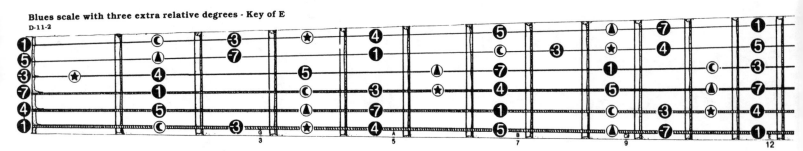

Blues scale with three extra relative degrees - Key of A
D-11-3

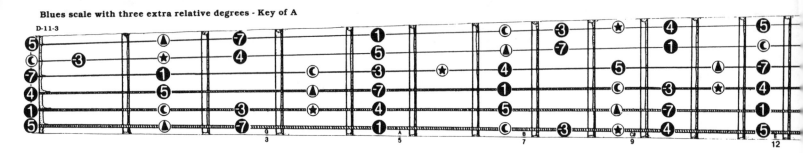

WINDOW #12

From One Box

Primary Objective Statement

To follow one box throughout the guitar's range

ometimes the guitar seems overly complex. The intricacies of the overlapping, repeating, symbol laden patterns pile up in your mind until you want to scream: ALL I WANT TO DO IS BE DANGEROUS ON ROCK GUITAR. DO I REALLY NEED ALL OF THIS GARBAGE? I am here to tell you that relief is an attitude. Keep in mind that no matter how complex it all seems at any particular moment, you only handle one part of the pattern at a time. Like driving a car, the map of the country might seem overwhelming, but the curve immediately ahead remains the challenge. The mark of a great musician, however, is the attaining of the acquired ability to *see around the corner;* to know ahead of time where the usable notes are waiting and to confidently run over them, bringing them to life at will. Blues boxes are like cockroaches, if you've got one, well, you know.

The reason that the six string guitar seems overly complex is that it not only spans four octaves in its range (6/0, 4/2, 1/0, 1/12, 1/24) but, unlike the piano, the same pitch frequency can appear in as many as six "unison" positions (1/0, 2/5, 3/9, 4/14, 5/19, 6/24). So, if you isolate just one box (or one riff), you will find the guitar always offers you two kinds of differentiation: the same box in another *higher or lower octave,* or the same box in a *unison octave.* The purpose of this WINDOW is to take just one box, the most primary box in the history of lead guitar, and go around the fretboard in the keys of E and A, and find where it repeats itself. Just to get tuned in, look at the diagram below of the blues scale at the root note fret in the key of A. The specific box we will study appears in the diagram at the right, and contains the four notes: 1, -3, 5, -7.

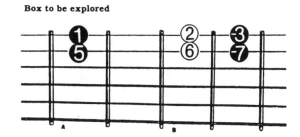

A blues scale across fifth fret

Box to be explored

D-12-1

The simplicity of this classic *four note box* is evident. The dimensions seem custom designed for the human hand. The index finger can easily play across two strings at once, holding down 2/5 and 1/5 simultaneously, with the ring or pinky easily reaching the upper two notes of 2/8 and 1/8. *What a great box.* The two primary musical notes (1, 5) are easily held with the most basic finger of the hand, and the two "blue notes" (-3, -7) which *make rock leads come alive,* just happen to be side by side, a sweet three frets above. If you center the riff in the key of E, things get easier still because the open strings take the 1st and the 5th, with the other two notes (-3, -7) being played *with just one finger!* See, I told you it was easy. Who needs invertible counterpoint? Give me the blues scale in E.

Okay, so now that you know a little bit about the basic box we are going to run down, I will first show you a few ways in which you can employ the box to produce various riffs. Then I will take you on a tour of the fretboard, pointing out where this box reappears again and again in the keys of E and A.

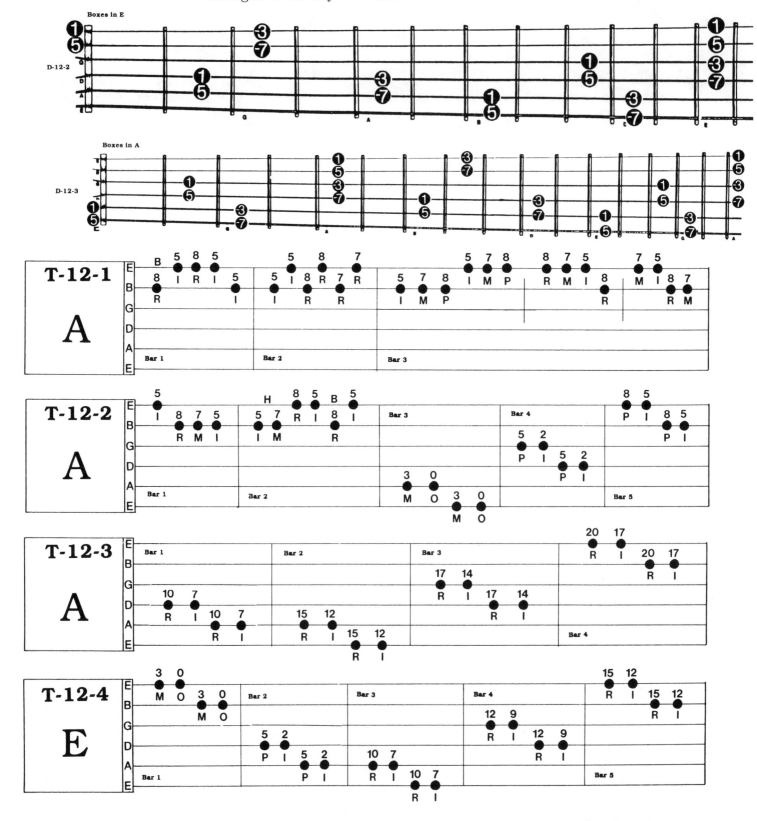

WINDOW #13

Running Bad

Primary Objective Statement

To demonstrate "tumble down" lead runs

Nothing beats a great lead break. Especially the kind that runs at breakneck speed and seem to tumble down, down, down into infinity. I'm not talking about those distinctive single note melodic breaks which are so clear and to the point. I'm talking about when you hear the guitarist pick up a motif and run down the scale with it. The first time I became aware of this type of playing was when I heard Good Times - Bad Times, the first cut on Led Zepplin's first album. It was clear from the first listen that Jimmy Page had applied some transcendental methods to his style of playing the electric guitar. Hearing that riff wind down the instrument's range was like throwing a rock into a deep canyon, it just kept falling. No longer was the guitar just for keeping the rhythm, or riff bopping on the beat, Chuck Berry style. Jimmy *ran with it.* It was a new perspective on scale usage: tune into a string of boxes, gear up a repeating riff, and keep it rolling through right on down the line.

I figure that running is a good way to get to know the boxes, increase your dexterity, develop a fluid style, and when the time comes for playing slower, you will have that covered. Let's start with descending triplets along the open position in the key of E. Each triplet will begin on a consecutively lower blues scale degree. Remember: the secret to speed playing lies in mastering the pull off, hammer on, and a clean, hard picking style.

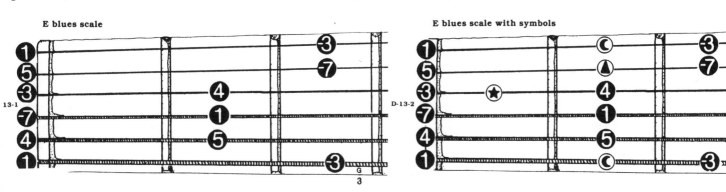

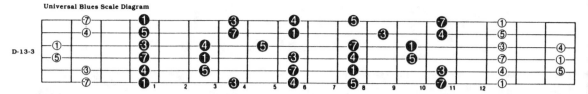

Universal Blues Scale Diagram

D-13-3

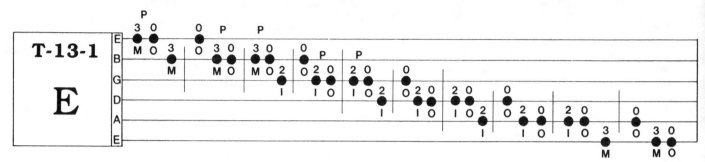

T-13-1 E

The reason for the use of a triplet is simple. It extends the movement of the passage so that the instrument's range is not "spent" too quickly. Oh, you can run every consecutive note in the scale, but you run through the mid-range in a matter of seconds. The transcriptions below will offer you three ways of playing through the C major scale. The first transcription will take you straight through the scale, one note after the other, across the two octaves of the open position. The second transcription uses an eight note "descending octave" figure which starts on the G note on 1/3 and runs down an octave to the G note on 3/0. The following figure starts on the note F 1/1 (the next degree down in the C major scale) and runs down to the F note on 4/3. The final transcription uses a descending four note figure through the same scale. Stretch your fingers and turn on the tape player.

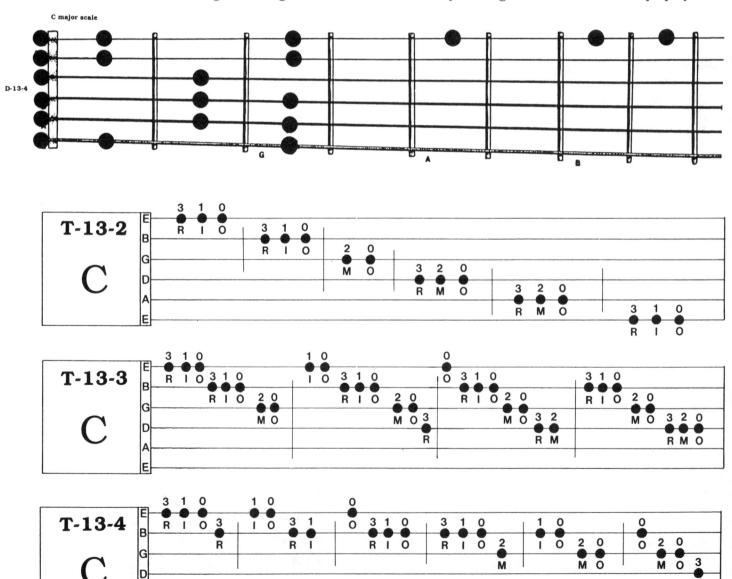

C major scale

D-13-4

T-13-2 C

T-13-3 C

T-13-4 C

There are two things to consider when running a descending or ascending "step" figure which repeats on a higher or lower scale degree each time it is played: the *territory* of the scale pattern which you plan to use to execute the passage, and the figure, or motif, which you choose to repeat. Repeating figures are practically infinite in their variety. Just put on the FM rock station and they start pouring out into the room in all shapes and forms. The following example in the key of A will use a triplet constructed by playing a blues scale note, then playing the next lower note, then repeating the original note. Three notes are sounded, two frequency pitches are used in each figure. Each figure starts on the next higher blues scale degree. Check out the extended box in which the passage takes place, and make sure to pull off and hammer on whenever possible.

Universal Blues Scale Diagram

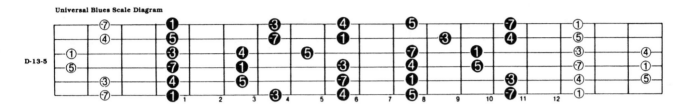

E blues scale

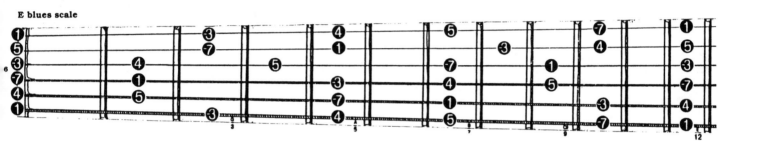

A blues scale

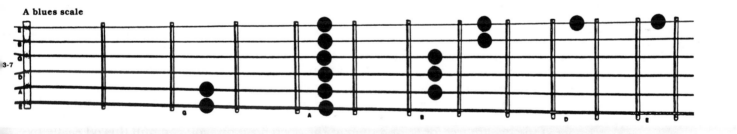

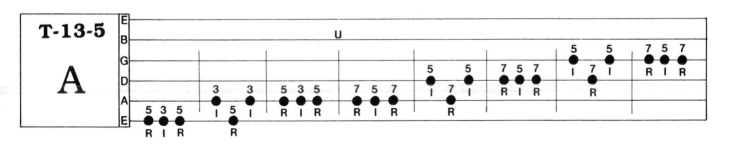

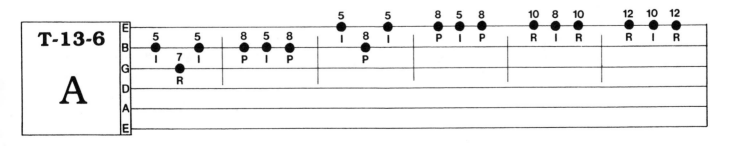

Next up is a double triplet which takes place twice in each octave. You really have to look carefully at the construction of this figure to get it. There are four triplets to the octave, at which point the last note of the final triplet is again repeated to open the first triplet of the next lower octave. All of this is done exclusively with blues scale degrees. Look closely at the extended box in the key of E which starts below the root note fret at the twelfth fret, and continues three full octaves down from 1/12 to 6/0.

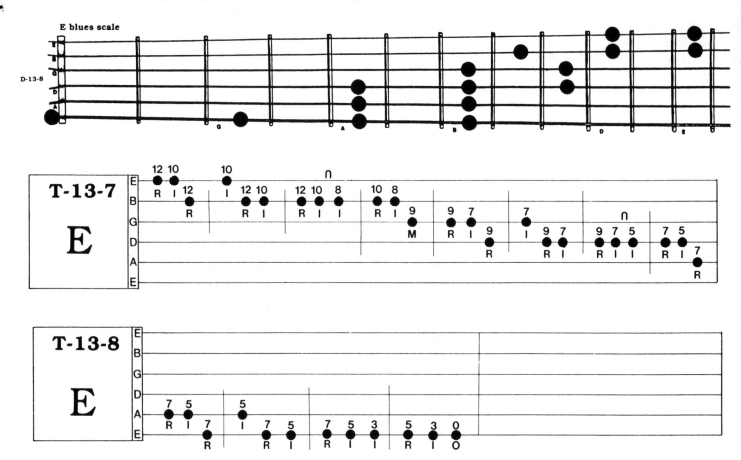

Remember when I told you that rock artists mixed in relative scale degrees with riffs which are based in the blues scale? Well, now we will explore precisely such a passage. The repeating figure is a double triplet, with the second note of the second triplet employing a relative scale degree. Transcribed first with the relative notes played below the root note at the twelfth fret for E, and then at the open position, you can pull this off easily by counting one, two, three to yourself four times.

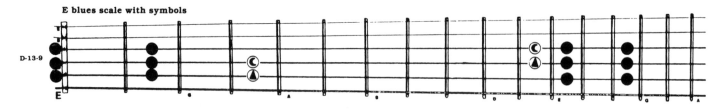

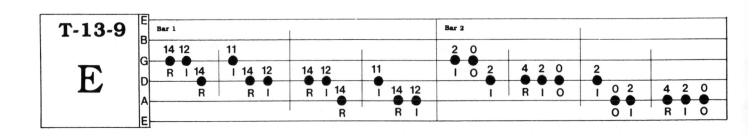

The repeated pull off hammer, employing the open string to sound the third note of a triplet, is a great move, and there are several different ways in which it can be employed. It can be repeated several times before being moved up to the next position, or it can be repeated on an adjacent string. The transcription below will work as a rough outline for the examples you will hear on the tape.

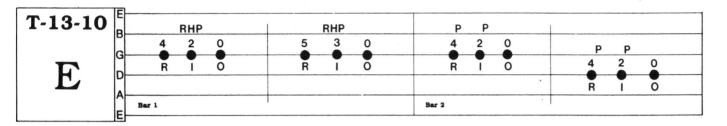

Repeating figures do not necessarily have to "step up" through the scale one degree at a time. Sometimes you will hear the figure *repeated several times* in one position before moving on, or you will hear the figure repeated in a higher or lower octave. This approach involves the use of boxes more than scales. Below you will find a few examples transcribed.

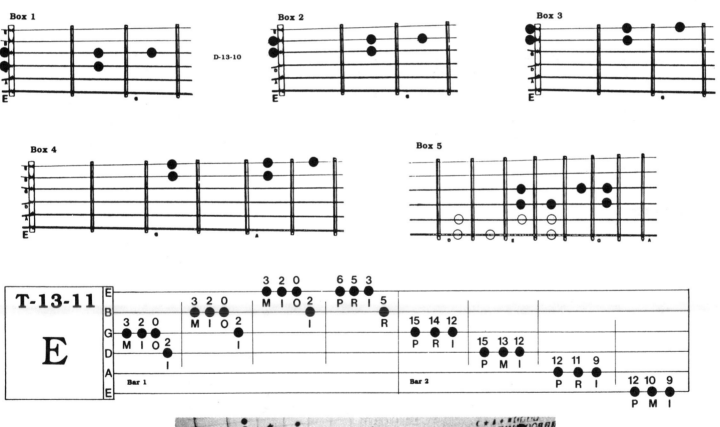

Another favorite move for the blues and rock guitarists alike, is to switch from the blues scale to the relative scale in the middle of a run. This not only affords a variation in tonal quality, but also allows for an interesting positional change. Don't ever forget: the relative scale pattern is identical to the blues scale pattern, only moved down three frets. The following transcription explores the possibility of changing between these two scales.

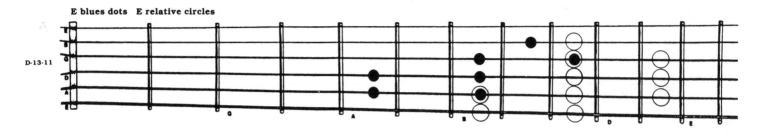

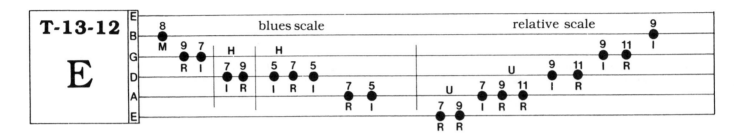

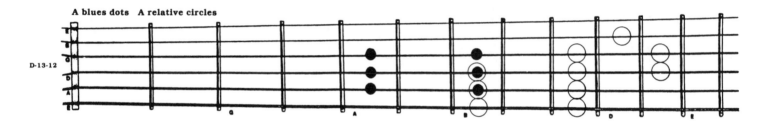

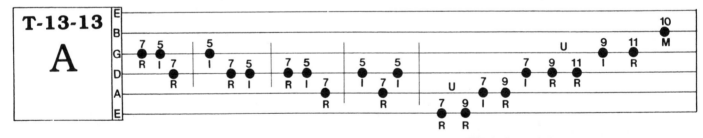

WINDOW #14

World of E

World of A

Primary Objective Statement

To present an overview of rock's two primary chords

A world is a self-contained universe — a place where things stay in relation to one another. Such is the musical world. Let me impress upon you two vital facts. First, the matter of key is one which concerns *centering* a tonic note on one of the twelve musical tones. Second, the guitar is *locked* by its very nature into a certain part of the musical range: namely the four octaves above the open low E string note of 82.41 hz. Everything else follows from these two facts. Once we have established these two truths, we can start to build *worlds within.* Because the open string adjacent to the low E string is tuned to A 110 hz, the relationship between the low E string (tonic) and the A string (a fourth above) will always remain *built into the guitar itself.* All adjacent strings are tuned a perfect fourth (five frets) apart from each other, except the 2nd and 3rd strings which are tuned a major third (four frets) apart from each other in pitch.

The singular musical relationship between the first and the fifth is the most fundamental *interval* in all of music. This is why the fifth is called the dominant tone. It is, however, the musical link between the triad built on the 1st and the triad built on the 4th which represents the most common *chordal relationship* in popular rock music. There are others, of course, which we could list and consider. But the mutuality shared by the first chord and the fourth chord is so strong that there is no way you can get very far into the subject of songwriting without reckoning with their magnetism for each other. The chordal center built on the fifth is the same story, but it seems that musical themes are built using the fourth chord, and are resolved or "come to cycle" when the fifth chord comes into play.

The first thing that I want you to check out is WHAT WE, AS GUITAR PLAYERS, ARE STUCK WITH: *the chromatic fretboard set to low E.* The notes that you see on the first five frets across all six strings are there to stay exactly as diagramed. THEY WILL REMAIN THE SAME NO MATTER WHAT KEY OR SCALE YOU PLAY IN.

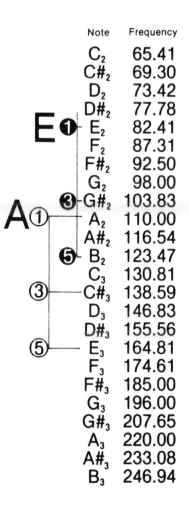

Note	Frequency
C_2	65.41
$C\#_2$	69.30
D_2	73.42
$D\#_2$	77.78
E_2	82.41
F_2	87.31
$F\#_2$	92.50
G_2	98.00
$G\#_2$	103.83
A_2	110.00
$A\#_2$	116.54
B_2	123.47
C_3	130.81
$C\#_3$	138.59
D_3	146.83
$D\#_3$	155.56
E_3	164.81
F_3	174.61
$F\#_3$	185.00
G_3	196.00
$G\#_3$	207.65
A_3	220.00
$A\#_3$	233.08
B_3	246.94

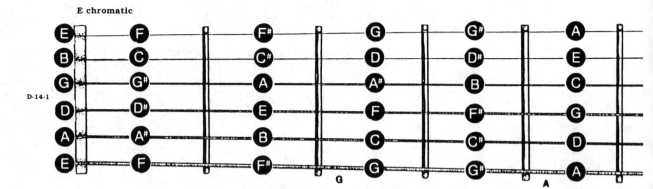

E chromatic

D-14-1

The above diagram represents the chromatic scale in the key of E. If we assign the number one to the note E, and use the interval pattern of W, W, H, W, W, W, H, WE ARRIVE AT THE MAJOR SCALE PATTERN FOR THE KEY OF E shown in the diagram below.

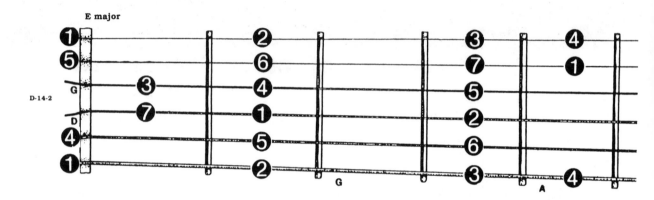

E major

D-14-2

Now, if you label each chromatic step not included in the major scale with a number relative to the major scale (same as the black piano keys in the key of C), you will come up with a diagram which looks like this.

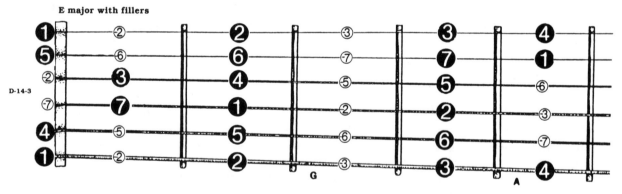

E major with fillers

D-14-3

The open strings span precisely two octaves from high to low string, with the intermediate octave note taking its place on 4/2. The major triad, consisting of the 1st, 3rd, and 5th, is actually a subset of the major scale. You already know the form of the E chord, but take a look at the major scale components of which it consists. A note appears on each and every string. Name them with your eyes closed.

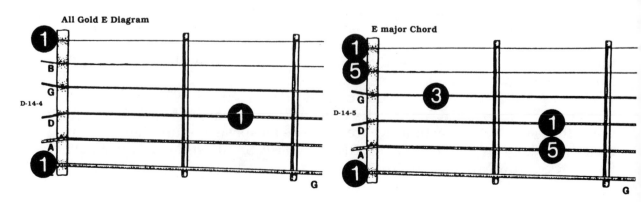

All Gold E Diagram

D-14-4

E major Chord

D-14-5

If you are going to be dangerous, it is not enough to simply know the whereabouts of the major triad. The E major chord outlined above is the primary skeleton on which other musical degrees, both major and altered, are added. Below you will witness the E major triad with all of the trimmings. These other degrees which you see "outside" of the major triad are represented in the most elemental way: (underline ibtp) identified by their position. The variety of ways in which they *can be used* is a whole other deal. They can be added to the triad, suspended over the triad's degrees, used in scales. You name it. You can do it. It's been done before. Sharpen up because we are going in with the *Universal World of E Diagram.*

Universal World of E Diagram

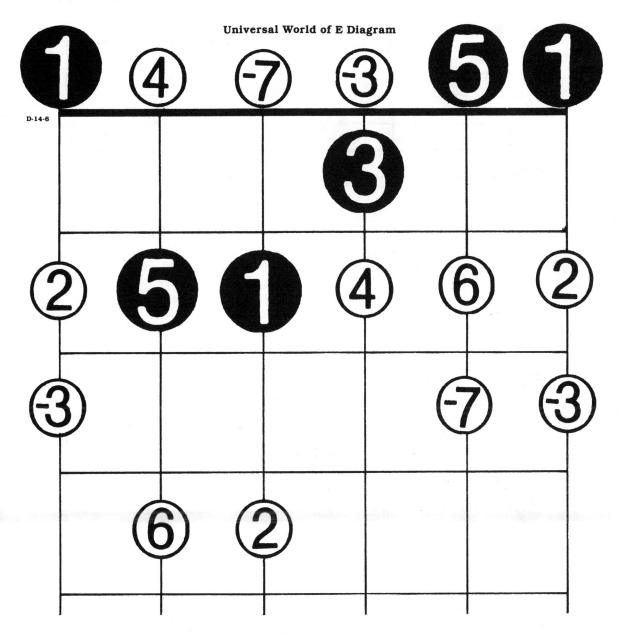

From this master diagram, one could teach for years. Let's start by looking at the three easy alternatives a blues guitarist has to play the E 7 chord. That is the "seventh" a whole step below the tonic (a flatted seventh). The leading tone is, of course, a half step below the tonic. The two easy positions to grab the flatted seventh degree are found on 4/0 and 2/3. The three diagrams below show one or the other, and even both. So forget E major and play these three.

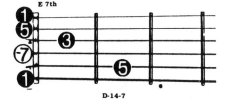

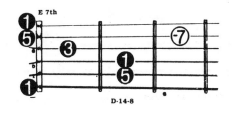

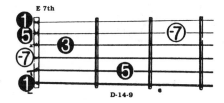

Next we will look at the sixth. To frame it, I always go back to the *Universal World of E Diagram* and locate the tonal centers available. No big deal, let me figure it out. Let's see now, C# notes are the sixth note for the key of E, so that means we have 2/2 and 5/4. So, here is what it looks like. *PRESENTING:* THE SIXTH CENTERS FOR THE KEY OF E WHICH ARE EASILY ACCESSIBLE AROUND THE MAJOR E TRIAD IN THE OPEN POSITION, BLAAAAAAA, BLAAAAAAA, BLAAAAAAA, DOES JIMI EVER USE A SIXTH CHORD???? PETE MAYBE, BUT, IT DOES NOT MATTER TO THE POWER CHORD, 1, 5, and 1, 5, 1″. But here they are anyway.

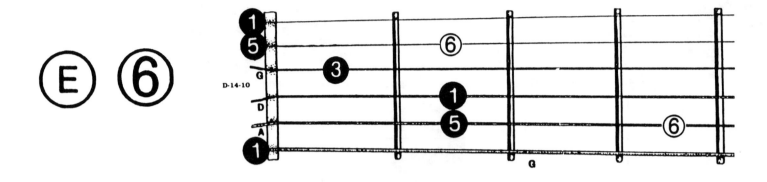

Moving right along, we will go to the 2nd center a whole step above the *famous tonic center*. You see, the ninth center is the same as the second, but the additional octave (seven numbers) tells us to look to the higher octave to find this little friend. Hey, please, wow, help me find this little critter. Seems to be a few out there somewhere. Yeah, on 1/2, 4/4, and 6/2 just two frets up from the *All Gold E Notes Diagram.*

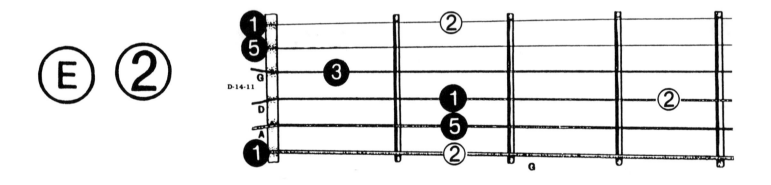

Gee, *what's left?* Just the big sus 4, that's what! I already told you that the 1 chord against the 4 chord is the most common chordal move. The same thing goes with the scope set at the scale level, when we are considering the individual interaction of the major scales degrees. Yeah, THE FOURTH, THE FOURTH, THE FOURTH. Quick, find all the A notes (5/0, 3/2).

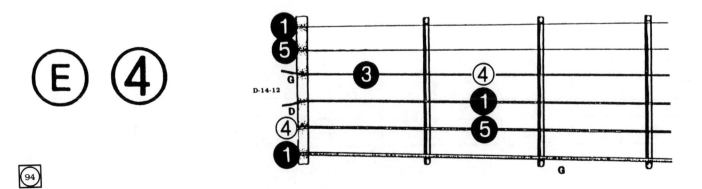

The flatted third is definitely the power behind a few things musical. For starters, the 1, -3, 5 is the minor triad. The flatted third is the primary "blues note" upon which the American blues tradition was founded, with the flatted seventh running a close second. The flatted third also finds itself into all of the diatonic, seven note, major altered minor modes of which there are four: natural (1, 2, -3, 4, 5, -6, -7), melodic ascending (1, 2, -3, 4, 5, 6, 7), melodic decending (1, 2, -3, 4, 5, -6, -7), and harmonic (1, 2, -3, 4, 5, -6, 7). But, more to the ultimate point, the flatted third is the second degree of the sacred FIVE NOTE BLUES SCALE. This is a blues note, for sure, just a half step above the second and a nine iron (three frets) above the tonic.

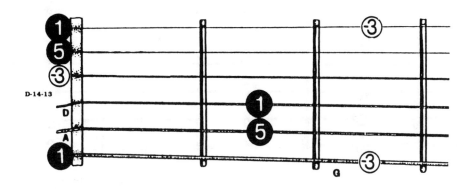

THE MAJOR SEVENTH

Funny thing about the E major 7th chord. There doesn't seem to be a really great open position where it can be made. This is because the low note of the guitar is an E, and the E flat note is, well, *missing*. The D# (E flat) note which you find on 4/1 is also "out of the easy line" which the hand uses to make the open E major chord. You're fooling with the formula just a little too much to go lowering the tonic just one fret. It's easy to put stuff on top of the ol' lazy boy, but lowering the tonic on 4/2 does not come as easy as when we lowered the third on 3/1 to make the minor chord. Sure, and try to pull off the regular open E chord while playing the D# note on 2/4 with your pinky. I don't know about you, but that seems like JUST A LITTLE BIT TOO MUCH TROUBLE TO ME. Doesn't matter anyway, because other chord forms accept the 7th degree in a way which we can easily utilize by barring.

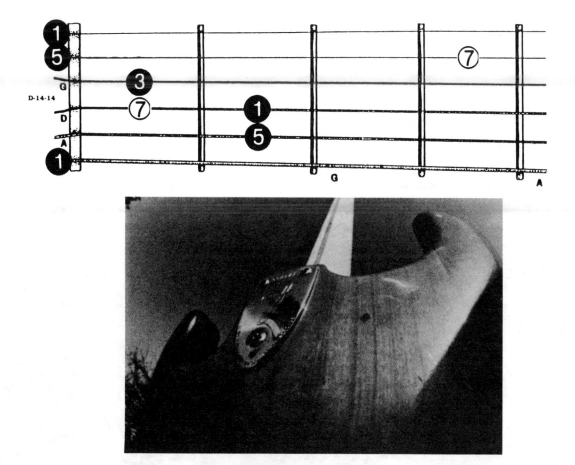

THE WORLD OF A

The study of music involves the comparison of related spheres of interaction. The World of A is identical *in proportion* to the World of E with A taking its position a perfect fourth above E in the musical range. This would be easier to see if our instrument covered the pitch range in a sweeping "open time line" like the piano. Thing is, we have to deal with six tonally staggered strings, and that infernal "tuning irregularity" between the 2nd and 3rd string. Even though the worlds of E and A take place five half steps apart from each other, there is one unchanging bond which they both share in common: the notes played on the six fixed strings.

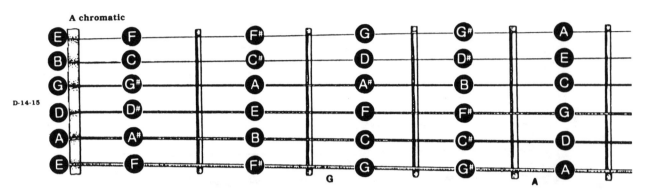

Let's proceed immediately to the diagram of the tonic notes for A, and the A major triad diagram in the open position. Now the tonic is centered on the fifth string open with the sequence of triad degrees we know from the E chord (1, 5, 1, 3, 5, 1), playing themselves out "one string over" towards the thinner strings. The configuration of the A chord would be identical to the E chord if it were not for the tuning irregularity, which brings the third degree in A up to 2/2 above 3/1 where it is found for E. One other thing I will point out: the low E note played on 6/0 is actually the 5th degree of the A major scale, but I did not include it in the line up for the sake of establishing the predominance of the tonic note.

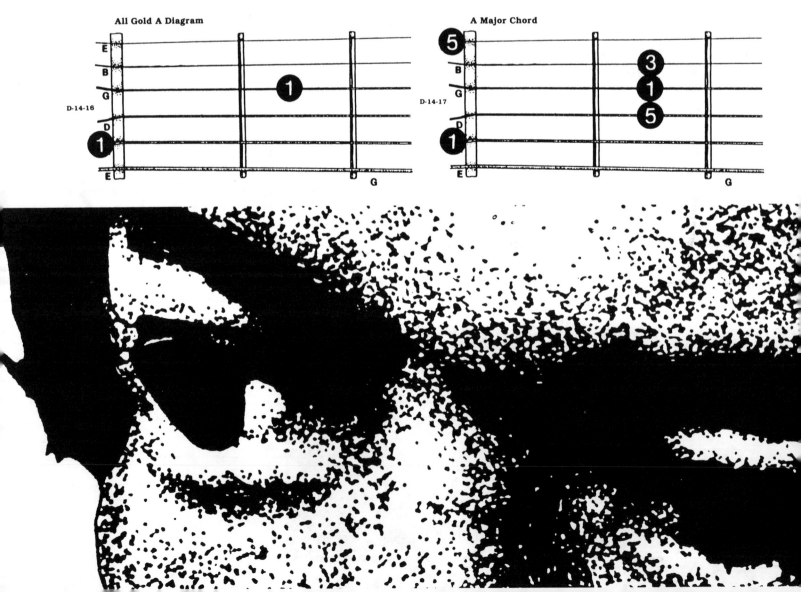

Next up is the *Universal World of A Diagram* which depicts the major A triad in large black dots, with all of the other useful musical tones in and around this chord shown in smaller outline dots. Enter the world of A.

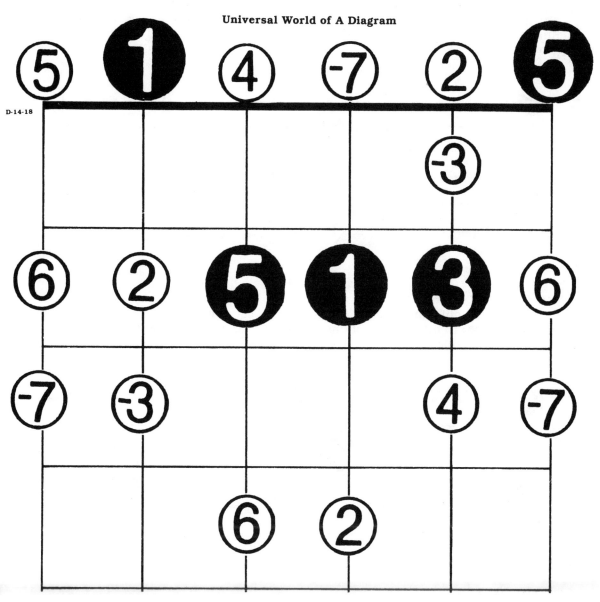

Universal World of A Diagram

THE SEVENTH

Just like in the key of E, there are two easy positions where you can grab the *flatted seventh* (commonly called the seventh) and add them to the components of the major triad. These two locations are on 1/3 and 3/0, and can be used separately or together to form the A 7th chord. For your information, there is also a -7th position for the key of A on 6/3.

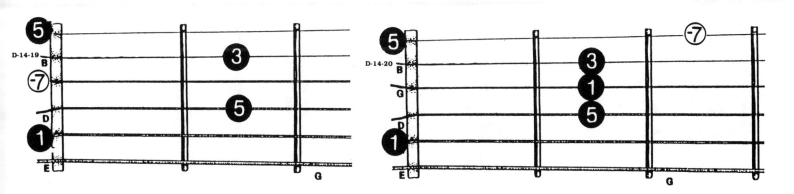

THE SIXTH

The sixth degree of the A major scale is an F# note, of which there are three on the first four frets of the guitar: 1/2, 4/4, and 6/2. The most common form of the open A sixth chord employs the major A chord with the note 1/2 added on top. The sixth located on 4/4 for the key of A, is comparable to the sixth degree of the E major scale found on 5/4. These "low" sixth positions for E and A are familiar to any rock guitarist as the "open position" hammer-ons above the fifth of the E and A chords in their respective positions. Look at them. Know them all.

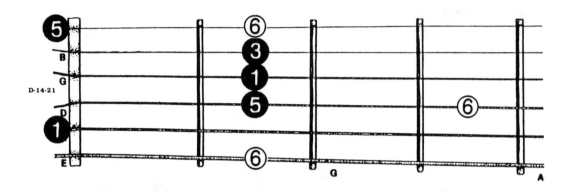

THE SECOND AND NINTH

There are three different "second" degree positions that you will find in the key of A under the first four frets. These positions are 2/0, 3/4, and 5/2. The centers on the 2nd and 3rd are unisons, while the guy on 5/2 is a useful step in a run up above the tonic on 5/0.

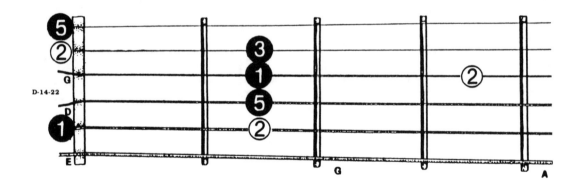

THE SUS FOUR

By this time you know that A is the fourth to E and D is the fourth to A. So if we are setting up the game for A, we will look to all of the D notes, found under the first four frets on 2/3 and 4/0. The happy little fourth add-on that you find on 2/3 is the all time favorite of all A chord players. The open fourth string is the logical place to start to build the D major triad. The importance of the fourth can't be overstated.

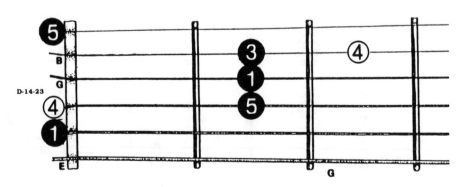

THE MINOR TRIAD AND THE FLATTED THIRD

There are two positions for the flatted third around the open A chord. These two positions are 2/1 and 5/3. The 2/1 position is used in the A minor triad and the 5/3 position is a great all around blues note for playing on and off of the A note on 5/0.

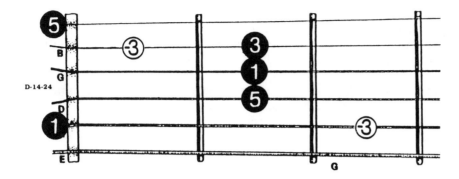

THE MAJOR SEVENTH

The three centers that we find for the major seventh degree in the key of A (G#) are located on 1/4, 3/1, and 6/4. The center on 3/1 is the common major seventh degree used in the open major seventh chord. This beautiful jazz chord is a great vehicle for sliding around the fretboard. The E major seventh chord can be fingered at 4/9, 3/8, 2/9.

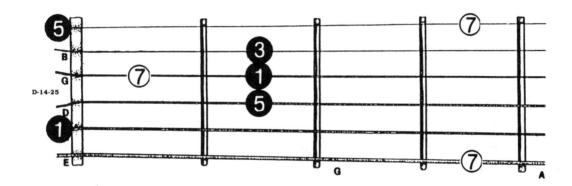

TO USE E AND A TOGETHER

It sounds too simple to believe. After all, the E and A major chords are the first thing that any guitar player learns (except for, perhaps, the C and A minor chord which are used to play such endless drivel as Row the Boat Ashore and Red River Valley). Even though these two chords are already familiar, please don't assume that you know all about their relationship, because you might miss a very important concept. The E and A are not just two chords, they are (with their respective barrings and alterations) *the vehicles of rock.* They are not just dry outlines; they are the *means to an end.* They are what a hammer and chisel were to Michelangelo, what a typewriter and paper are to a writer. And all this time you thought they were just two chords. HA!

The diagram below shows the components of the E chord in solid black dots, with the degrees of the A chord shown in larger circles. This will help us see which notes the two chords have in common, and which ones they don't. The transcriptions will provide a few ways in which these two chords work together.

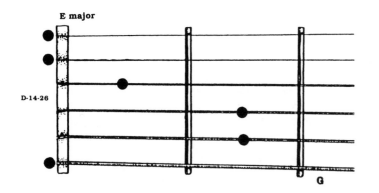

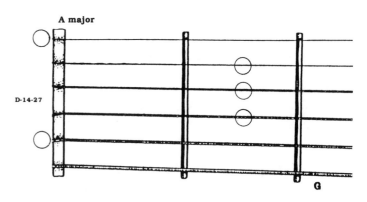

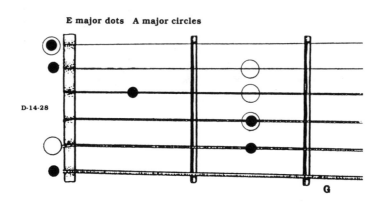

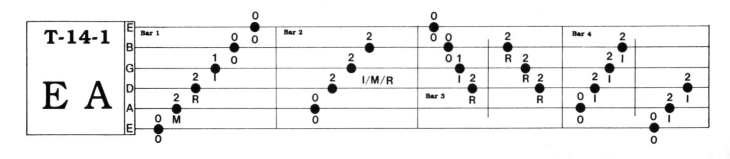

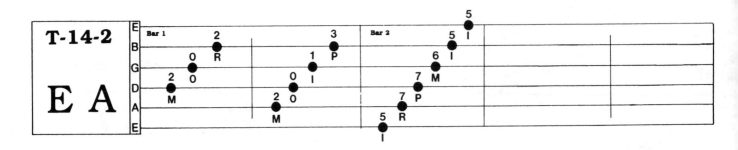

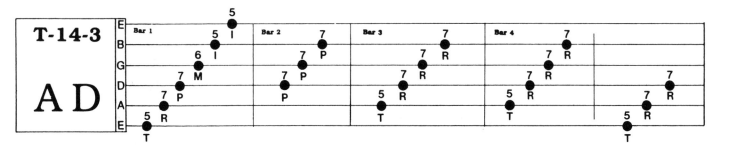

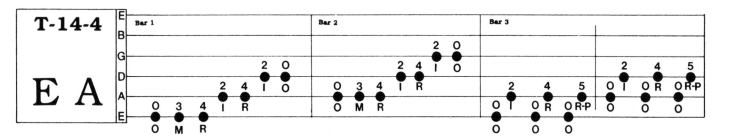

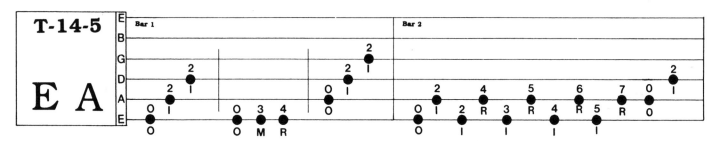

TO USE E AND A TOGETHER WITH THE BLUES SCALE

Now is the time to look at how the E and A chords work together with the five note blues scale. The marriage of these three elements is essential to good rock, no matter what particular style or form it takes. The transcriptions and diagrams below will tune you in.

The worlds of E and A are polar. They are not the same, because they occupy two different positions relative to each other (and a whole lot of other stuff). They are identical in proportion, yeah. I knew they were identical somehow. It is their inner divisions which are the same. Remember, you establish a tonic center, and that is it. Then you take ratio numbers, and establish notes. So, why would it matter if you establish a new tonic, say *a fourth above the starter?*

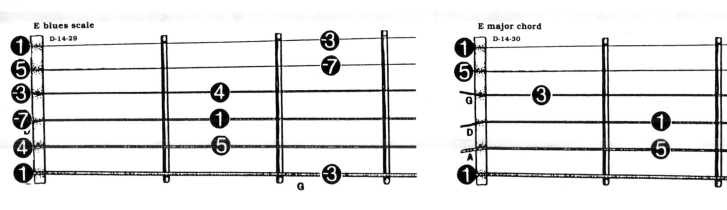

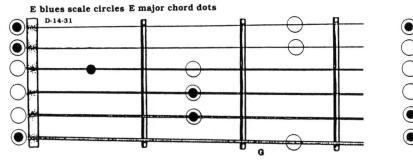

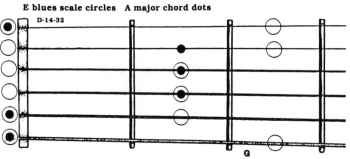

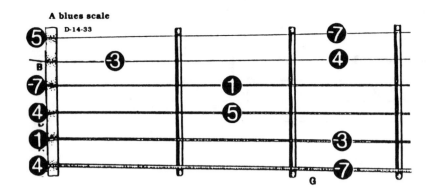

A blues scale

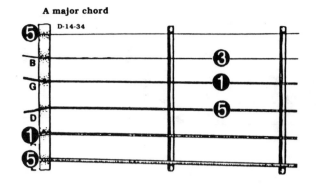

A major chord

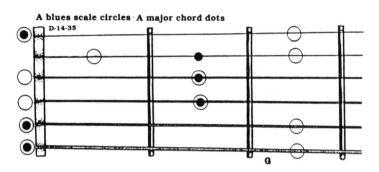

A blues scale circles · A major chord dots

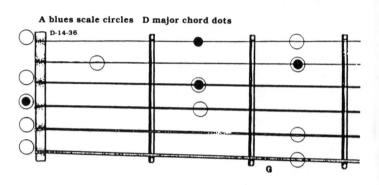

A blues scale circles   D major chord dots

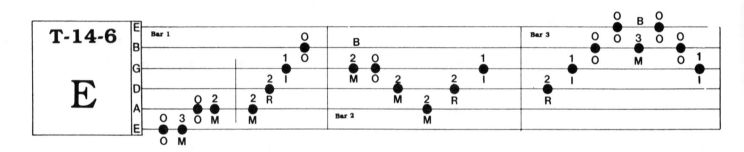

T-14-6

E

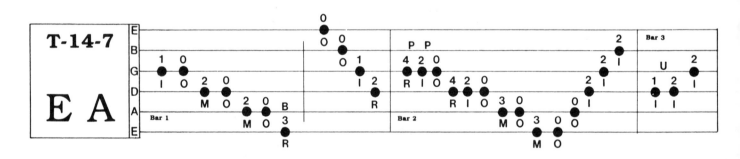

T-14-7

E A

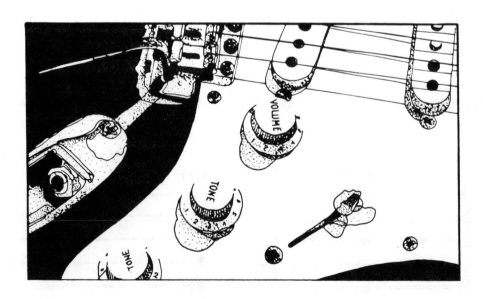

WINDOW #15

The Others

Primary Objective Statement

To present the notes in and around the open D, G and C chord

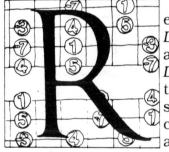

Remember back to the *Universal Major Chord Inversion Diagram?* That was the one that had just the 1st, 3rd, and 5th segregated out of the *Universal Major Scale Diagram* which gave us all of the possible inversions of the major triad on the guitar's fretboard. Yes, if you stare at the diagram directly below, you will see the E chord built above the first fret, with the A chord built above the seventh fret. Keep staring and you will also identify the basic chord forms of the D, G, and C major chords. We already talked about how the chords which appear across the twelve frets of this *Universal* pattern are actually all the same major chord, but in different inversions. The "other" chords, like the E and A, are found in the open position on the guitar when their "tag" degree name (D, G, C) is assigned to the number 1 slot.

Universal Major Chord Inversion Diagram

D-15-1

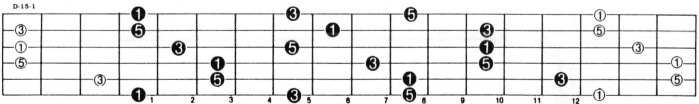

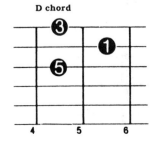

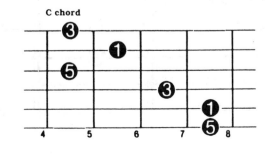

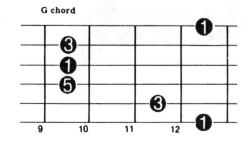

These are rock's "other" chords. They are not less important than E and A, because they are indeed major chord forms. It is just that when you build a fourth above D (G), G (C), or C (F), you do not find the "natural chemistry" that you find with the E and A relationship. This especially pertains to the way the E blues scale works its root note fret directly under the E and A chord.

One of the nice things about the way these "other" chords have been laid out for you, is that ALL TRIAD DEGREES ARE NAMED, not just those you find in the common chord form from the chord chart. For instance, check out how the D major chord plays itself out over the guitar's three bottom strings with 6/2, 5/0, and 4/0. The C chord has that suprising 5th on 1/3, along with the note two octaves below on 6/3. The G chord can be played with the second string open, or played on 2/3 with the same finger which you use to hold down 1/3.

I am sure that you can plainly see the degrees of the major triad laid out in black dots, but take a close look at how all of the "outside" degrees (both major and altered or "chromatic") have been laid out in smaller single line circles. With these degrees (2, -3, 4, 6, -7, 7), you can go forth into the world of music playing seventh chords, sixth chords, ninth chords, sus four chords, minor chords, and major seventh chords on your guitar. Take your pick.

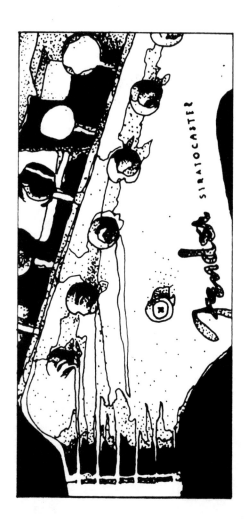

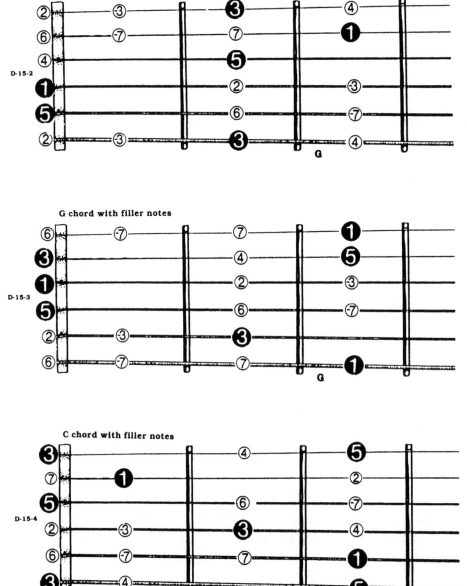

WINDOW #16

Roll the Sixth

Add the Seventh

Primary Objective Statement

To demonstrate the position and use of the sixth and seventh

Here is how you roll the sixth. Tune your guitar. Play the low string open with a pick and leave the string ringing. Then hold 5/2 with your index and pluck it. *Then, on top of that note,* play 5/4 with your ring finger. In the key of E, that is a big 1, 5, 6. The open E sixth chord is usually composed of all of the major triads degrees (1, 3, 5) across the lower four strings, with the sixth note added on 2/2. The chord is constructed in this way in order to establish the dominance of the triad in the lower register, while adding the distinctive, yet meeker, sixth from the upper register on top. The sixth which we are about to consider, however, is a full octave below this mark, taking its position on 5/4. With this note, you can play "off the top" of the standard E major chord, *rolling the sixth.* This special sixth note takes its place just a whole step above the fifth. The sixth's proximity to the fifth in the octave range allows it the sanctioned privilege of "carrying the coattails of the king."

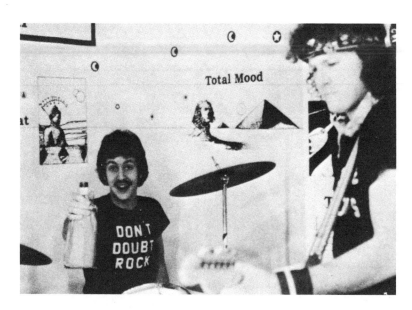

Total Mood

Using the rhythm to repeatedly and regularly signal the hammering of the sixth above the fifth, is another technique which rock inherited from the blues era. It's an easy one finger move, but the number of variations offered up to us in that vast ocean — *the records of rock*, is staggering. This common rhythm guitar technique is utterly convertible, adapting to any number of movable situations. In addition to this, you have the seventh (-7) just a half step above the sixth, along WITH THE SEVENTH'S POSITION ALONG THE ROOT NOTE FRET. These add-on notes are just little red lights, like on an airplane landing field, which bleep on and off above the major triad.

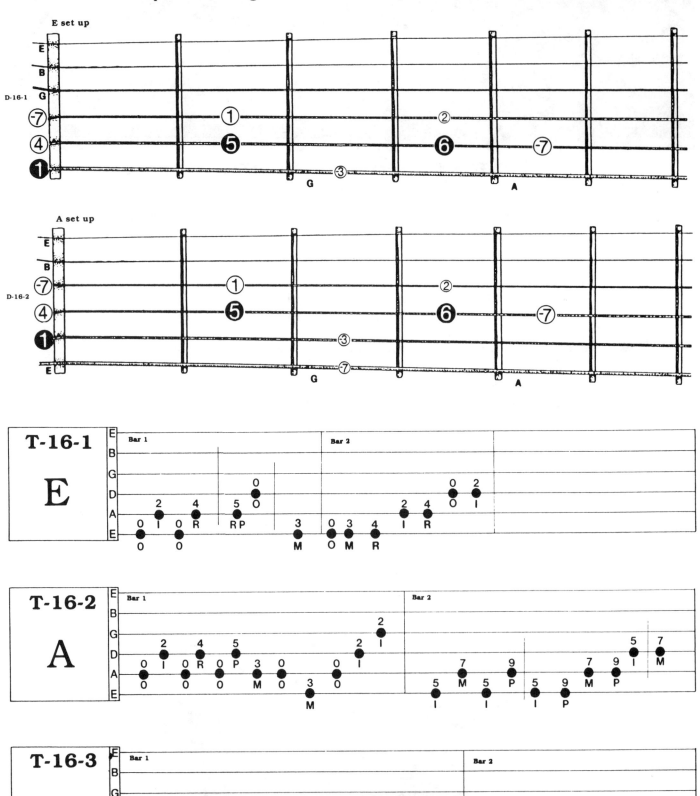

WINDOW #17

Suspend the Fourth

Primary Objective Statement

To study inversions of the suspended fourth chord

The relationship between the first and the fourth just will not quit. I'm trying to get to Sliding Power Chords, and we are just going into the matter of *sus four.* The reason I do this is because of the important role which this arresting chord plays in the rock guitar picture, and because, like so many others, the sus four position can also be slid in power chord fashion. So sit back for a minute and listen to the story of the "add on" fourth. The word "suspended" is used because the fourth degree is held over the third. On an instrument like the guitar, playing the fourth tends to "hog up" the third, just one fret below, reducing the use of thirds to the higher or lower octaves, out of the considered range. Sooooo, you "suspend" the fourth. The word means so much. You can hammer it on, build it into a full chord from the get go, pull it off, roll it over quickly, or *build a triad above the fourth degree.* Let's take a look at the common voicing of the sus fourth through the eyes of the rock guitarist. First, we will go right down the line through E, A, D, G and C. Then we will shoot for throwing the fourth around using bar chords.

Universal Major Chord Inversion Diagram

 First Octave   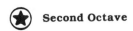 Second Octave    Third Octave

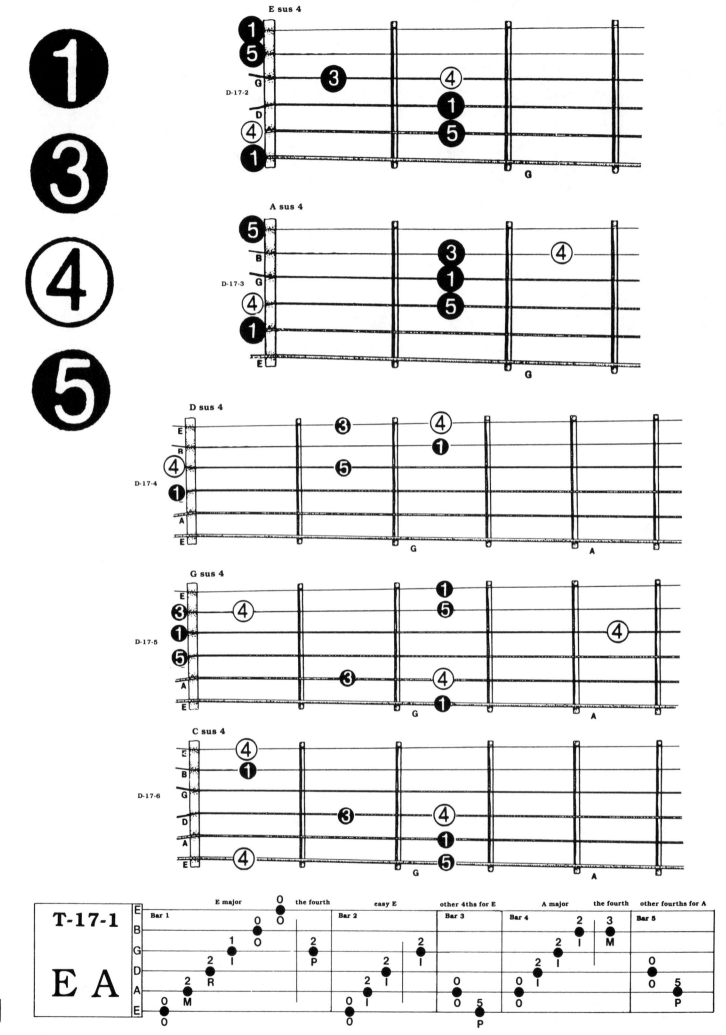

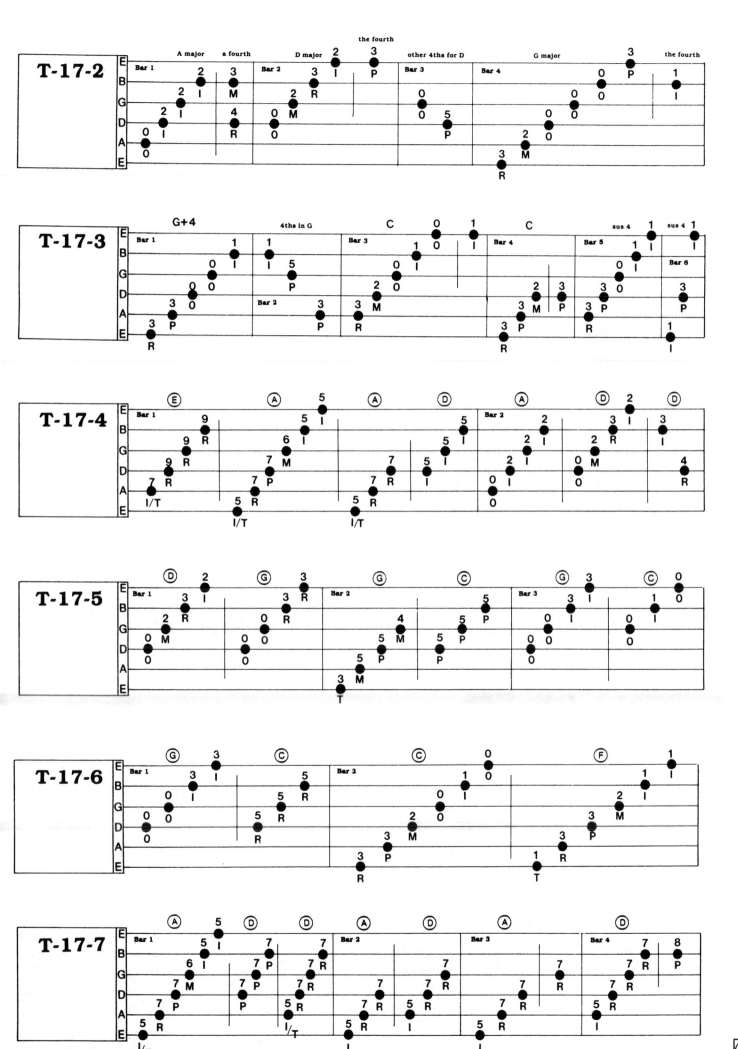

WINDOW #18

Augment the Ninth

Primary Objective Statement

To study inversions of the augmented ninth chord

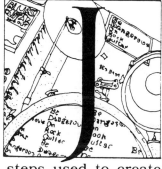 imi really used the augmented 9th chord to its full potential in his famous signature tune, Foxey Lady. You see, the two degrees that you add over the common triad (1, 3, 5) to get the augmented 9th chord are those ever-familiar blues scale degrees: -3 and -7. Those two "blues notes" keep popping up when you study rock. Yes, the flatted third and the flatted seventh have been known throughout musical history as minor "altered" steps used to create dissonance, *particuly when played against each other*. Hey, that is precisely the formula for the augmented 9th chord. The term "augmented ninth" refers to a raised 2nd played in the octave above where you sound the basic triad components of 1, 3 and 5. No matter what you call it, a flatted 3rd, a raised 2nd, or an augmented 9th, they are all names for the same note, a minor third above the tonic.

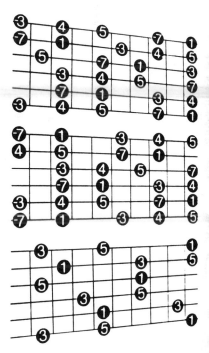

According to standard chord building "rules", whenever a chord's name contains a number higher than seven, the chord "automatically" carries the -7th degree in its makeup. Obeying the rules, the degrees of the augmented 9th are as follows: 1, 3, 5, -7, -3'. What happens when you run into one of these "stacked" chords is that they have so many components that several configurations are possible. The two that I will show you are both voicings of the E augmented 9th chord. The first one takes the basic E major chord and adds the notes on 1/3 and 2/3, with the -3rd on the first string, with the -7th on the second string. A cousin to this open position is shown diagrammed with the -7th on the fourth string open, with the -3rd on the third string open. These two notes take place directly on the "root note fret" for the key of E on the open strings, an octave below their respective positions on 1/3 and 2/3. By the way, when Jimi recorded Foxey Lady, he used the F# position for the augmented 9th across 1/5 and 2/5. He slammed just those two notes out of the chord.

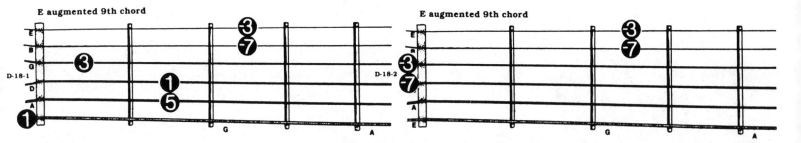

E augmented 9th chord

D-18-1

E augmented 9th chord

D-18-2

In contrast with the fixed open position, the second place I want to show you the augmented 9th chord is highly movable. Built on the Universal C major position, this fifth string root bad boy is portable to any chord center. If we want an E augmented 9th out of the deal, we have to center the chord to the E note on 5/7 with the -3 on 2/8, and the -7th on 3/7. By the way, if you want to make a sixth chord out of this, just lower the note on 2/8 to 2/7.

E augmented 9th chord

D-18-3

B augmented 9th chord

D-18-4

WINDOW #19

Sliding, Hammering,

Attacking, Sustaining:

The Power Chord

Primary Objective Statement

To explore the position, cause and effect of power chords

Power chording is one thing that rock did not inherit from the blues. We thought of doing it all by ourselves, thank you. It was the strictly timed blues form, with its relentless rocking and strumming, which spawned rock's creative use of those tonal clusters called *chords.* If you want to, music will always allow you to go deeper and deeper into its working order. Music schools are full of paper pushing people trying to get an "A" on the next test (a lot of fine violinists, too). But in order to understand power chords, you really have to " get the timing," you really have to "get the feel," you really have to "get it." A lot of the structure is simple, unchanging, unmistakable boxes that we move around, to create the desired effect. Most power chords are simply 1, 5, 1, or more to the point, just the interval of 1 with the 5th above. The way this interval can be casually moved is now rock history. It has a lot to do with the right hand. You can pound that one interval relentlessly with the drummer, then just hit it once hard, and let the drummer go. Sliding around the 1, 5, 1' configuration is certainly a good way to introduce yourself to the field. On the transcriptions below, you will find that on a few bars I condensed "all three sliding notes" down to a single representative dot — just to keep things uncluttered.

After rock guitar became an established trade in the late sixties, each artist shook down the fretboard to find the easiest moves which they could incorporate into their personal style. They would all borrow from each other, but each had their own distinctive "favorite" set of moves, which, of course, would change over time. All of this "research and development" eventually turned out a "school of power guitar moves." The big groups were the think tanks for refined style. The public bought the records, now everybody knows the moves. I will catagorize the basic outline of these power chord moves for you in the transcriptions and diagrams which follow.

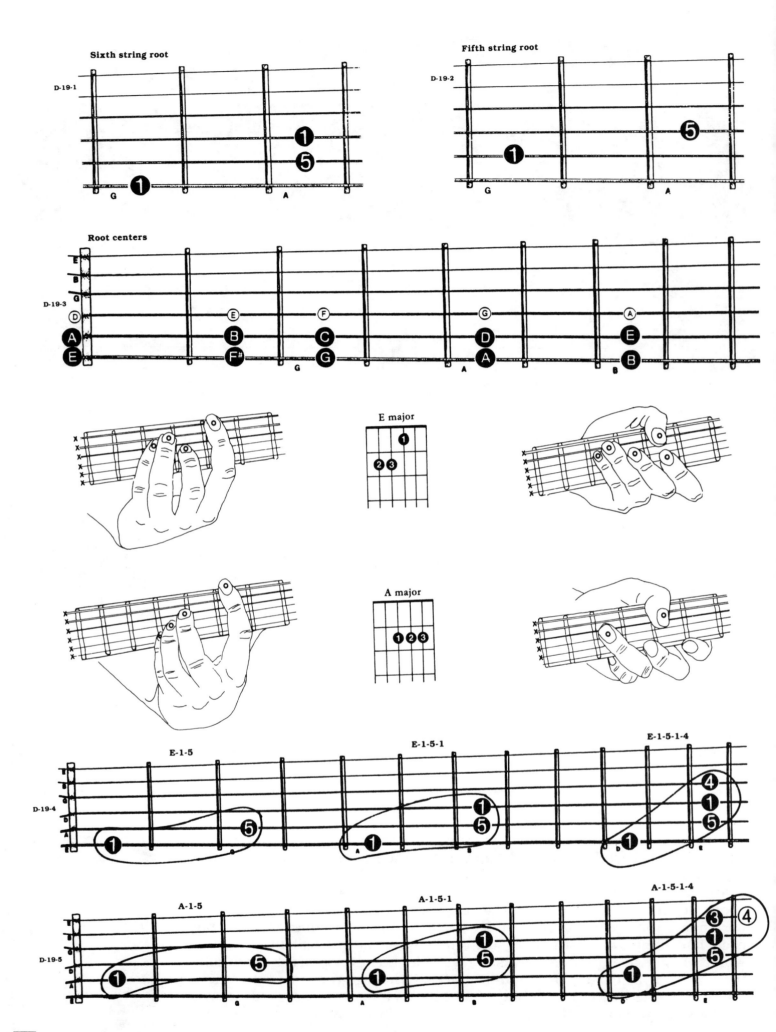

T-19-1

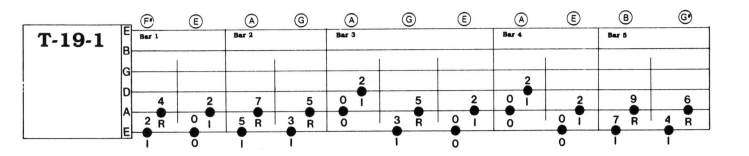

T-19-2

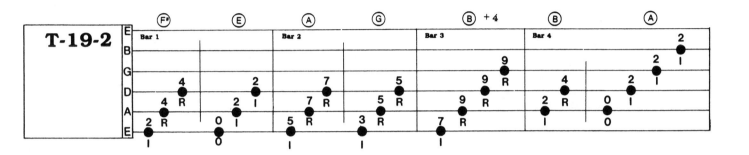

T-19-3

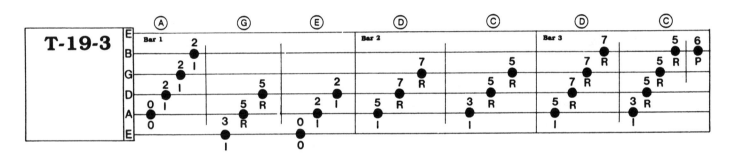

T-19-4

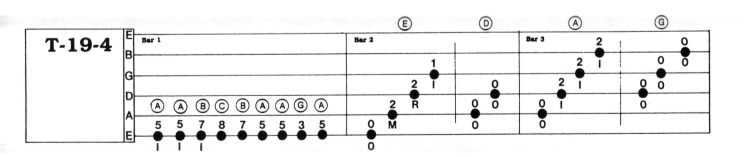

T-19-5

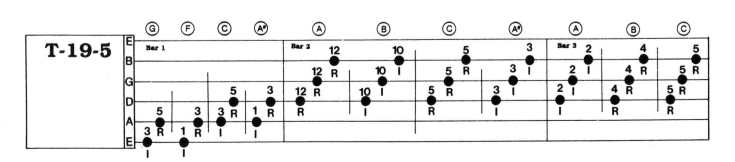

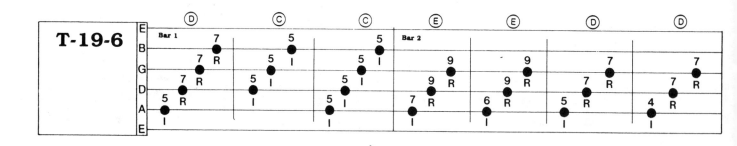

T-19-6

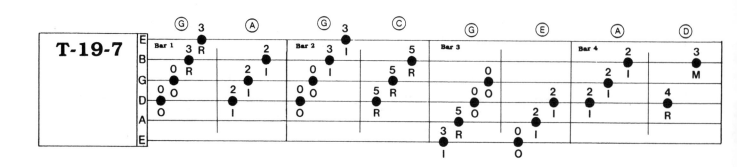

T-19-7

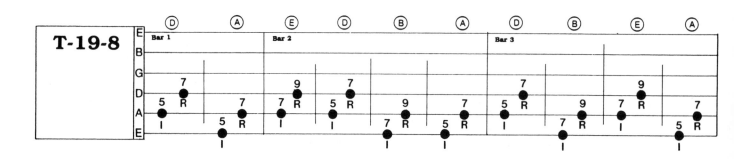

T-19-8

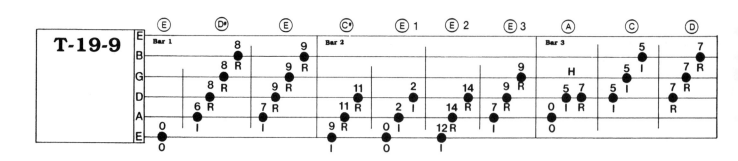

T-19-9

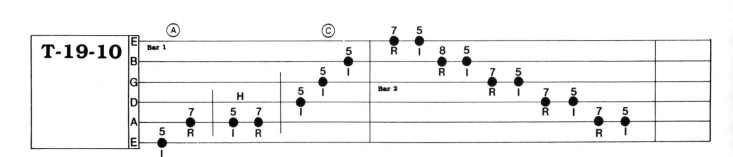

T-19-10

WINDOW #20

Harmonics

Primary Objective Statement

To study the position and use of harmonic overtones

Harmonic overtones are natural to the vibrating fixed string. Since they "come with the territory" of playing the guitar anyway, we will set out to use them to our great advantage. The strings' inherent overtones are always higher pitched than the singularly identifiable fundamental tone, and together form a subtle "chorus" effect described as the *timbre* of a note. Although the fundamental partially "hides" the spectrum of overtones under its greater amplitude, once the string is sounded, *all overtones are constantly in effect.* There is no way to get away from this fact: the string shakes in full, halves, thirds, fourths, fifths, sixths, sevenths, and eighths ALL AT ONCE — ALL THE TIME IT IS SOUNDING. You have to keep this in mind if you are going to truly understand the ways of harmonic overtones. This is because the characteristics of overtones are often different, and sometimes opposite, from the properties exhibited by only the fundamental notes of open or fretted strings.

Let's clear up one thing right off the bat. The fundamental is called the first harmonic, so the first overtone is the second harmonic and so on. All references in this book will be to numbered overtones. Now, if the fundamental, or the common sound of the open string is identified as the tonic, or simply 1, then the first seven overtones of the fixed string produce tones in this order of sequence:

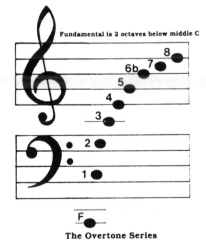

Fundamental is 2 octaves below middle C

The Overtone Series

Fundamental 1	First Overtone 1'	Second Overtone 5'	Third Overtone 1"	Fourth Overtone 3"	Fifth Overtone 5"	Sixth Overtone -7"	Seventh Overtone 1'''

The first overtone divides the string into two modes of vibration and has one free node. The second overtone divides the string into three modes of vibration and has two free nodes. This progression continues throughout the overtone series(<u>Harvard Brief Dictionary of Music</u> lists up to the sixteenth overtone), but we will consider only up to the seventh overtone, which divides the string into eight vibratory modes and produces the "triple octave" above the fundamental.

The study of overtones on the guitar starts with locating all of the available nodal points on the strings, and the practice of setting a chosen overtone "ringing" at will. First, let's take a look at how the harmonic nodes take their place along the length of the fixed string.

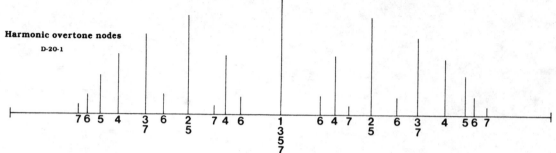

Harmonic overtone nodes
D-20-1

Notice how the nodes cut a "mirror" image on either side of the center mark created by the first overtone's single node. Also note that the higher numbered overtones often share "common nodes" with lower numbered overtones. Let's try pinning down the basics of this complex subject with a list of facts which concern the position, sounding, and interrelationship of the guitar's harmonic overtones.

1 *****The "bringing out" of a harmonic overtone by lightly touching a singing string does not actually increase the amplitude of the chosen harmonic, but allows the chosen harmonic to dominate by "knocking down" the amplitude of the fundamental, and all other lower overtones.

2 *****A chosen harmonic can be sounded by lightly touching the string and immediately removing the finger either *as the string is plucked* or *after* the string has already been sounded.

3 *****A *second* chosen harmonic can be sounded by lightly touching the singing string at a second higher numbered harmonic node, *after* you have already sounded a lower numbered harmonic on the same string.

4 *****Harmonic overtones produced on an open singing string can be "bent" by "pushing" on the neck or body of the instrument, or by going down on the "wa" bar once a harmonic has been sounded.

5 *****Harmonic overtones can be brought out of a fretted string in a fashion identical to that of the open string, except you "move up" the nodal point on the string one fret for each fret that you move above the nut with the left hand. These are known as artificial harmonics and can be slid or bent like any other fretted note.

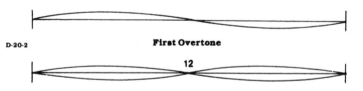

D-20-2   **First Overtone**

6 *****The *first overtone* is the easiest to "ring," and probably the most used of all harmonic overtones. Its only free node is located over the twelfth fret. The tone produced by this overtone is one octave above that of the fundamental, and is identical in pitch to the fretted note at the twelfth fret.

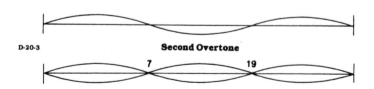

D-20-3   **Second Overtone**

7 *****The *second overtone* produces a note a 5th above the first overtone, and has free nodes above the seventh and nineteenth frets. Sounding the harmonic or fretting the string will produce the same letter named note in either of these two nodal positions, but the 7th fret harmonic will produce a note an octave above the fretted note, while the 19th fret position produces identically pitched notes for both the fretted and harmonic tones.

number indicates overtone

8 *****An identically sounding tone is produced on both of the second overtone's nodes over the 7th and 19th frets. The tone produced at the twelfth fret by the first overtone is lower in pitch than the two aforementioned identical harmonic overtones, which take their positions both above and below the 12th fret. This deal goes against the grain of what we learned about fretting, which was, if you fret the notes on the 7th, 12th, and 19th fret, you are going to get progressively higher tones.

Equidistant Harmonic Nodes

D-20-4

9 *****The nodes of the second overtone at the 7th and 19th frets are both equidistant from the nut and bridge respectively. The same two positions are also equidistant from the twelfth fret position. You see, we are dealing with dividing the string into partials, not with a number of frets. This does not mean that the frets are not important, because they do actually cut the string off into carefully considered lengths. Overtone nodes just don't "count up" the same way as fretting. Think distance.

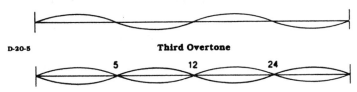

D-20-5   **Third Overtone**

10 *****The *third overtone* produces a double octave of the fundamental and has open nodes above the 5th, 12th, and 24nd fret. The most common position for bringing out this overtone is over the fifth fret, where it can easily be used along with fretted notes. All three nodal points sound the same named note as the open string, but . . .

11 *****When overtones share common nodal positions, like the first and third overtones share the node over the twelfth fret, the lowered numbered overtone will always predominate. This reduces the available nodal positions for the higher numbered overtones. Yes, the tones from the open strings sound an octave higher if we ring the overtones above the 12th fret, and an octave above that over the 5th fret. Our instrument runs six of these fixed strings *right next to each other*, so the game always works *across all six* the same way.

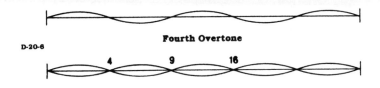

D-20-6   **Fourth Overtone**

12 *****The *fourth overtone* produces a tone a 3rd above the double octave of the third overtone, and has four free nodes above the 4th, 9th, and 16th frets, along with a node somewhere over the pickup area. The 4th fret is the usual position where this overtone is sounded. Please notice that this overtone, along with the sixth overtone, does not share any common nodes with lower numbered overtones. This is because the numbers five and seven (the number of string subdivisions from the 4th and 6th overtones) are not divisible by 2 or 3. All four nodes of the fourth overtone produce the same high pitched tone.

13 *****The common position for the *fifth* and *sixth* overtones are over the 3 1/4 and 2 2/3 fret positions respectively. You will find several nodal positions where these overtones can be produced on the <u>Be Dangerous On Rock Guitar Wall Poster</u>.

14 *****The *seventh overtone* produces a tone three octaves above the fundamental known as the "triple octave." The common nodes for this overtone take place along the string "about a third" of the way between the second and the third frets (the last position diagramed), and also a real sweet position above the eighth fret.

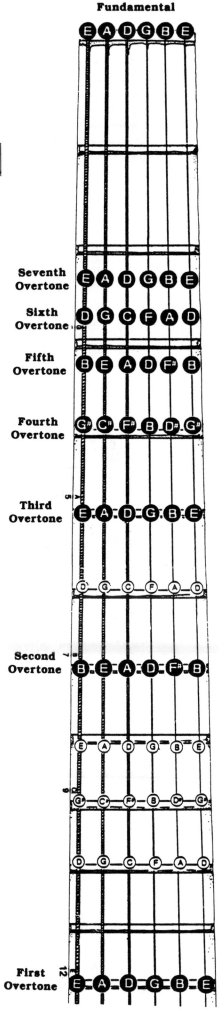

15 *****The common centers for the first seven overtones are shown across all six strings in LARGE BLACK DOTS starting with the first overtone's single node directly over the twelfth fret, working down to the seventh overtone over the 2 1/3 fret. Here is how they all stack up:

First seven overtones

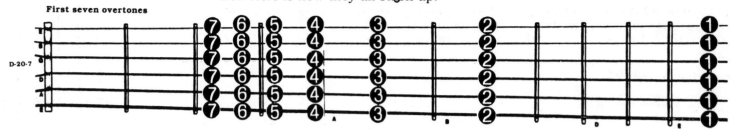

These are the common positions used by lead guitarists to pick up harmonics. Although we are only looking closely at the first seven harmonics, you should remember that many other higher overtones are also in effect, and will often pop out by accident as you hunt for the nodal centers that you really want. Just like a yo-yo, you can talk about it forever, but there is only one way to really get good (keep staring at the wall poster for guidance).

16 *****Harmonic overtones can be sounded "one after another" up and down, as well as across the six strings. In this way, you can play a "passage" of harmonically sounded notes, or introduce overtones singularly into a succession of fretted notes.

17 *****Harmonic overtones can be used to produce "chords" *across* two or more strings which coincide with the formation of the common open chord forms. The A chord is the biggie, with notes played straight across the 2nd, 3rd, and 4th strings. The open E chord is also useful with notes straight across the same fret on the 1st and 2nd, and also the 4th and 5th strings.

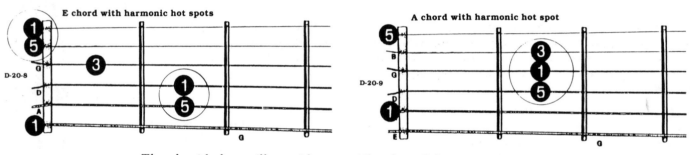

E chord with harmonic hot spots   A chord with harmonic hot spot

The chart below will provide you with a few of the most commonly obtained "harmonic chords." The easiest and most popular harmonic chords are the G chord sounded across the 2nd, 3rd, and 4th strings above twelfth fret (same chord sounds above the 5th and the 8th fret) and the D major chord on the 2nd, 3rd, and 4th strings above the seventh fret.

Harmonic Chord Chart		
Fret	Strings	Chord
12	2-3-4	G'
7	2-3-4	D'
5	2-3-4	G"
2-1/3	2-3-4	G'''
12	4-5	D'
12	1-2	E'
7	4-5	A'
5	4-5	D"

Harmonic overtones are tricky business. They require a light touch and a determined attack in order to bring them out. Sitting quietly and practicing their sounding, and working them into your style are two different things. They have been around as long as stringed instruments. There is a centuries old classical violin technique which requires the performer to "hold" his finger on a harmonic node (not touching the string to the board) while the bow moves across the string sounding the desired harmonic overtone.

The first time I ever heard purposely sounded harmonic overtones in a rock format was the opening two notes of Jimi Hendrix's <u>Stone Free</u> released in the spring of 1967 as the flip side of his first single <u>Hey Joe</u>. The master of modern day harmonic technique is, of course, one Edward Van Halen. His records have spawned a nation of axe wielding aspirants who look to him for overdriven example and harmonic inspiration.

WINDOW #21

Proven Places

Primary Objective Statement

To explore fretboard positions used in rock

After all is said and done, and all of the overtone diagrams have gone to bed, it boils down to this: rock *is* music, the guitar *is* an instrument, and to a certain degree it is absolutely necessary to study the basics of musical phenomena and form in order to approach playing the six string guitar in any fashion or style. The thing is, after you wade through the basics long enough, you will inevitably come to the same fundamental conclusion arrived at by thousands before you: ALL I REALLY WANT TO DO IS PLAY ROCK GUITAR AND HAVE FUN. I DON'T WANT TO PLAY CLASSICAL GUITAR. I DON'T CARE ABOUT FIFTY-SEVEN WAYS TO FINGER THROUGH THE MAJOR SCALE. I JUST WANT TO PLAY ROCK GUITAR.

Yes, it is time to put down *The Big Picture* and concentrate on how rock guitarists move around the fretboard. During the research of <u>Be Dangerous On Rock Guitar</u>, I threw together a really great tape of 1001 rock songs all strung together one after the other. I edited the songs down so only the characteristic opening bars, chord cycle, and outstanding lead breaks went down onto the tape. All the endless verses stayed on the record. The whole tape is about an hour, and it's just clips. I really poured over our rock record collection with a fine toothed comb. It took a few days of listening and recording, but I did not stop until the tape was complete with ALL OF THE GROUPS THAT COUNT, with only their best stuff edited down. It has a thousand moods, and to hear the clash of reality when one song just cuts out cold and the other one blasts in, always gives you a feeling for how deep the well truly is. No need to go into names, really, its just the whole clan.

I kept playing the "rock encyclopedia" tape over and over, stopping it, starting it, *figuring it out*. After a few hours of picking apart each song and lead break, certain patterns began to emerge again and again: PATTERNS COMMON TO ROCK. These "proven places" are simply positions to which the style of rock guitar has adapted itself. Certainly the same boxes are there for any type of music, but it took the rock style to fit the guitar fretboard so well, in so many ways. These are the places where rock has already been written. So go to them to create more.

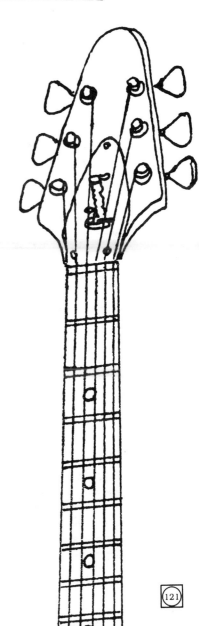

Below find a catalog of positions, each with its own special place on the board. Some are movable, but some with open string moves are locked into one key.

POSITION 1-E presents the "open" E blues box used so often by the early blues players. The E (1) and A (4) chords fit into the blues scale box so naturally that it is almost unbelievable. This box is totally moveable to any other fret position for use in other keys.

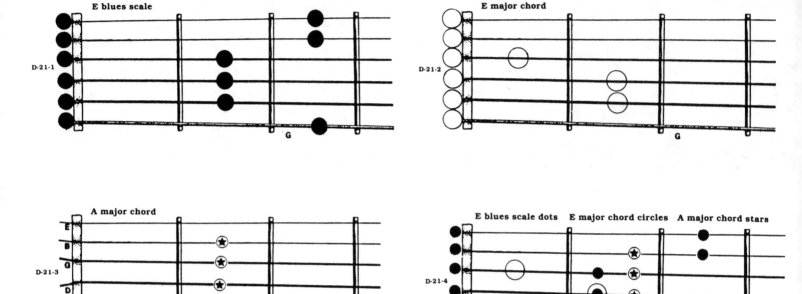

POSITION 2-E uses the low E string open, along with the next higher E note on 5/7, to form a cool E blues box. You can work out along the fifth fret and jump up to slam the E major chord across the 9th fret whenever you want.

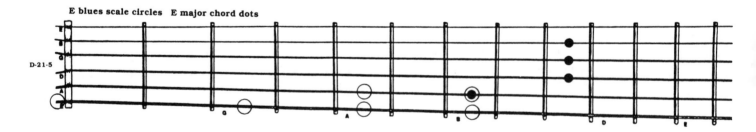

POSITION 3-E uses the relative "root note fret" in E to run the E relative scale, while obtaining easy access to the F# and E bar chords across the 11th and 9th frets. The C# major chord is also shown on the two low strings, along with the open E position down at the bottom.

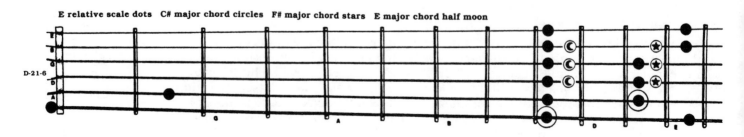

POSITION 4-E lifts position 1-E up to the 12th fret, exposing the underside of the root note fret to playing from beneath. The D and E bar chords have also been outlined.

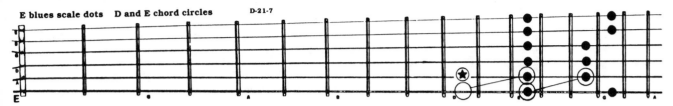

POSITION 5-E uses the extended open E blues box on the first three frets just over the open strings, along with the common 1, 5 bar chords for E and A built above the 5th and 7th frets.

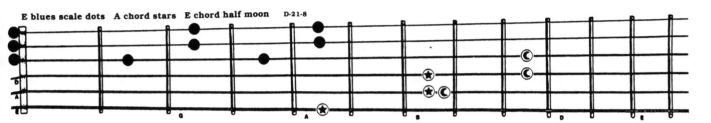

POSITION 6-E shows the E chord barred to the fourth and fifth frets. These fret centers represent the common places where you can build moves for the 1st, 4th, and 5th in the key of E.

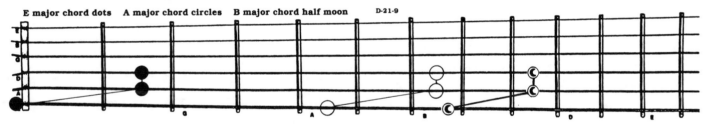

POSITION 7-A gives the A blues box across the 5th fret, with the A major and D major chords superimposed. Please note the A major chord which has been diagramed in the open position.

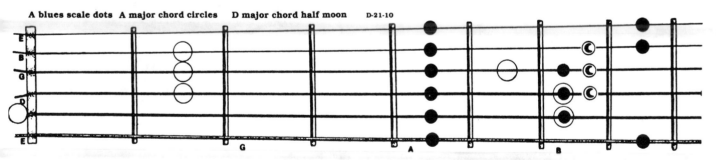

POSITION 8-A takes you along the open position for the key of A, demonstrating the blues scale in black dots, the A major chord in hollow circles, and the D major chord configuration in stars. Tonic notes are located on 5/0 and 3/2.

Tape Side	Window
1 A	1
1 B	1 cont. 2, 3
2 A	4, 5, 6
2 B	6 cont. 7, 8
3 A	8 cont. 9
3 B	9 cont. 10, 11, 12, 13
4 A	14, 15, 16, 17
4 B	18, 19, 20
5 A	20 cont. 21, 22
5 B	22 cont.
6 A	23, 24
6 B	24 cont.

A blues scale dots   A major chord circles   D major chord stars   D-21-11

POSITION 9-A is a cousin to the E shot from position 2-E. This time around you get to use all of those easy one finger bar chords which you see across the second, fourth, fifth, and seventh frets.

A blues scale dots   A bar chords circles

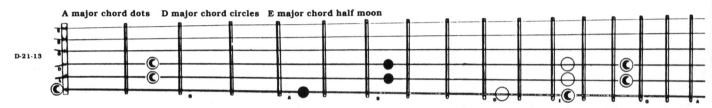

D-21-12

POSITION 10-A gives you the three fret position where you can build moves for the first, fourth and fifth chords for the key of A. Note that the E chord takes place at both the 12th fret and the open position.

A major chord dots   D major chord circles   E major chord half moon

D-21-13

POSITION 11-A shows the relative scale for the key of A along the second fret, three frets below the blues scale root note fret at the fifth fret. Please note that if you add the 4th and 7th major scale degree to this scale, you get the major scale itself.

A relative scale with fillers

D-21-14

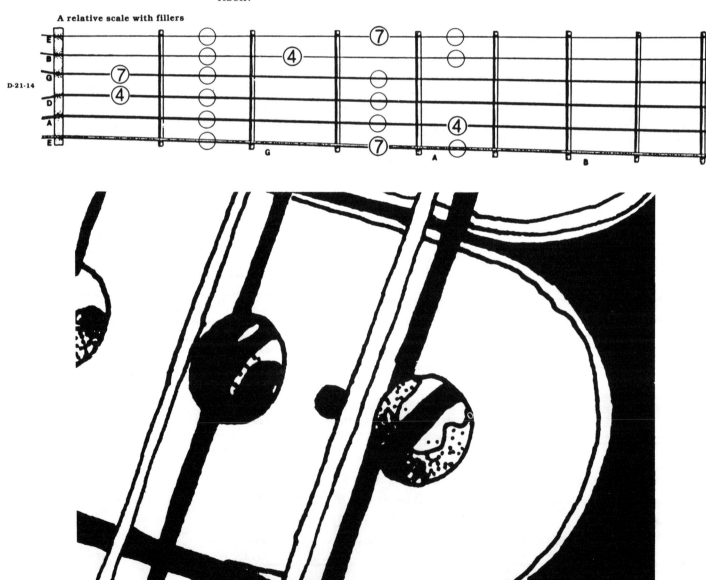

POSITION 12-G shows the basic blues scale, 1st chord and 4th chord set up for the key of G. One of the advantages of using this position is that the relative scale for G is the same as the familiar E blues box across the open strings, three frets below the G blues scale position.

G major chord dots   G blues scale circles   C major scale half moon

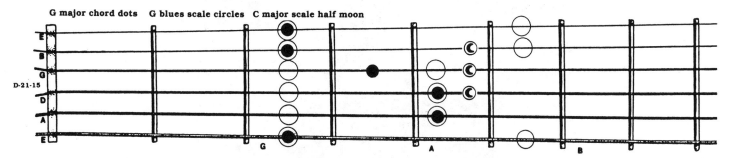

POSITION 13-G is a study of whole step bar moves using the E and A bar just above the open strings. The guitar is very rich and full in tone at this position, and these same chords can be found used with each other in the keys of G, C, or F.

F major chord dots   G major chord triangle   A# major chord diamonds   C major chord stars

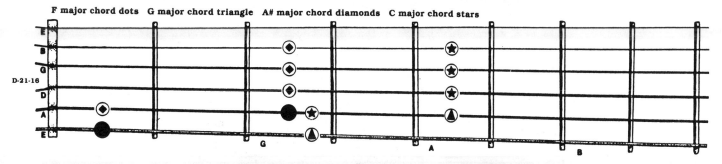

POSITION 14-D shows the relationship between the basic box of the blues and relative scale in the key of D. The dots with circles around them are either the first or the fifth from the major scale, two degrees common to both of these rock scales.

D blues scale dots   D relative scale circles

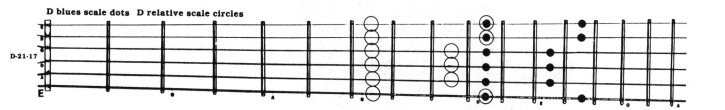

WINDOW #22

Bag-O-Tricks
for
Flash Lead

Primary Objective Statement

To investigate 21 flash techniques

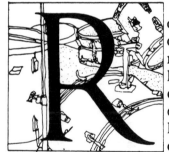

Rock technique, ah, my favorite subject! For a while early on, rock and roll was sort of an accelerated blues rhythm. For the bottom, the 6th was hammered regularly over the 5th in rhythm with the tonic, and it didn't matter much if it was the guitar or the piano doing it: *it was rock and roll.* Yes, the world of music has always recognized the ability of the guitar to successfully carry out a low range rhythm, but it was not until the forties that Charlie Christian made everybody aware that the electric guitar could handle a *full line* that directly competed with the horn section. This was when the bag-o-tricks for lead guitar started to fill up. And, it hasn't stopped since. The shining "single line with double stop" leadwork put down by Elmore James and Chuck Berry were on the ball, but were only hints of things to come: *outstanding examples of veiled potential.*

The wonders of the overly sensitive electric guitar were independently and repeatedly discovered by anybody who cared to overdrive the guitar's signal. The exceptionally creative string techniques used by today's artists were spawned ten and twenty years ago when the cards were first on the table. Call it what you will: overdriven, distorted, sustaining. It all means that the "driven" electric guitar sings with such sweet harmonics and sustains such continual acoustic presence, that it has now earned a long standing reputation as an instrument with tremendous aural capabilities. Greater volumes created the "feedback" cycle, which causes the output of the guitar to directly increase the vibration of the fixed strings. This causes an ever increasing output, which drastically changes the nature of the instrument. It can get to the point that you either have to *play now,* or *shut it down.* If you just stand around with the thing on, it's going to start to make wierd noises *on its own!* Once this "full cycle" style of amplification was discovered, hundreds of great rock records were recorded, each with a different slant on the art. The six string guitar will go down in music history as a sleeping giant that rock awoke. You see, the guitar has been capable of pulling off the tricks all along. It just took a few generations and a lot of electricity to make it happen.

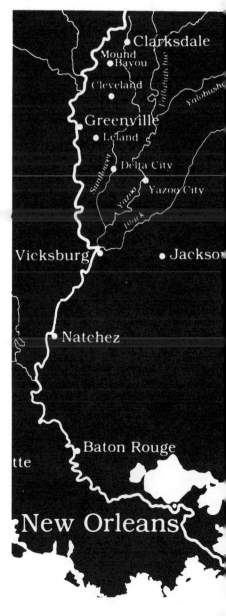

TRICK 1 — THE TIP OFF

As simple as it seems, quickly pulling the tip of the finger off of the fretted string is a big part of flash lead technique. Concentrate on a "light touch," and a "flowing" approach. Set your goals for tomorrow. EXPLORE NEW PLACES EVERY DAY. You will become a fast, accurate, diverse lead guitarist when you become *filled with intent* to do so. Push yourself to the next level, pulling off every available note.

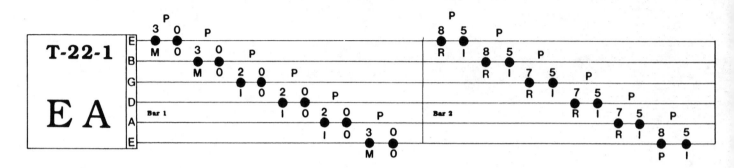

TRICK 2 — THE HAMMER ON

The hammer is another rock technique which cuts down on the number of times you actually have to pick the string. The repeated hammer is directly linked with the pull-off technique. Try a repeated hammer anywhere you are playing an interval above a note held with the index finger.

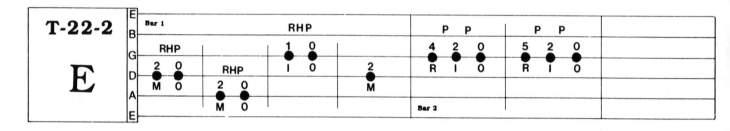

TRICK 3 — WILD BENDS

We're not talking regular old half-step bends taken out of the scale pattern. We're talking about *going for it.* Try working an exaggerated bend note into your next break. You know, *plan it.* The transcription below will give you a sample of some of the more outside techniques you can use, including the giant ride, the wavering bend, the descending step bend, the bass slide, and the world famous vertically moving unison bend.

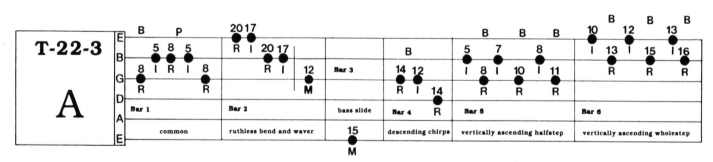

TRICK 4 — RIGHT HAND ON BOARD

Eddie Van Halen was the first guy that I heard use his right hand on the board. I was listening to the record, and all of a sudden there was this incredible high note that was entirely out of the range where the left hand was apparently working. Then I saw this guy in town do it, and I went home to practice. What a great idea! Even Jimi wasn't into this stuff. I show you two ways to employ this technique, although I know that there are certainly many more, including using more than one finger on the right hand. Bring the finger down confidently onto the string for both the single and repeated note technique. The right hand notes have a little star above them.

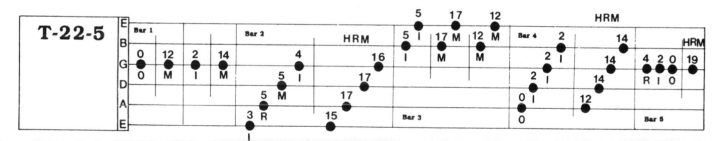

TRICK 5 — OPEN STRING HARMONICS

The open strings are so nice. Hard to tune, but nice. The harmonic overtones of the fixed string are easy to set "singing" on the open string. All of the nodes that you see on the life-size harmonic diagram on the wall poster are waiting for you to find them, dig them out, and let them go. If you try, you can sound the first overtone over the 12th fret, and then pick up a *second*, higher overtone by again touching the singing string over the 7th, 5th or 4th fret. Lots of funny sounds also inevitably result from slightly "flexing" the body and neck of the six string electric guitar, after an open string harmonic has been sounded.

TRICK 6 — ARTIFICIAL HARMONICS

There is nothing artificial about artificial harmonics. That's just what they call them. Think about the hammer on technique for a second. You pluck an open string, and then bring the fretting finger sharply between the first and second fret. You'll immediately hear a higher note. Try to imagine how fast the steel string adjusts to a new fundamental mode of vibration (and a whole new set of "artificial" harmonic nodes), the split second that the steel of the string touches the fret metal. Yes, fretted or not, a singing string shakes in full, halves, thirds, etc. You will find that artificial nodes are just as sensitive to the touch, and just as difficult to sound, as the open string harmonics.

To "adjust" the open string nodal positions that you see on the wall poster to an artificial position, simply add the number of frets that you are fretting above the nut with the left hand, to the open string nodal position — and you have it. As things move with the left hand, so do the nodal positions move. The advantage to using artificial harmonics is that they can be bent, slid, and textured by movement of the fretting finger on the string.

TRICK 7 — HAMMER ON FRET HARMONICS

On the whole, both open and artificial harmonic nodes take place over a fret. The trick here is to hammer a finger of the right hand down onto the string, bringing it down hard onto the fret metal. This single action sounds the string and rings the chosen harmonic at the same time. The result is a subtle "struck chime" effect like you get on a door chime. This technique is particularly effective if you chime the harmonics over a major chord.

TRICK 8 — RUNNING HARMONICS

Harmonic overtones can be sounded "one after another" just like fretted notes can be put into a passage. You can "play" different harmonics one after another on a single string, or across several strings. Another thing you can do is add a single harmonic note into a passage of fretted notes. In WINDOW 1 - The Big Picture, you will find detailed information about which frets you can expect to obtain the same note from either fretting or sounding the harmonic (the 12th, 19th, and 24th frets).

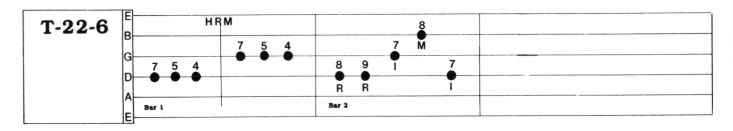

TRICK 9 — BENT OR SLID HARMONICS

Once an artificial harmonic overtone has been sounded, it can be bent or slid around just like a fretted note, as long as the string is firmly held down to the fretboard.

TRICK 10 — TRI-PICK TECHNIQUE

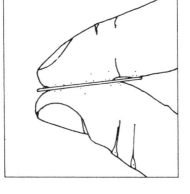

The tri-pick technique is an important little harmonic move which allows you to sound high pitch harmonic "chirp" notes at will without taking time out to purposefully "touch" a particular harmonic node. The technique is performed by choking up on a hard pick with the index and thumb, in such a way that the pick does not extend past the tips of the fingers. After grabbing the pick tightly in this fashion, don't just pluck, but BEAR DOWN on the string with a quick singular action which plucks the string one, two, three; first with the nail or flesh of the index, then pick, then the tip of the thumb. You really have to work at this for a minute before you "get the knack." The action of both fingers and the pick on the string serves to pluck the string into action, and then immediately mute the fundamental in a single move. You can use this technique to chirp just one note, but it works equally as well to chirp all of the notes in a fretted passage. Try picking away from the bridge a little further than usual where the nodes of the higher overtones begin to stack up.

TRICK 11 — STRING RAKE

You hear this move all over Hendrix's albums. Simply take the pick firmly in hand and, with the amp's gain turned to ten, run the pick down the length of the guitar's wound strings. You can also do this with the palm of the hand, or anything that happens to be on top of the amp.

You can also rake the strings with the pick after they have passed over the nut at the very top of the guitar, or on some models, down at the bottom after the bridge. The plucking of these little shorties results in a high pitched tingling sensation used by Eddie Van Halen to open Running With The Devil.

TRICK 12 — AGAINST THE STAND

Another Hendrix move, pushing the guitar's strings up against the mike stand serves as the ultimate slide technique and a sure crowd pleaser. Try sounding the strings open running the stand across all six strings for the full length of the string. The frequencies will scream into the ultra high range as you approach the end of the string.

If you happen to be playing Johnny Be Goode in the key of B, hold the mike stand with the left hand, and bring it up to the two thin strings directly over the seventh fret and hammer away with the pick on just those two strings. Now, if you can only figure out how to do this and the duck walk at the same time . . .

TRICK 13 — RAPID PICKING

Try bearing down on just one of the thin strings with a fast, alternate up and down picking style. This sounds a stacatto attack consisting of only one note. Works great with thin string bends, as well as on the lower strings played open.

TRICK 14 — HIT BACK

Try taking your hands entirely off the guitar and let it just hang from your shoulders. Now take the knuckles of your left hand and rap on the wood of the head stock from the back. Listen to what happens. This sounds all six strings without touching them. This technique works to a lesser extent by striking the body of the guitar. I rarely set the strat to the bass positions on the pickup selector, but I have discovered that with the selector switch in this position, if I rap the back and walk up in front of the amp, the bass tones produced are somehow particular (and peculiar) to this technique, and cannot be derived by plucking the string.

TRICK 15 — THE POWER SLIDE

The power slide has got to be unique to power rock. Sure, a lot of you might say, "Give me an accoustic guitar and I will make it come alive with the feeling of a good power chord slide." Well look, it took the overdriven electric to *get it.* The Spanish guitar of centuries past was wonderful. It was dreamy, outstanding and overwhelming in its ability to carry emotion. Complex classical technique was in full evidence a long time ago. BUT DO YOU REALLY THINK THERE WERE ANY POWER SLIDES? HELL, NO! The rock guitarist slides around 1 and 5 together, and 1' is added if it is desired. The blues scale degrees 1 and -3 are used as individual notes or as the base for further triad building for power chord usage. The triad built on -7 is used to bounce back and fourth between the tonic. In between and over these described centers we perform dangerous power slides by MOVING A CONFIGURATION DOWN THE STRING LENGTH IN A ROAR. The Spanish guys may have done it in a series of sophisticated steps, I don't doubt that. It is just that the use of the tube amp was responsible for the *power slide* and not the acoustic guitar.

TRICK 16 — CREATIVE WA BAR TECHNIQUE

You sort of have to go to the tape for this one. Just be gentle with the thing. If someone who doesn't have a wa bar on their guitar is about to play your guitar, be ready for overbearing use of the bar. It just seems that when people first try to use it, it has to be to some gross order. Sure you say, Jimi put his to the wood every time and HE stayed in tune. Yeah, BUT HE WAS JIMI HENDRIX. Truth is, the lightest touch affects the frequency.

Let's start off the tape with a passage that ends on a bent note, while we go to the wa bar to gently lift it from underneath the bar to slightly, yet truly, *raise the note.* A steady and light touch can enable the wa bar to be used throughout the lead, rather than just for exaggerated effect. On the red strat, I arranged for the bar to swing "closed" by moving over the strings and bridge and sort of tuck down onto the wood of the guitar beyond the bridge. It even goes into the case that way. One time I tuned the guitar to the tuner a few times with the wa bar tucked away. When I went to use the wa bar (on the first song), I swung it around. But all of the strings jumped up in frequency when I brought it away from the body it was pressed against. Oh well, now I know.

TRICK 17 — FANCY EACH NOTE

If you ever feel uninspired, just try playing the tonic. Then, just tune up relative to that for a while. Then play another note (eleven left) and study the interval. Then just add in rhythm and melody, change it, and you are back on your way again.

TRICK 18 — CHUGA

Chuga is a friend who comes around whenever you are riding the rhythm on the lower three strings. Maybe even mute the strings a little with the right hand leaning on the bridge, you know, just to make chuga thud a little. When chuga comes to town, you become the metronome, your pick distinctly driving out the subdivided beat.

TRICK 19 — PINKY PULL OFFS

You at least have to look at it, you know, just to give it some consideration. Violin players are trained from square one to play a *half step* and *whole step* above the note held by the ring finger in order to reach the next higher degree of the major scale. Their whole world of playing is planned around the fact that you *can and will* get it with the pinky, if you reach for it. There are two schools of thought, really.

The first thinks, unless it is easy, don't bother. Concentrate on feeling the blues, don't get all wrapped up in theory. The second thinks, I want to go way out, and I need the pinky to do it. B. B. King doesn't really need to use the pinky except in chording. While some jazz masters use it for the fast pull offs above the index to grab a minor third, so they swear they can't live without it. Who knows?

Jeff Beck explored rip-roaring rock/fusion music on his historic album <u>Blow By Blow</u> which educated a lot of old school rockers with the realization that *there was more beyond.* Jeff smiles when he thinks of it because he remembers the half-a-decade he spent as a rock/blues star before he put it out. So, jazz guys use the little finger more than rockers. Big deal. Metal Masters go to the mountain, jazz masters go downtown.

TRICK 20 — HOW HARD TO PICK

I was watching this guy in the spotlight the other night and the band was cooking hard for a long time. I thought to myself, "How is this guy going to come out of this? What do you do after you have been riding hard? Oh he needs a transcending move now," I thought. The guitarist went into this quarter note thing, but it was not the passage so much as the *regularity* and *softness* with which he played that accepted the change of pace. He knowingly laid back and let the steam blow off the top. It was great! He was playing soft *on purpose.* When he finally did come up for air and started to distinctly pluck the string again, he didn't have to increase the volume on the amp. By doing nothing more than increasing the amplitude of the strings' vibration, the guitar once again became alive.

TRICK 21 — RETURN TO BASICS

Have you ever noticed that it is the beginning of rock songs that truly grab you? When the first bars of a great work break into the room, you sort of salute the piece by bracing for the world that it offers. Improvising is fine as long as it grows from that base. If you feel it is too thin at any one point, just turn to the drummer, close your eyes, and get back to the time.

Did you ever notice that another great part of the rock song is when it comes back into the regularity of the signature riffs right after the fantasia of the lead break? This is just another example of the return to the clock. Remember now, whenever in doubt, *return to the basics.* When trying to make it right, *return to the basics.* When you are taking it down, come up at one point, and *return to the basics.*

E blues scale first twelve frets

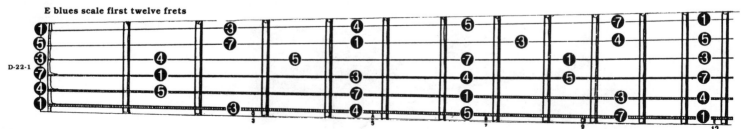

D-22-1

WINDOW #23

Primary Objective Statement

To present a method for deciphering any recording

When I wrote Jimi Hendrix - Note for Note, I sort of stuck my neck out. I kept telling everybody that I was going to write this great book. I started by writing a biography of Jimi's life, spent weeks getting underground Hendrix recordings, wrote a lead guitar primer, drew the cover portrait, selected the twelve songs that I wanted to transcribe. But the bottom line question was still unanswered: HOW IN THE WORLD WAS I GOING TO FIGURE OUT JIMI HENDRIX NOTE FOR NOTE? I knew the procedure, really. It was just difficult to actually GET DOWN TO DOING IT. Writer's block, I guess. Then one fine day I simply bit the bullet and set up the music room for the task. I said to myself, "What's the problem? There is nothing hidden on the musical recording. The tones are recorded one after the other. Jimi had a six string guitar that was set up just like mine. I only had to IDENTIFY THE OBVIOUS. I mean, if I was responsible to cracking the secret recipe for Kentucky Fried Chicken, I would be in BIG TROUBLE. But, to identify and list a passage of frequencies — how hard can it be?" I found out.

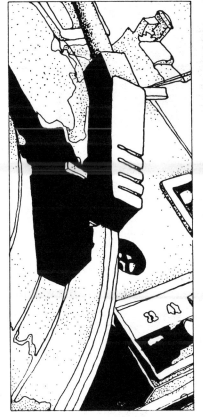

TYPES OF PLAYBACK SYSTEMS

There are three basic ways to play recordings for the purpose of copying guitarwork: the turntable, the cassette player, and the reel-to-reel tape deck. The problem with the turntable is that you cannot stop the recording in its tracks to play back short segments. The problem with the cassette machine is that it does not have variable speeds which can be used to slow down the music to half speed. The problem with the reel-to-reel machine is that very few people have them. The reel-to-reel is by far the best piece for breaking down the music. We are not talking about super high-tech recording decks, here. We are talking about old, used, beat, half worn out, pawn shop quality stereo reel-to-reel decks. We are not really concerned with *recording* anything, just with *playing it back*. The cassette deck is good for copying, but the record player takes a distant, yet acceptable, last place.

THE PROCEDURE

The following list of pointers will help you learn how to copy any recording that you want. The most important thing that I can tell you IS TO ACTUALLY TRY TO DO IT. Once you break down your first lead break you will be filled with confidence and will come to the same conclusion that I did: *you can teach yourself guitar.* The list is slanted towards those fortunate enough to have access to a reel-to-reel recorder, but will also assist you in copying from a turntable or cassette.

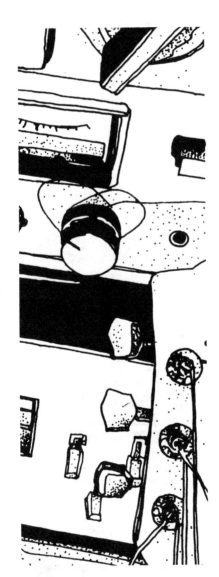

- Get your guitar ready. Put on new strings and clean up the board. Tune up the instrument to a metered tuner if possible, and make sure you have enough good hookup chords.

- Tape just the piece of music that you want to figure out onto the cassette or reel-to-reel, pressing the tape counter to zero on the first note of the lead break, or the beginning of the song, if that is what you want to figure out.

- Set the volume between the recording and your guitar to a good balance. There are a number of ways to wire up the deal. On my home use Sony TC 399, I plug the strat right into the front of the deck (source) and use earphones to monitor everything. By flipping the monitor switches to different settings, I can hear just the recording, just my guitar, or both. Believe it or not, I find it preferable to use a distortion box to overdrive the signal of the guitar. It gets rid of that "flat" up front sound, giving the live guitar a distant feel that better matches the recorded guitar.

- Play the opening bars of the song and try to figure out the opening chord or bass note on the low string. Tune this string perfectly to the recording. Then turn the recording off and tune up the other five strings, run the machine down to the zero point on the tape counter and get ready.

- Get ready to PLAY SHORT SEGMENTS AND REWIND. This is the key. This is the secret. This is the one, single, most important point that my experience can tell you. You must DOMINATE OVER THE MACHINE'S CONTROLS. Get to know each one — especially PLAY, PAUSE and REWIND. Play just the opening notes that you want to figure out. I do not mean opening bars — I mean opening *notes*. Forget the song. Forget the break as a whole. Just GET THOSE FEW NOTES. Run them ten times if you have to, because after the recorder is off and you have to go to your guitar to pick them up, you must have them fresh in your mind. I don't know what it is about the first few notes, but everything seems to fall into place after you get them behind you.

- The single note lead break is the best type with which to start. The question of position, which box was used, immediately rears its dangerous head. The secret to which box the artist used is to be found right ON THE TAPE. You just have to know what to listen for. If a note is hammered on, it is obviously above another fretted note rather than below it on a higher string. All of the finer points will become evident as soon as you TRY HARD TO ACTUALLY DO IT. After you teach yourself the breakdown process on your own equipment, then you can teach yourself any type of guitar style that you want.

- The portable battery operated cassette players have a lot of good features for tape copying. Many newer models have a great feature called "cue review". This allows the quick rewinding of short segments of tape without "breaking" the machine out of the play mode. That's the game: quick, accurate, specific reviewing of the musical frequencies.

- If you have a reel-to-reel, try slowing down a piece of tape by recording the original on the middle speed for slow playback on the low speed. This procedure introduces half as much tape over the playback head for any time period, and results in the frequencies of the original signal sounding one octave below their "real" pitch. Slowing the tape down is a great way to isolate short segments of tape because everything is slower, lower, and easier to deal with.

- If you want to figure out chords, isolate the chord in question and play it several times over the head, on the slow speed if possible. This will plant the chord's components into your mind. Unlike the piano, the guitar's notes are not really sounded "simultaneously", but in quick succession. By playing the chord in question enough times on the tape machine, you can become familiar enough with the chord's degrees to shut the machine off and "sing the notes to yourself." At this point YOU CONTROL THE PLAYBACK SPEED. Just sing them slowly, pick up your guitar, AND FIND THE RIGHT NOTES.

Hey, I'm not going to tell you again: DO IT YOURSELF. I once had a student who just could not figure out the lead to Honky Tonk Woman. He telephoned me and said, "It's just too hard, too fast. I can't pin it down." The first thing I said to him was, "How long on the clock did you actually try to do it? Did you just give the hell up after ten minutes, or did you really try?" He never really answered me. I agreed to help him if he promised that we would take the phone off the hook, lock the doors, and not leave the room until we had figured out each and every note of the song in question.

About three hours later, after I had forced the guy to PIN IT DOWN USING THE REWIND BUTTON, he shook his head affirmatively at me across the wires, guitars, tape recorders, and beer cans — and I knew he was set for life.

WINDOW #24

40 Classic Rock Moves To Turn You Into A Dangerous Guitarist

Primary Objective Statement

To demonstrate 40 great rock passages

Nothing compares to a real-life example. Scale studies, acoustics, chord inversions, octave structure and fingering principles are all very nice in their proper place. But the truth of the matter is that rock guitarists pick up bits and pieces of playing style from wherever they can and then COP THE RIFFS FOR THEMSELVES. Don't get me wrong. I know that true knowledge of the total fretboard is ultimately important because it will, in time, lead you to true musical invention and domination over the instrument. It is, however, just as important for the student to be presented with a slew of tiny, tasty tid-bits that one can go home and chew on, have fun with, and use to flat-out amaze both friends and neighbors with great rock riffs.

So here they come — all forty of them. Make sure to listen closely to the forty moves as they are recorded on the cassette tape. The printed transcription works well to convey information about where the correct notes can be found on the board, but the true phrasing of the riffs, along with multiple aural effects, can be heard only on the cassette.

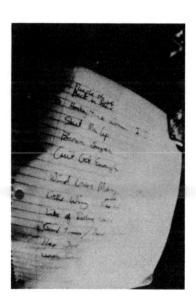

MOVE 1 — Move 1 takes you into the open E chord for a closer look. Take special note of the final bar which studies each of the six strings across this open position.

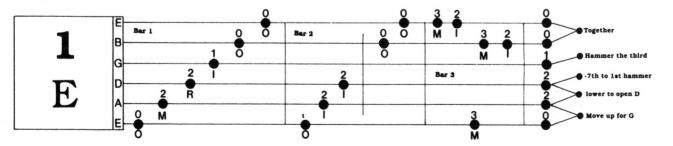

MOVE 2 — Move 2 takes you into the open A chord for a closer look. The final bar shows you little tricks you can perform across all six of the open strings in this position.

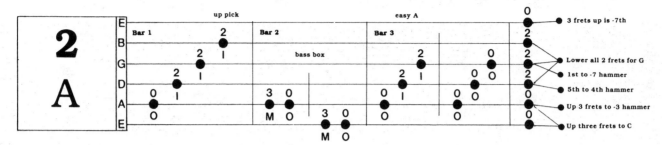

MOVE 3 — Now we move the E chord up and bar it at the fifth fret. Notice the three individual riffs that you can play right on and across this position. Octave position is also shown.

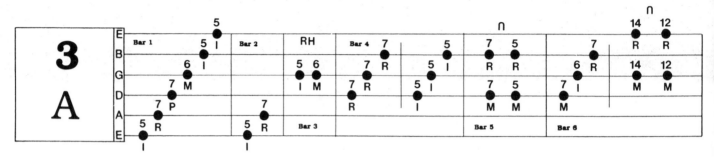

MOVE 4 — The trick here is to be fast and steady with the pick. Hard to get this guy down at first. You will be better at performing it the third day you try. Trill those notes fast and evenly, back and forth.

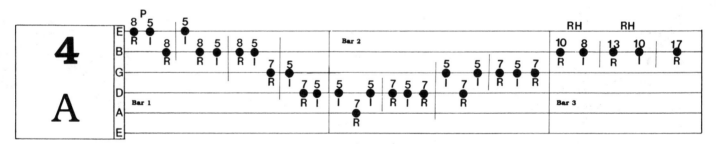

MOVE 5 — Now I am going to show you all of the beautiful little grace notes that fit so quaintly *in and around* the E chord formation. These are shown in both the open and movable bar position.

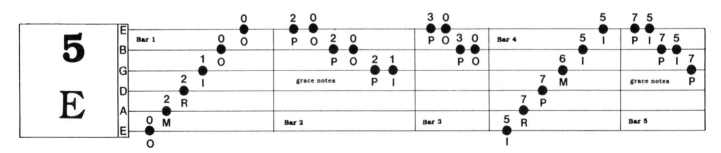

MOVE 6 — Now you get to find out all about the grace notes that you can play *in and around* the A chord position. The open A position is shown in the first bar, with a barred minor position following in the 2nd and 3rd bar.

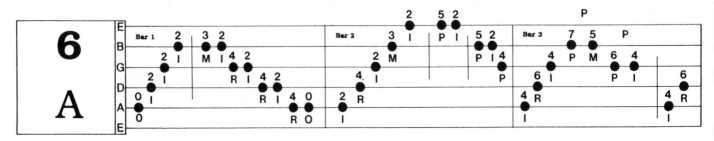

MOVE 7 — Here is one of my all-time favorite blues licks in A. Get the bending smooth, then wind this dude all the way down until that low range third on 5/4. The final bar demonstrates a seventh chord built on the fifth (E).

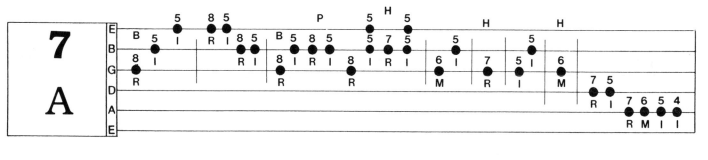

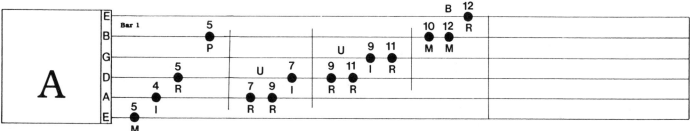

MOVE 8 — Here is an A major scale passage sprinkled with a few minor notes. This one will give you a good idea of how guitarists use the major scale. Real classy riff.

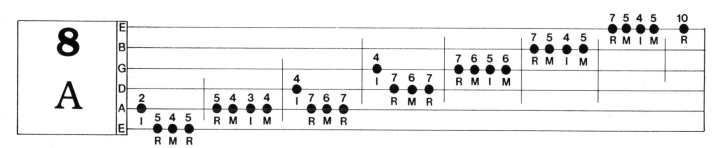

MOVE 9 — Double string resolution time is here. You get examples in different octaves for both E and A. Get ready to slide two notes at once, and to pick "over" any unused string.

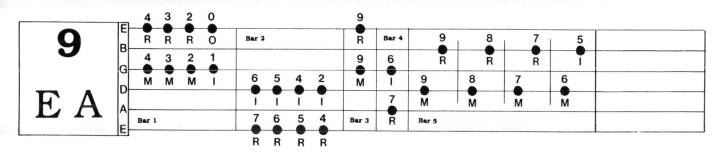

MOVE 10 — Move 10 takes you through a few ways to employ a seventh position which takes place on the top three strings. Play all three strings as if they were one.

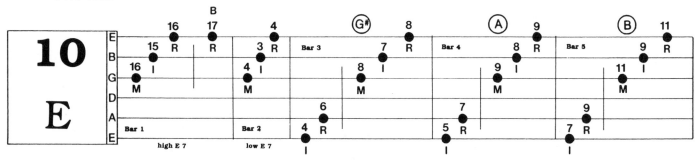

MOVE 11 — The famous 1-5 position on the two low strings is expanded upon in this important move. Note closely the positions for the 6th, 7th, 2nd, 9th and 4th.

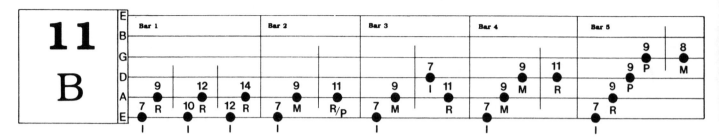

MOVE 12 — Move 12 starts off by slamming the one finger A bar around before you go into a great power chord riff using open chords.

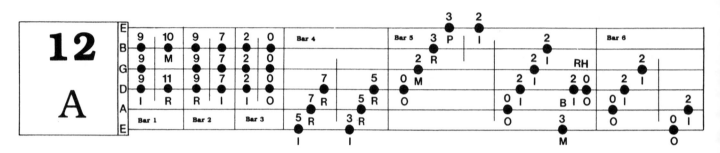

MOVE 13 — Here is a classic blues lick which starts you off on the root note 5th fret in A, only to take you up to the next higher box up around the 12th fret. Note the two string resolution.

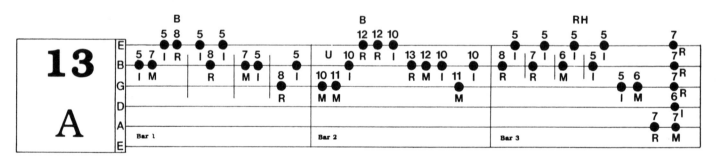

MOVE 14 — Here is a famous low range "step" riff perfect for heavy metal execution. Try it a few times to get the ascending positions correct, then try the final chromatic climb.

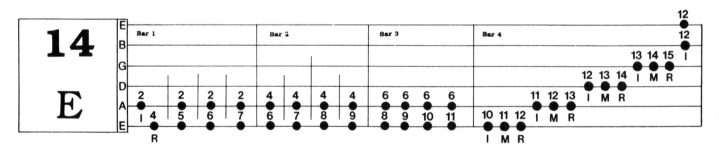

MOVE 15 — This move shows you how to hammer on the barred E 7th chord in two different positions. The final bar brings you a low range step-down.

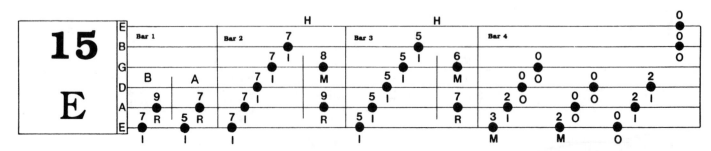

MOVE 16 — Time for multiple pull-off double triplets. Try to make the final octave riffs soar into the upper range.

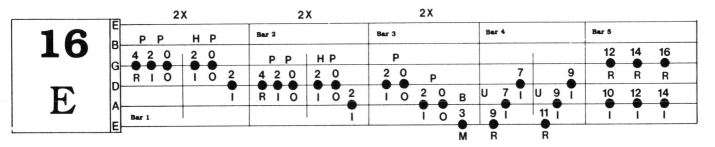

MOVE 17 — Here is a fast bend and pull. The transcription can fool you into thinking you have time to get them all, but listen to the tape to understand how it sounds.

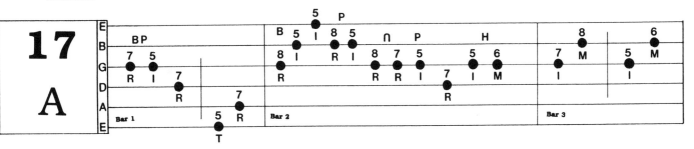

MOVE 18 — Harmonic overtones can be used to create chords or single tones built into a normally fretted passage. Both techniques are shown here with the G chord over the 12th fret, and the D chord over the 7th fret.

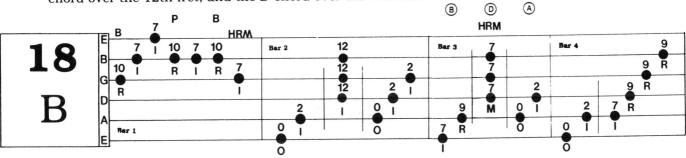

MOVE 19 — This is a trill move which takes you all the way down the first string using whole steps and half steps, and degrees from the blues and relative scales. The ending has a little twist down on the low three strings.

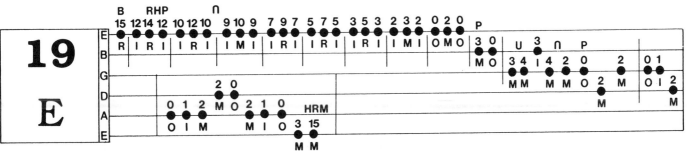

MOVE 20 — Starts off with descending double string unison bends, then heads into two descending double triplets. Ends up with open position power chords (G, A, E.)

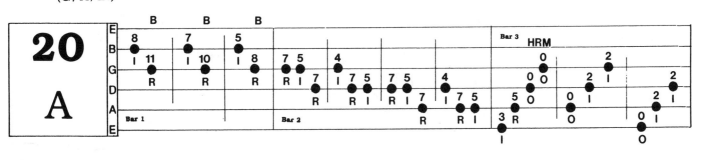

MOVE 21 — Here is a take-off on the famous Chuck Berry opening used so many times throughout rock history. Slide the high note down with the right hand, and play across the 2nd fret relative position for A in the final bar.

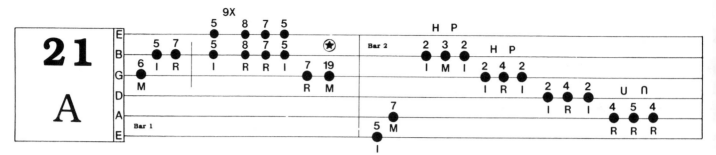

MOVE 22 — Here is an example of fast climbing two-finger pull-offs with notes from the right hand regularly sprinkled in. Get it going fast, then push it up.

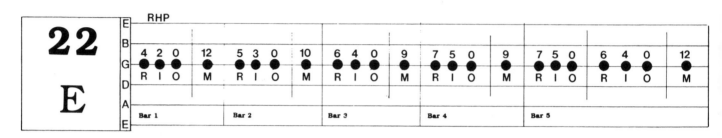

MOVE 23 — Move 23 takes the repeated step pull-down through consecutively descending steps on the third string. Watch for the single right hand notes which have small stars above them in the transcription.

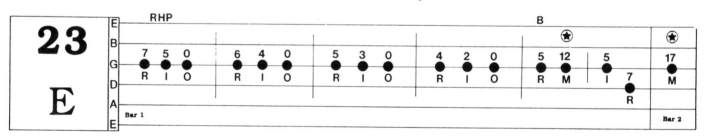

MOVE 24 — This is the basic boogie box in the open A position. Notice the slide up for the A chord from the open strings, along with all of the usable add-on notes that you find above and adjacent to the open chord.

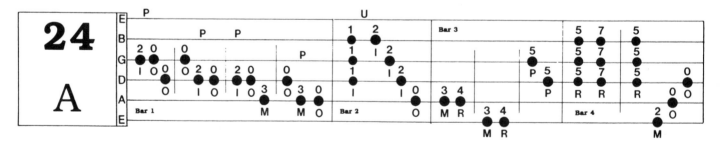

MOVE 25 — Here is a real mover which combines both the major chord and bass lead line along four different positions. Notice how the final bars demonstrate an upper lead position for each of the four bass positions.

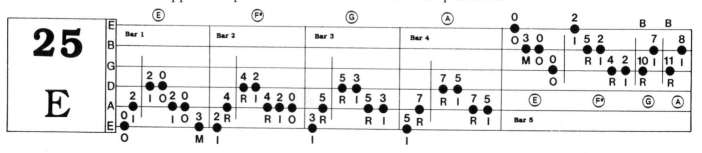

MOVE 26 — The great thing about this riff has got to be that one artificial harmonic note. The final bar shows you a terribly dissonant descending passage for use during "bombing raid" imitations.

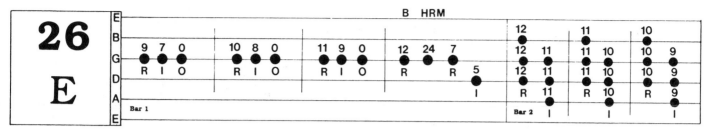

MOVE 27 — Along the open string position, this move takes you through hammering, pulling and bending techniques involving the E major chord and the E blues scale.

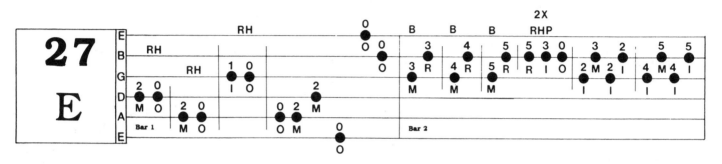

MOVE 28 — Starts with lightning quick chromatic pull-offs across the 3rd, 4th and 5th strings. This is followed by open and octave positions for the A chord, along with a sliding sus 4 configuration.

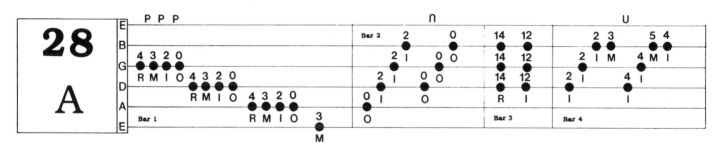

MOVE 29 — This move shows you a few nice add-on trills that you can play along the ever-movable root note fret. Ends with a pretty Major seventh slide between G and F.

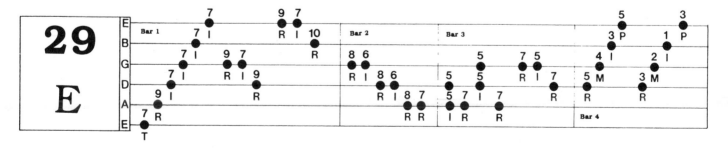

MOVE 30 — Move 30 opens with pick attack on just the second string. This is followed by repeating motif and final trill down the third string.

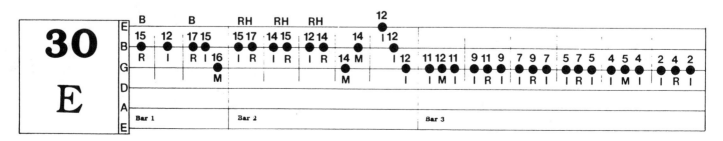

MOVE 31 — Here is the heart of three great rock positions. Each one will offer you a new insight into how rock artists apply their art to the instrument. All are based around the E major chord across the 9th fret.

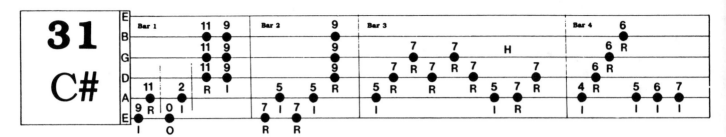

MOVE 32 — Here is a slick fast moving riff right out of the blues box along the 12th fret in the key of E. The final bar will show you two lower octave positions where you can play the same riff.

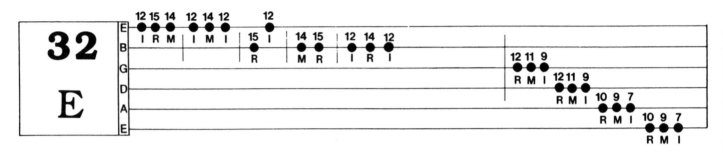

MOVE 33 — Take your index finger and place it across the two thin strings at the fifth fret. Then get ready to execute this easy blues lick as it moves down to a lower position. The final bar hammers on the E chord notes above the fifth fret bar.

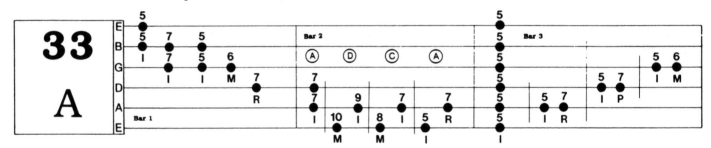

MOVE 34 — Pound the one finger A chord in different positions around the board — OR ELSE.

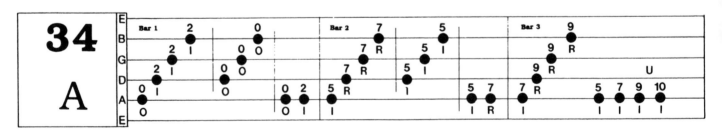

MOVE 35 — This move shows you a few things you can do to spice up the E augmented 9th chord. This is such a classic rock chord that I felt obliged to show you a few ways in which to highlight its use.

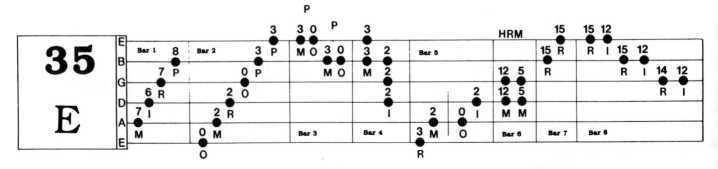

MOVE 36 — Move 36 shoves around the lower string 7th chord position in the key of E around the 5th and 7th frets. The middle bar shows you the common blues box for use with this chord sequence. The final bar demonstrates a classy slide-in move.

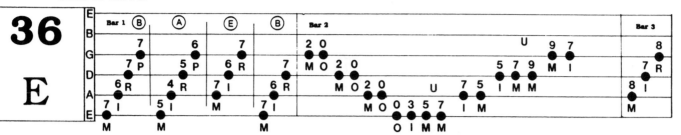

MOVE 37 — How does one get familiar (and I mean *really familiar*) with the range of their instrument? Well one way to do it is to take a motif box and play it across the six strings on each of the first twelve frets of the instrument.

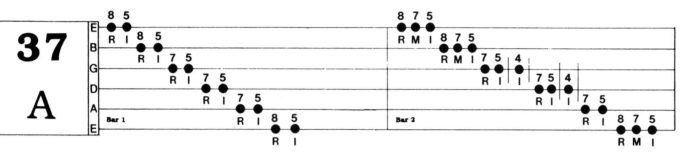

MOVE 38 — Find in this move a series of fast trills, each executed in three different positions on ascending strings. The final bar will take you up in steps to the twelfth fret.

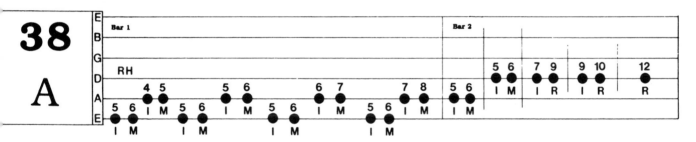

MOVE 39 — Here you get "across the strings" consideration of the two string box bending technique. Keep moving it down, watching for alternative bent notes set off by small mini-bars.

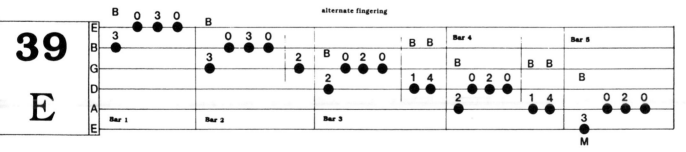

MOVE 40 — Double string techniques abound in this short study on the thin strings in the key of G. The second bar is an evenly paced step down, with the final bar showing a high position bent string riff.

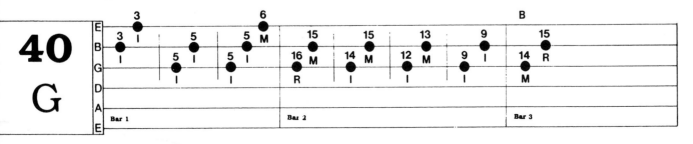

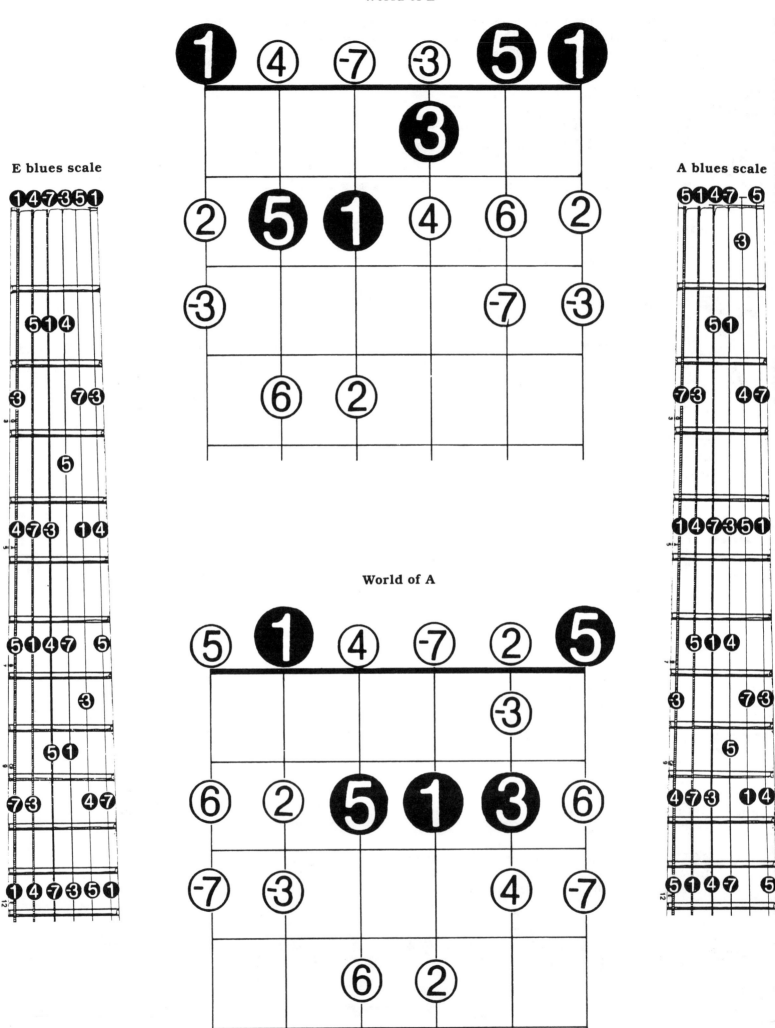

Notes

Notes

Notes

Get Further Into
Be Dangerous On Rock Guitar

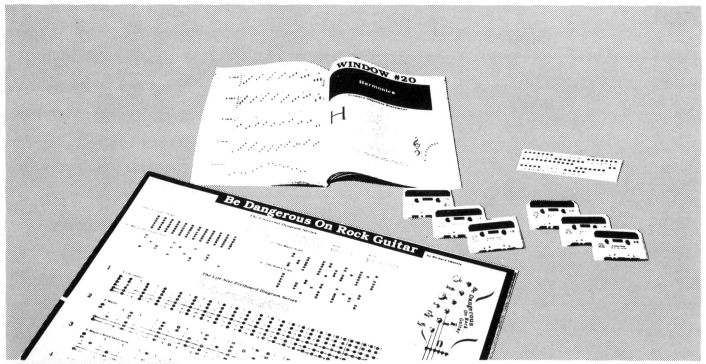

reat guitarists are made. Although at times we all feel that we were born to play, a growing guitarist has to have direction, instruction, examples and inspiration from other musicians. The great Jimi Hendrix, fresh out of the U.S. Army paratroopers, played the gritty "chittlin circuit" of the South and the clubs of New York's Harlem for five long years — HALF A DECADE — before he forged his own style on his first landmark album **Are You Experienced?**, produced in London. During this developmental period, Jimi worked directly with hundreds of other guitarists and musicians. The young master was always pushing, sharing, asking, jamming and talking about the guitar, day and night. Then, using his prior knowledge as a base, *he did it his way.*

I believe that you can develop your own talent. After I was done writing this book, I recorded six hours of cassette tape, laid out a 30" x 40" wallposter, and made Helpful Fretboard Dots, all of which supplement the methods put forth in the primary 24 chapter book. Here is your chance to get a deeper look at **Be Dangerous On Rock Guitar.** Because I made the tapes, wallposter and dots *after* I made the book (which took over two years) I really had a chance to reflect on the material and bring the most important facts to the surface. If you enjoyed this book, and have come along this far with me on the adventure, I can assure you that the rest of the **Be Dangerous** package will provide you with valuable insight.

The Heavy Guitar Company started in 1975 with a small ad in the back of **Rolling Stone** magazine. Since this time we have grown to accomodate demanding guitarists from across the nation and around the globe, developing a world of satisfied customers. We are waiting to carefully fill your order for any part of the **Be Dangerous** package that you want to order now. A free catalog will be included in your first purchase.

Be Dangerous

Richard Daniels

Richard Daniels
Owner/Operator
The Heavy Guitar Company

Book

The **Be Dangerous On Rock Guitar** book is 150 pages and contains 24 WINDOWS which will take you, step by step, through the procedure of becoming a DANGEROUS GUITARIST. Inside this book you will find the story of rock guitar brought to you by incisive text coordinated with over 200 fretboard diagrams, 132 six line "guitar tab" transcriptions, 75 chord figures along with dozens of charts, photos and illustrations — *altogether a visual encyclopedia of rock guitar technique.*

6 Tapes

The six 1-hour **Be Dangerous On Rock Guitar** cassettes follow the same 24 WINDOWS found in the book, allowing the varied subject matter of the course to *come alive with sound.* The tapes comprise an "audio version" of the book, passing through the WINDOWS one at a time, sounding out all of the numbered transcriptions found in the book. The real beauty of the cassette tapes is their ability to *teach by sound example* — which no book can do. You can tune your guitar precisely to the "tuning tone" given on the tape, allowing you to experience first hand all of the finer points of the delicate art of playing rock guitar — speed playing, harmonics, string bending, pulling, hammering, sliding, muting, flash lead techniques — everything you read about in the book.

This time Richard went all out to provide you with the finest rock guitar instruction tapes. From the collection of custom strats, to the rack mount digital delay, to the stack of screaming amps, nothing was spared during the production of the **Be Dangerous** tapes. Designed for repeated listening in short segments, you will find the six cassettes chock-full of helpful hints, hot licks, and high tech guitar moves. On top of everything, you get a verbal rant — directly from the author of the book — that will encourage you to explore new musical boundaries with your new found knowledge.

Wall Poster

The **Be Dangerous On Rock Guitar Wall Poster** is 30″ wide and 40″ tall. At the top of the poster, you will find the four part **Universal Diagram Series** (chromatic, major, major chord inversion, blues scale) which charts out the 12 fret repeating foundation patterns used by all modern guitarists. The Universal Diagrams can be applied to any key. The heart of the wall poster is the twelve part **Full Size Fretboard Diagram Series** which display the rock guitarist's most powerful weapon; *the scales that cover the board.* Imaging the actual size of these twelve printings! We're talking about a dozen **24 fret layouts**, precisely marked to scale degree printed THE SAME SIZE AS YOUR GUITAR FRETBOARD for the chromatic, major, blues, major triad inversion and rock hybrid scale for the keys of E and A. Just sling on your guitar, pin this poster to the

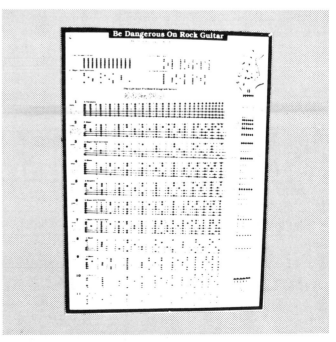

wall, and things start to get clearer immediately. This GIANT makes it so *easy* to see where the most used rock scales and chords appear that you will find yourself easily commanding the entire fretboard as never before.

In addition to all of this, on the right side of the poster in a vertical position you will find the unique, fullsize "nut to bridge" Harmonic Overtone Diagram which shows all positions of the first seven overtones over the full length of the string. You can search the world over if you want- but you will never find anything like the BE DANGEROUS WALL POSTER.

_____**Please read this before using order blank** _____

The Heavy Guitar Company is now ready to fill your order for **all** or **any part** of the **Be Dangerous On Rock Guitar Package**. To properly fill your purchase order, it is important that the order blank below is carefully filled out in full. If you order the **Whole Package**, you will receive the BDORG book, the six BDORG tapes, and the BDORG wallposter. If you order **The Rest of the Package**, you get everything named above *except the book*.

You can order all six tapes together for $48.00, but if you want to order one or more tapes separately, please check correct box (1 through 6). All individual tapes are $10.00 each. After you arrive at the subtotal, please include **$3.00 shipping charge** for all orders up to and including $18.95, and **$5.00 shipping charge** for all orders $19.00 and over. Virginia residents please add 4% sales tax.

Foreign Orders send check or money order in U.S. funds only, no C.O.D.s. Canada and Mexico please order same as U.S. All other countries require extra postage. Send for free postage information and catalog. Make checks and money orders payable to The Heavy Guitar Company. Credit chard phone orders are taken on The Heavy Guitar Phone/FAX Hotline: 1-610-869-5885.

The Heavy Guitar Company

School of Guitar

Box 129, West Grove, PA 19390
Heavy Guitar Hotline: 1-610-869-5885

		Qty	Price	Amount
	Whole Package (book, 6 tapes, wall poster, dots)		$59.95	
	The Rest of Package (6 tapes, wall poster, dots)		$52.00	
	Book Only		$15.95	
	Wall Poster		$6.95	
	To buy tapes separately, **PLEASE SPECIFY TAPE(S)** (1 through 6)			
1	**Tape One** (covers WINDOWS 1, 2, 3)		$10.00	
2	**Tape Two** (covers WINDOWS 4, 5, 6, 7, 8...)		$10.00	
3	**Tape Three** (covers WINDOWS 8 cont., 9, 10, 11, 12, 13)		$10.00	
4	**Tape Four** (covers WINDOWS 14, 15, 16, 17, 18, 19, 20...)		$10.00	
5	**Tape Five** (covers WINDOWS 20 cont., 21, 22)		$10.00	
6	**Tape Six** (covers WINDOWS 23, 24)		$10.00	
ALL 6	**All Six Tapes**		$48.00	
			SUBTOTAL	
	Send Check, Cash or Money Order	Virginia residents add 4% sales tax.		
		Shipping Charges per order of $18.95 and less, add $3.00 Shipping Charges per order over $19.00, add $5.00		
		TOTAL AMOUNT ENCLOSED		

VISA

MasterCard

Name _____

Address _____

City/State/Zip _____

Check Out The Heavy Guitar Company's Homepage
http://www.heavyguitar.com

Feel free to contact Richard through his personal E-mail
richard@heavyguitar.com

We are now happy to take your credit card order over the phone on the
HEAVY GUITAR HOTLINE:
1-610-869-5885
The HOTLINE rings directly into Richard Daniels office. Feel Free to call anytime and order books tapes or videos directly from the author, or to ask any question about Richard's work, to make a comment or to request a free catalog. The HOTLINE number accepts all incoming FAX (use same number). A complete product line FAX ORDER FORM is also available: Call In!